THE STRUCTURED LITERACY PLANNER

The Guilford Series on Intensive Instruction
Sharon Vaughn, *Editor*

This series presents innovative ways to improve learning outcomes for K–12 students with challenging academic and behavioral needs. Books in the series explain the principles of intensive intervention and provide evidence-based teaching practices for learners who require differentiated instruction. Grounded in current research, volumes include user-friendly features such as sample lessons, examples of daily schedules, case studies, classroom vignettes, and reproducible tools.

Essentials of Intensive Intervention
Edited by Rebecca Zumeta Edmonds, Allison Gruner Gandhi,
and Louis Danielson

Intensive Reading Interventions for the Elementary Grades
Jeanne Wanzek, Stephanie Al Otaiba,
and Kristen L. McMaster

*Intensifying Mathematics Interventions
for Struggling Students*
Edited by Diane Pedrotty Bryant

*Literacy Coaching in the Secondary Grades:
Helping Teachers Meet the Needs of All Students*
Jade Wexler, Elizabeth Swanson, and Alexandra Shelton

*Structured Literacy Interventions:
Teaching Students with Reading Difficulties, Grades K–6*
Edited by Louise Spear-Swerling

*The Structured Literacy Planner: Designing Interventions
for Common Reading Difficulties, Grades 1–9*
Louise Spear-Swerling

THE STRUCTURED LITERACY PLANNER

Designing Interventions for Common Reading Difficulties, Grades 1–9

Louise Spear-Swerling

Series Editor's Note by Sharon Vaughn

THE GUILFORD PRESS
New York   London

Copyright © 2024 The Guilford Press
A Division of Guilford Publications, Inc.
370 Seventh Avenue, Suite 1200, New York, NY 10001
www.guilford.com

Printed in the United States of America

This book is printed on acid-free paper.

Last digit is print number: 9 8 7 6 5 4 3

Library of Congress Cataloging-in-Publication Data
Names: Spear-Swerling, Louise, author.
Title: The structured literacy planner : designing interventions for common
    reading difficulties, grades 1–9 / Louise Spear-Swerling.
Description: New York, NY : The Guilford Press, 2024. | Series: Guilford
    series on intensive instruction | Includes bibliographical references
    and index. |
Identifiers: LCCN 2023040857 | ISBN 9781462554317 (paperback) |
    ISBN 9781462554324 (cloth)
Subjects: LCSH: Reading—Remedial teaching. | Reading (Elementary) |
    Reading (Middle school) | Reading disability. | Reading comprehension. |
    Response to intervention (Learning disabled children) | BISAC: EDUCATION
    / Special Education / Learning Disabilities | EDUCATION / Professional
    Development
Classification: LCC LB1050.5 .S638 2024 | DDC 372.4—dc23/eng/20231011
LC record available at https://lccn.loc.gov/2023040857

About the Author

Louise Spear-Swerling, PhD, is Professor Emerita in the Department of Special Education at Southern Connecticut State University. She helped prepare both general and special educators to teach reading using Structured Literacy approaches for many years, including supervising a public school tutoring program that paired teacher candidates with struggling readers. Her research interests include children's reading development, reading difficulties, and the knowledge and skills needed to teach reading effectively, especially to struggling and at-risk readers. She has presented and published widely on these topics. Dr. Spear-Swerling is author or editor of several books, including *Structured Literacy Interventions: Teaching Students with Reading Difficulties, Grades K–6*, and is an editorial board member for several journals, including *Annals of Dyslexia, Teaching Exceptional Children,* and *Reading Psychology.* She consults often for K–12 school districts, mostly on students with severe or persistent literacy difficulties and ways to improve their achievement.

Series Editor's Note

How many of you have wondered how to develop Structured Literacy lessons for your students? Even if you are currently using a Structured Literacy curriculum, you often need to refine the lessons you are using to fully meet the needs of specific students. If you are *not* using a Structured Literacy approach but are interested in learning more, this book is the right one for you.

I am excited to share that this book provides the practice knowledge needed to both design your Structured Literacy lessons and refine the ones you are currently using. What is truly unique about this book is that the knowledge of Structured Literacy is made so accessible to us. Using the information provided, we can design and modify lessons with ease and confidence.

You will relate to the case studies provided and find them useful as examples for the students you teach. Then you can seamlessly utilize the clear and organized instructional procedures to address your students' challenges. What I really like about this book is the reliance on common reading profiles. This permits us as educators to think about clusters of students, their learning strengths and needs, and then the specific mechanisms for meeting these needs. The detailed description of poor reader profiles gives us a visual image of students and then a well-documented pathway for intervention. Because the practices are linked to scientifically based research, we have confidence in using the lessons provided.

How does the Structured Literacy approach link to the science of reading? As described in the Preface, all aspects of the comprehensive approach to Structured Literacy as represented in this book are specifically and directly derived from the best and most current scientifically based research available. This research is translated in ways that are completely accessible to educators, so that we have specific lessons and instructional practices we can map right on to the students we teach. This includes practice exercises aligned with the focus of each chapter. I am eager to use *The Structured Literacy Planner* in my classes as well as to share it with the range of educators with whom I work. I am confident you will return to it regularly as a guide for further developing your knowledge, skills, and expertise.

SHARON VAUGHN, PhD

Preface

In the graduate program that prepared me to become a special educator in the late 1970s, I was lucky to have strong preparation from some highly capable teacher educators. By contemporary standards, there were important gaps in my training, especially in the areas of comprehension and writing. Still, my classmates and I were very well prepared to teach a wide range of foundational literacy skills successfully to struggling or at-risk readers. We read scientific research of the time from luminaries such as Isabel Liberman and Donald Shankweiler. We learned about how to teach basic skills explicitly and systematically, using course texts such as Engelmann (1969). And we applied what we were learning in practice experiences with struggling readers, experiences supervised by knowledgeable mentors.

This book describes a set of explicit approaches to teaching reading that have become known as Structured Literacy (SL; International Dyslexia Association [IDA], 2019, 2020) and that are especially effective for struggling readers. While these approaches share many commonalities with the way that I was initially trained so many years ago, they are also informed by over 40 years of research on reading since then, with much more to say about language and reading comprehension, as well as a better understanding of how children learn to read and spell printed words. The content of SL involves the language and literacy skills that research has shown are important in learning to read and write, both foundational and higher-level literacy skills. The instructional features of SL—not only explicit, systematic teaching of key skills and concepts but also other features detailed in the chapters of this book—have been informed by decades of direct evaluations of specific instructional practices and interventions in reading, the research that is essential to drawing conclusions about the best ways to teach students (Shanahan, 2020).

The research base for SL is one part of what is sometimes called the *science of reading* (SOR). In addition, SOR research encompasses a vast array of other studies, including basic scientific research on reading from many fields, such as neuroscience, cognitive psychology, communication sciences, and linguistics. This latter research is also very valuable but cannot, by itself, permit conclusions about the most effective instruction and interventions, because it was not designed or intended to do so. Furthermore, in recent years, the term *science of reading* has acquired an additional meaning, that of an advocacy movement (e.g., The Reading League [TRL], 2022). Members of this movement, comprised of educators, parents, researchers, policymakers, and others, are deeply concerned about how children in the United States learn to read and about how many educators are prepared to teach reading. These reading reform advocates maintain that given the importance of proficient reading in educational and occupational attainment, as well as the many negative social and economic consequences of poor reading, learning to read is a fundamental human right. These movements exist not only in the United States but also in other English-speaking countries, such as Canada (Ontario Human Rights Commission, 2022).

There are certainly good reasons to be concerned about the reading achievement of students in the United States, especially—but not only—the achievement of poor and minority children, students with disabilities, and English learners. For example, in 2019, one-third of U.S. fourth graders performed at the lowest, below-basic level in reading on a widely referenced measure of students' achievement across states, the National Assessment of Educational Progress (NAEP). For Black fourth graders, the corresponding percentage was 52%; for Hispanic fourth graders, 45%; for those with disabilities, 70%; for those eligible for the National School Lunch Program, an indicator of students' family income, 47%; and for fourth-grade English learners, 65%. Most of these percentages of fourth graders at the below-basic level increased in the 2022 NAEP assessment, in the wake of the COVID pandemic (National Center for Education Statistics, 2019).

Consistent, appropriate application of what is now known from research about how to prevent reading problems, why some students struggle in reading, and how best to help them, could make an enormous difference in many students' outcomes. Unfortunately, however, application of this research both in public schools and teacher preparation is far from universal (Adams et al., 2020; Ellis et al., 2023; Moats, 2017; Porter, Odegard, McMahan, & Farris, 2021). Moreover, misapplication and misunderstandings both of SOR and SL occur frequently, particularly in public discourse and the popular press. For example, professional groups with an interest in SOR (e.g., IDA, 2019; National Center on Improving Literacy, 2022; TRL, 2022) have emphasized that effective reading instruction is not just about teaching phonics, or about using one particular method or commercial program in instruction or intervention. Nevertheless, on the Web or in public discourse, references to SOR are used to support claims about the unequivocal superiority of a particular program or method, often one heavily focused on phonics skills, as a cure-all for reading difficulties. Some of the debates are highly antagonistic. Contentious debate in the field of reading, in which people with different viewpoints have sometimes been likened to combatants in "reading wars," is nothing new (see Stanovich, 2000, Chapters 19–21, for a thoughtful and prescient summary of these issues pre-2000). However, the current debates may be even more combative, fueled by social media and a hyperpartisan political climate.

Likewise, although this is often not reflected in the public discourse about SOR and SL, professional groups have emphasized that SOR research is ongoing and that knowledge about reading continually evolves. This is particularly true for findings at the edge of new discoveries rather than well-established, consensus research findings supported by extensive studies. In the future, research will almost certainly *not* show that the best intervention for poor decoders is to teach them to memorize word shapes, or to look only at the first letters of words and then guess based on pictures. However, research might well show that specific details of phonics or comprehension interventions, as yet unidentified, are more or less effective for different subgroups of students.

Beyond simply being unpleasant, why are these conflicts a problem? Among other issues, misunderstandings of SOR may lead to overly rigid prescriptions for teaching that are ineffective or unnecessary, channeling scarce resources, including instructional time, in the wrong direction. Misunderstandings of SL approaches may lead educators or parents to be overly wedded to one particular program, when a different one might be better for a given student; or to emphasize phonics intervention to the exclusion of other key components of intervention that a student requires, such as in vocabulary or comprehension. And although reasoned debate is a normal part of science, when debates become personal or unduly antagonistic rather than impartial and focused on evidence, they may lead practitioners to think that all research is just a matter of someone's opinion. When it comes to major, well-established consensus findings in reading, nothing could be further from the truth.

This book defines SL in relation to research-supported language and literacy content and instructional features, similar to the original definition advanced by the IDA (2019, 2020) and the one described in Spear-Swerling (2022b); that is, SL is conceptualized as an umbrella term that includes a variety of programs and methods sharing this content and these features. Many of the instructional activities in the book are modeled after ones described in published intervention studies (e.g., Clarke, Truelove, Hulme, & Snowling, 2014; McCandliss, Beck, Sandak, & Perfetti, 2003; Roberts, Vadasy, & Sanders, 2020) or in Institute of Education Sciences practice guides (e.g., Baker et al., 2014; Vaughn et al., 2022), adjusted to suit the needs of the students described in various chapters. The book makes ample use of case examples of individual students, because these are often highly relatable and meaningful for practitioners. All of the case examples are authentic, in that they are based in some way on actual students whom I have assessed, taught, or encountered in my work in schools. However, I have based cases on composites or altered details, so that individual students' identities cannot be discerned and their privacy is protected.

In addition to its emphasis on SL, the book is organized around another concept that I believe can be extremely helpful in teaching struggling readers, but one that unfortunately seems to have made limited inroads in education. This is the concept of common types of reading difficulties, which involve three patterns: difficulties based only in word reading, only in language comprehension, or in both areas. An understanding of these patterns can greatly improve assessment and intervention practices in reading for students with and without disabilities, as well as those across the K–12 grade range. A substantial, interdisciplinary research base supports the existence of these common patterns of reading problems (e.g., Capin, Cho, Miciak, Roberts, & Vaughn, 2021; Catts, Adlof, & Weismer, 2006; Catts, Compton, Tomblin, & Bridges, 2012; Cutting et al., 2013; Lesaux & Kieffer, 2010; Spencer & Wagner, 2018), often termed *poor reader profiles* in research studies.

The book devotes two chapters to each profile, one for students functioning at early stages of reading, and the other for those at more advanced stages of reading. Readers should not interpret the term *stage* too literally. It is only intended to convey the range of reading achievement that teachers of poor readers may encounter across the elementary, middle, and early high school grades, and to ensure that activities valuable for the full range of students are included. For example, middle–secondary educators often see poor readers with problems involving multisyllabic word reading, reading fluency, and higher-level comprehension; however, they can also encounter more severely impaired poor readers who function at early stages of reading and require intervention in basic phonics or comprehension skills. Similarly, elementary teachers encounter poor readers who vary in achievement, with milder as well as more severe problems in word reading or comprehension. The goal of the book is to help educators plan SL interventions for all of these poor readers.

This book is aimed primarily at an audience of practitioners who work with, or are being prepared to work with, struggling readers in grades 1–9. That audience includes general and special educators, reading specialists, reading interventionists, and, in some cases, speech–language pathologists. Multiple case examples, intervention activities, lesson plans, and application activities are used to make the content of the book clear and practical for this audience. School leaders who manage systems of tiered interventions, as well as district administrators engaged in professional development with inservice educators, may also find the book helpful. It can potentially be paired with a previous edited book on SL (Spear-Swerling, 2022c), but it can also stand alone, if desired, depending on the background of the audience and other resources in use.

The first three chapters of the book provide information necessary to understand later chapters. Chapter 1 explains in detail the two main themes, involving SL and poor reader profiles, and why they are important to successful teaching of poor readers. Chapter 2 describes the structure of English at multiple levels—words, sentences, and longer discourse—a grasp of which is essential for SL teaching of both word reading and comprehension. Chapter 2 includes multiple structure-of-English practice activities (e.g., counting phonemes or morphemes in words, identifying varied sentence structures, recognizing different passage structures), embedded in the chapter to assist readers in learning this important content. There is also a cumulative structure-of-English knowledge assessment available online for Chapter 2. Chapter 3 focuses on assessment of poor readers—specifically, how to determine poor reader profiles and target interventions properly for individual students, as well as how to use diagnostic assessments to further identify specific skills to address in intervention.

The remainder of the book describes interventions for the common patterns, or profiles, of reading difficulties. Chapters 4 and 5 focus on students with a profile of specific word recognition difficulties (SWRD), that is, difficulties specific to word reading. This pattern of poor reading is often associated with dyslexia but can also be found in many struggling readers who do not have disabilities. Chapter 4 describes interventions for students with SWRD at early stages of reading, those learning to read basic, one-syllable words, whereas Chapter 5 focuses on interventions for advanced-stage readers with SWRD, involving students who need work on reading two-syllable and multisyllabic words. These chapters also include a format for intervention lessons for students with a profile of SWRD, as well as sample lesson plans for specific students described in the chapters.

Chapters 6 and 7 address students with a profile of specific reading comprehension difficulties (SRCD), which involves students who have poor reading comprehension despite at least adequate word reading. This type of reading problem becomes more common beyond the primary grades. It can be found in some English learners, students with certain disabilities (e.g., some students with autism spectrum disorders), and other poor readers as well. Chapter 6 focuses on intervention activities for students at relatively early stages of SRCD; Chapter 7 details activities for students at more advanced stages of SRCD, such as some poor readers in middle school and early high school. These chapters include a format for intervention lessons tailored to these students' needs, with sample lessons.

The topic of Chapters 8 and 9 involves students with a profile of mixed reading difficulties (MRD), who have difficulties both in word reading and language comprehension. MRD is a common pattern of reading difficulty among students with relatively severe reading comprehension problems, students from low-income backgrounds, and some students who are English learners. These chapters follow the structure of previous ones, with Chapter 8 devoted to early-stage readers with MRD and Chapter 9 to advanced-stage readers. A format for intervention lessons with these students is also provided. The final application activities for these chapters involve planning a sample lesson for one of the students described in each chapter.

Evidence-based reading interventions, implemented by well-prepared, knowledgeable teachers, matter greatly in poor readers' outcomes. Moreover, by improving students' reading, effective teachers can alter the trajectory of many students' lives for the better. Most educators aspire to be this kind of teacher, successful in reaching all of their students. I hope this book will help its readers—both current and future teachers—to achieve such aspirations.

Acknowledgments

In my experience, the old proverb that "it takes a village to raise a child" applies to writing books, too. Many people have contributed, directly or indirectly, to this volume. First, I would like to express my sincere gratitude to Sharon Vaughn of The Meadows Center for Preventing Educational Risk, at the University of Texas at Austin, and Rochelle Serwator of The Guilford Press for their enthusiastic support of this work. They provided guidance on many issues, from planning the organization of the book to coming up with a good title—always my nemesis—and their wise suggestions shaped the book in important ways. Many others assisted in the process of preparing the manuscript for publication, including Laura Patchkofsky, Jacquelyn Coggin, Jared Greenberg, Katherine Lieber, and Katie Leonard. Thanks to Paul Gordon for designing a beautiful cover.

I would also like to acknowledge the numerous researchers whose work has informed and influenced my own for many years. These researchers are cited in this book, as well as in my previous writing. My work in education would be impossible without the wide array of scientific studies of reading to inform it that so many capable investigators have done.

My colleagues in the "LD Guidelines" group in Connecticut, whose mission was to revise the state's guidelines on identification of learning disabilities, have been very receptive to my writing on Structured Literacy and poor reader profiles. They are Alycia Trakas, Donna Merritt, Claire Conroy, Perri Murdica, and Lisa Fiano. I appreciate all their ongoing encouragement during the long process of writing this book and their understanding on the occasions when a writing deadline meant that I had to miss one of our virtual meetings.

As always, many thanks are owed to my family—my husband, son, and daughter. My husband's longstanding support and encouragement, stretching back decades to when our children were small and finding time to write was especially challenging, has greatly facilitated my pursuit of an academic career. My son and daughter have also been supportive of and curious about my work. With my son, who is himself a special educator, "talking shop" about the nitty-gritty of reading assessment, instruction, and intervention is a great joy. My conversations with my daughter about our shared interest in the craft of writing—sometimes interspersed with discussions of fanfiction and analysis of characters in our favorite streaming series—are often different, but no less joyful. I am so grateful to have all of you in my life.

Finally, I deeply appreciate the interest of so many practitioners in my work. I admire these educators' commitment to helping struggling readers and their pursuit of continued professional development, often in the face of many challenges: mediocre pay, reams of paperwork, worries about school shootings, the COVID-19 pandemic and its aftermath, and now even book bans in some districts. These are the classroom teachers, special educators, and reading interventionists who come up to me after a talk, their brows furrowed in concern, to ask questions about the best way to help a student who is struggling. They are the administrators who know that their district literacy practices are problematic for many students and are trying to improve them, despite the difficulties of doing so. They are the teacher educators who understand how important substantive, evidence-based teacher preparation is, and who are trying to improve teacher education from within. Many thanks for all you do.

Contents

CHAPTER 1

Introduction

How Structured Literacy Interventions Can Help Students with Varied Reading Problems

Alysha Bentley, a reading interventionist at a diverse, urban K–8 school, sighed as she looked at a recent round of progress monitoring data for her most challenging group of students. All fifth graders, this small group had started intervention at exactly the same level on the school's reading comprehension assessment, which is why the students were grouped together. The progress monitoring data confirmed what Ms. Bentley thought. None of the students was progressing well, not at all. Furthermore, despite having considerable assessment data for the students, Ms. Bentley was having trouble coming up with a good plan for how to help them, although she very much wanted to do so.

Ms. Bentley was in her third year as a reading interventionist, with some experience teaching struggling readers. In her teacher preparation program, she had taken several courses on how to help poor readers. Her courses had generally emphasized the importance of developing higher-level comprehension abilities through motivating, engaging activities that would lead students to make important inferences on their own. Both Ms. Bentley's teacher preparation coursework and the core Tier 1 English/language arts program in her school tended to view teacher-led, explicit instruction negatively, as drill-and-kill that would quash students' interest in learning. However, this group of fifth graders was especially hard to engage, and the work she had done on comprehension to this point did not seem to be having much effect.

Furthermore, Ms. Bentley was expected to work on grade-level standards, with grade-level texts, and for all of these students, grade-level standards and texts were very difficult. For instance, one standard involved determining the theme of a story from details in the text, and one of the required texts at Ms. Bentley's school was *The*

1

Black Stallion (Farley, 1941). This classic novel tells the story of a teenaged boy, returning from a visit to his missionary uncle in India, who is shipwrecked with a wild black stallion on a desert island; the stallion turns out to be a thoroughbred racehorse. Two of the students in Ms. Bentley's intervention group have little idea what a *stallion*, *missionary*, or *thoroughbred* are, what *pedigree* means, or why pedigree matters in horse racing. One of these students has additional limitations in background knowledge. He has never seen a horse race or been on a boat, and he does not understand words such as *deck*, *rail*, or *gangplank* in describing parts of a boat. Ms. Bentley does her best to explain, and occasional problems with vocabulary and background knowledge are to be expected. However, these students' limitations are extensive, weighing them down and getting in the way of their ability to become engaged in the story, let alone determine the theme. Another student in the group has different challenges. Although he met expectations on a basic phonics assessment, when reading text, he repeatedly stumbles in reading words like *stallion*, *missionary*, and *thoroughbred*. He also is overwhelmed by the demands of the text, though for different reasons.

Ms. Bentley is a caring, capable, and dedicated teacher. However, she could substantially improve her effectiveness with a broader range of students, including the fifth graders who have her so concerned, through two key ideas. The first idea involves common types or patterns of reading difficulties, sometimes called *poor reader profiles*, which could help her better understand and plan for individual students' needs. The second involves using Structured Literacy (SL) interventions to teach students more effectively. Both key ideas can help all practitioners who teach poor readers, not just Ms. Bentley. This chapter explains each idea in detail, as well as their value for teachers and their students.

Common Poor Reader Profiles

Research on Poor Reader Profiles

Common poor reader profiles relate to the simple view of reading (SVR; Gough & Tunmer, 1986; Hoover & Gough, 1990), a widely referenced scientific model of reading, which says that good reading comprehension involves two broad types of abilities: (1) reading printed words and (2) oral language comprehension, understanding what has been read. Each broad ability involves numerous component abilities. Reading printed words requires skills such as knowledge of grapheme–phoneme (letter–sound) correspondences, phonemic awareness (PA; e.g., the ability to blend sounds into whole words), and the ability to read words automatically as well as accurately. Oral language comprehension requires knowledge of vocabulary, the ability to understand syntax or sentence structure, and background knowledge, among other areas. These abilities underlying reading development also interact and become more tightly interconnected over the course of development (Scarborough, 2001).

Both word reading and language comprehension are essential to reading comprehension, and good readers must be strong in both of them. From the SVR, it therefore follows that reading problems can relate specifically to word reading, or specifically to language comprehension, or to both areas. The three poor reader profiles have been termed (Catts et al., 2006) specific word recognition difficulties (SWRD), specific reading comprehension difficulties (SRCD), and mixed reading difficulties (MRD). Research supporting the existence of the different poor reader profiles is extensive and multidisciplinary in nature, from fields such as reading, cognitive psychology, special education, communication sciences, and neuroscience (e.g., Capin, Cho, Miciak, Roberts, & Vaughn, 2021; Catts et al., 2006; Catts, Compton, Tomblin, & Bridges, 2012; Cutting et al., 2013; Fletcher, Lyon, Fuchs, & Barnes, 2019; Leach, Scarborough, & Rescorla, 2003; Lesaux & Kieffer, 2010; Spear-Swerling, 2004).

Why Should Teachers Know about Poor Reader Profiles?

Researchers who have studied experts and novices in numerous domains, including not only teaching (e.g., Hattie & Yates, 2014), but also many other areas such as chess, chemistry, physics, and medicine, have identified some fundamental characteristics in which experts and novices differ (Chi, Glaser, & Farr, 1988). Across all domains, experts are much more likely than novices to recognize important patterns of data and to grasp their implications. They organize their knowledge around core concepts and big ideas, not lists of individual facts. Expert teachers perceive large, meaningful patterns that include being able to anticipate and plan for difficulties that students are likely to encounter in the future. They understand individual students' difficulties at a deeper level that enables them to plan instruction more effectively (Hattie & Yates, 2014).

For practitioners who work with struggling readers, poor reader profiles represent key patterns that are both *meaningful* and *actionable*. The profiles are educationally meaningful because they are valuable in making educational decisions, including planning instruction. They are actionable because they involve skills that can be improved through appropriate instruction and intervention. Furthermore, they are useful for understanding a wide variety of reading problems across the K–12 range, in students with and without disabilities.

Knowledge about the profiles facilitates teachers' abilities to choose appropriate reading assessments and to integrate data across those assessments, not just interpret each assessment in isolation. This knowledge would enable Ms. Bentley to see that even though the students in her intervention group started intervention with very similar reading comprehension scores, as well as similar performance on silent reading fluency and basic phonics assessments, they had different underlying patterns of reading problems—that is, different reading profiles.

The reading skills of Ms. Bentley's three students—Drew, Marcus, and Eli—are displayed in Table 1.1. If one looks only at the first three left-hand columns of the figure—the assessment data available to Ms. Bentley—the students look quite similar, and it seems to make sense to group them together. Nevertheless, the students differ substantially in their underlying component skills for reading, as shown in the three right-hand columns. Drew, a student with dyslexia, has serious difficulties in reading

TABLE 1.1. Performance of Three Fifth-Grade Students in Reading

Student (profile)	Reading comprehension	Silent reading fluency	Basic phonics assessment	Phonics assessment—multisyllabic words	Oral vocabulary	Oral language comprehension
Drew (SWRD)	Below basic	Below benchmark	Met benchmark	Well below benchmark	Above average	Average range
Marcus (SRCD)	Below basic	Below benchmark	Met benchmark	Met benchmark	Well below average	Low end of average range
Eli (MRD)	Below basic	Below benchmark	Met benchmark	Below benchmark	Below average	Below average; especially weak background knowledge

multisyllabic words but has strengths in his oral vocabulary knowledge and oral language comprehension—a profile of SWRD. In contrast, Marcus's skills for decoding multisyllabic words meet grade expectations, but he has significant weaknesses in oral vocabulary knowledge—a profile of SRCD. Eli, with a profile of MRD, has weaknesses in all of these areas—multisyllabic word reading, vocabulary knowledge, and broad language comprehension. He is also the student with significant weaknesses in background knowledge.

However, Ms. Bentley was not fully aware of these differences in her students' component skills because the necessary assessments for detecting them had not been administered. Poor reader profiles have implications for the types of assessments to administer in reading evaluations, which can improve assessment practices. Furthermore, the profiles provide an important starting point for planning interventions. A crucial initial consideration in intervention planning involves deciding whether a student's reading comprehension or reading fluency difficulties are based in word reading, language comprehension, or both areas. Yet sometimes this seemingly obvious step is overlooked. For instance, students with SWRD, whose difficulties center mainly on word reading and do not involve language comprehension, are sometimes given comprehension interventions because they score poorly on measures of reading comprehension, when word reading, not comprehension itself, is at the root of their poor reading. In fact, this was true for Ms. Bentley's student Drew, who was receiving comprehension intervention that did not address his true needs in multisyllabic word reading, which had not been detected by the basic phonics assessment, focused mainly on one-syllable words, in use at Ms. Bentley's school. Profiles also help teachers identify and plan instruction for multiple components of literacy in which a given student may be weak, a very useful aspect of profiles, because most poor readers' intervention needs go beyond a single component of literacy. This was true for Drew: He needed intervention in not only multisyllabic word reading but also spelling multisyllabic words and reading fluency.

In addition, poor reader profiles have implications for academic domains beyond reading. The profiles involve underlying patterns of strengths and weaknesses in different components of language, and these patterns tend to affect poor readers' performance in written expression as well as reading. For instance, Ms. Bentley's student Marcus had a profile of SRCD that was linked heavily to limitations in vocabulary, which also affected his word choice in written expression. Effective intervention for Marcus's vocabulary weaknesses might therefore help improve his written expression, as well as his reading comprehension.

Finally, information about poor reader profiles can help a teacher anticipate and prevent, or at least lessen, problems that students are likely to encounter in the future. For example, Marcus's oral vocabulary weaknesses dated back to his earliest years in school. Vocabulary limitations did not impact his reading comprehension greatly at first because the texts he had to read were relatively simple and did not place heavy demands on vocabulary knowledge. Furthermore, he progressed appropriately in learning phonics skills, which led his teachers to think that he was not at risk in reading, a common experience for students with SRCD (Clarke et al., 2014). However, as Marcus advanced in school and the expectations for reading comprehension increased, his underlying weaknesses in vocabulary began to have a much more negative impact on his reading comprehension. If teachers had recognized his vocabulary weaknesses and his profile of SRCD sooner, then earlier intervention could have been provided, which might have helped to prevent or at least lessen some of the reading difficulties that Ms. Bentley observed in him (Clarke et al., 2014).

The next section of the chapter considers each poor reader profile in depth. Table 1.2 summarizes the three profiles in detail.

Detailed Description of the Poor Reader Profiles

As shown in the top row of Table 1.2, students with SWRD have problems that are specific to reading printed words; these students have at least average oral vocabulary knowledge and average oral language (listening) comprehension. Although these students may demonstrate poor performance on measures of reading comprehension, their difficulties are due entirely to problems with word reading, and not actually to comprehension, as was the case for Drew. Even when students with SWRD have some accurate word-reading skills, nonautomatic word reading may drain their comprehension as they read text because the effort they have to put into reading words leaves fewer mental resources available for comprehension.

When students with SWRD are reading texts they can decode well, or when they are listening to texts read aloud, their comprehension is average or better. Interventions for these students need to address individual students' weaknesses in word reading, in areas such as PA, basic decoding skills, and strategies for reading long words (e.g., structural analysis and morphology). Interventions for SWRD must also address spelling. Because SWRD are usually based in phonological weaknesses, spelling interventions often must include teaching the phonological aspects of spelling, for example, being able to segment and correctly sequence sounds in words. Typical phonologically based spelling errors in students with SWRD include omissions of sounds (e.g., misspelling *flap* as *fap*) and incorrect sequencing of sounds (e.g., misspelling *desk* as *deks*).

TABLE 1.2. Description of Common Poor Reader Profiles

Profile	Out-of-context word reading	Oral vocabulary/comprehension	Text reading fluency	Reading comprehension	Examples of underlying causes	Typical intervention needs
Specific word recognition difficulties (SWRD)	• Below average in reading real words, nonsense words, or both • Difficulties may involve accuracy, automaticity, or both • Phonemic awareness (PA) often weak	• Oral vocabulary at least average • Broad oral language comprehension at least average	• Typically below average due to problems in accuracy and/or automaticity of word reading	• Often below average compared to peers due to problems in word reading • Good in texts student can decode well	• Dyslexia • Inadequate teaching or curriculum in PA, phonics, or other word-reading skills	• Phonics and other word-reading skills (e.g., structural analysis of long words) • PA if PA is weak • Spelling • Text reading fluency (accuracy and/or rate)
Specific reading comprehension difficulties (SRCD)	• Real word reading, nonsense word reading, and PA all at least average • Automaticity as well as accuracy at least average	• Oral vocabulary, broad oral language comprehension, or both, often below average • Weaknesses may be mild, not sufficient for student to qualify for SL services	• May be in average range or higher • If below average, fluency problems *not* related to word reading (e.g., student may read slowly because he or she is trying to understand the text)	• Below average • Weaknesses in language areas (e.g., vocabulary, syntax, and so forth, *not* word reading) • Student often has similar comprehension difficulties in listening as in reading	• Limited exposure to academic language or background knowledge • Certain disabilities (e.g., some cases of autism spectrum disorders) • Inadequate curriculum or instruction	• Individual students' specific comprehension weaknesses (e.g., background knowledge, syntax, vocabulary) • May need nonphonological spelling skills (e.g., morphology)
Mixed reading difficulties (MRD)	• Below average in reading real words, nonsense words, or both • Difficulties may involve accuracy, automaticity, or both • PA often weak	• Oral vocabulary, broad oral language comprehension, or both, often below average • Weaknesses may be mild, not sufficient for student to qualify for SL services	• Typically below average • Poor fluency may relate to both word reading and language comprehension	• Below average • Poor reading comprehension relates to both word reading and language comprehension • Listening comprehension often relatively better than reading comprehension	• Dyslexia combined with limited exposure to vocabulary and academic language • Broad language disabilities • Inadequate curriculum or instruction	• Phonics and other word-reading skills • Spelling • Individual students' specific comprehension weaknesses • Text reading fluency, if weak • PA, if weak

Students with SRCD, shown in the middle row of Table 1.2, have the opposite profile to that seen in SWRD. These students have at least average word reading, including at least average phonological skills such as PA and nonsense word reading, but nonetheless have difficulties with reading comprehension. Poor reading comprehension in these students is often linked to the second domain of the SVR, problems in oral language comprehension, for example, limited vocabulary knowledge, difficulties with complex syntax, and/or problems with inferencing that may relate to lack of background knowledge (Elleman, 2017; Oakhill, Cain, & Elbro, 2015). Similar types of comprehension difficulties may be evident whether the student is reading a text or listening to it, as in a teacher read-aloud. However, in many students with SRCD, oral language weaknesses are milder than the students' reading comprehension difficulties, perhaps reflecting differences between oral and written language, such as the fact that academic texts tend to make greater demands on vocabulary, syntax, and background knowledge than does oral language (Spencer & Wagner, 2018).

Students with SRCD may have grade-appropriate reading fluency, but if their fluency is poor, this is not due to problems in word reading; rather, slow rate of reading may relate to problems in language comprehension, such as a student reading slowly in order to try to comprehend. Students with SRCD need interventions focused on their specific weaknesses in language comprehension, which may vary across students. Ms. Bentley's student Marcus had a profile of SRCD, linked mainly to weaknesses in vocabulary knowledge, but students with SRCD can have weaknesses in many other language areas.

Spelling may or may not be weak in students with SRCD. However, these students have grade-appropriate phonological skills, so any spelling weaknesses usually relate to other aspects of spelling, such as difficulties with morphology, meaningful word parts (e.g., misspelling *psychology* as *sikology*) or with spelling generalizations (e.g., misspelling *hoping* as *hopeing*). Because the phonological aspects of spelling are intact, the intended word is generally obvious even when the word is misspelled. Spelling intervention may need to address aspects of spelling other than phonology, such as teaching about morphology, rules for adding endings to a base word, or semantic knowledge about homonyms, depending on the student's specific needs and grade placement.

As shown in the bottom row of Table 1.2, students with MRD have difficulties in both broad abilities of the SVR, word reading and language comprehension, and intervention needs to target both areas. Ms. Bentley's student Eli had a profile of MRD, with language comprehension weaknesses linked both to vocabulary and background knowledge, but with his poor reading comprehension further complicated by difficulties with multisyllabic word reading. As is true for students with the first two profiles, in MRD, individual students' specific weaknesses within the areas of word reading and language comprehension may vary.

Students with MRD frequently have poor reading fluency, related both to poor word reading and difficulties in language comprehension. Likewise, poor reading comprehension in these students relates to both areas, word reading and language comprehension. Unlike students with SWRD, who have good reading comprehension when reading texts they decode well, students with MRD may struggle even when reading texts they can decode because of language-related weaknesses such as limitations in vocabulary knowledge. Often, students with MRD will comprehend relatively better when listening than when reading because when listening, they do not have to cope with decoding demands. However, weaknesses in language areas such as vocabulary still contribute to listening problems, with these students' listening comprehension often somewhat below grade expectations, and reading comprehension even lower, due to the influence of poor decoding. Also, spelling is frequently a weakness in students with MRD and may include weaknesses in phonology as well as in other types of spelling knowledge.

For students with MRD as well as SRCD, it should be noted that language comprehension weaknesses can be mild, not at a level that would make them eligible for speech–language services (Nation, 2005). Mild difficulties may not have much impact on reading when children are in the earliest grades, reading relatively simple text, but have a bigger impact on reading as students advance in school and the comprehension demands of reading increase. Without appropriate assessment of oral vocabulary and oral language comprehension, milder difficulties in these areas may not be noticeable to teachers. However, more serious language comprehension weaknesses may be evident even without formal assessment, and their impact on reading comprehension may manifest earlier.

Executive Function, Reading, and Poor Reader Profiles

Recent research on reading development and reading difficulties has highlighted the potential importance of certain reading-related abilities beyond those captured by the SVR (Wagner, Beal, Zirps, & Spencer, 2021). One area that has received considerable attention from scientific investigators is executive function (EF), which has been defined in a variety of ways, to include working memory, for example, the ability to hold words in memory during reading to understand a long, complex sentence; cognitive flexibility and shifting processes, such as the ability to think about multiple ideas in a text at the same time and shift focus as needed; inhibitory processes, including the ability not to be distracted by information in a text that is irrelevant to understanding key points; and higher-level planning and monitoring processes, such as monitoring one's comprehension during reading to think about whether what has been read makes sense (Cartwright, 2015; Nouwens, Groen, Kleemans, & Verhoeven, 2021). EF and language abilities interact, with each area influencing the other, but EF generally is conceptualized as involving a set of specific cognitive abilities distinct from the abilities in the SVR.

EF appears to contribute both to decoding and reading comprehension (Nouwens et al., 2021) but has been studied especially in relation to the latter. EF may contribute to reading comprehension even after decoding and language comprehension are accounted for (Spencer & Wagner, 2018; Wagner et al., 2021), and it may be a key precursor to the development of skilled reading (Spencer, Richmond, & Cutting, 2020). Also, the importance of EF appears to increase with grade level (Cutting, Materek, Cole, Levine, & Mahone, 2009; Sesma, Mahone, Levine, Eason, & Cutting, 2009), perhaps because of increases in text demands across grades. Nevertheless, findings about the role of EF in reading have been somewhat conflicting, likely in part due to methodological differences among studies, such as the ways in which EF is defined and measured, as well as the age of the participants and other sample characteristics.

So, what is the relevance of research on EF to poor reader profiles and to teachers? First, research supports the importance of certain abilities conceptualized as part of EF, such as working memory, cognitive flexibility, and higher-level planning and monitoring processes, to success in both reading (e.g., Foorman et al., 2016; Shanahan et al., 2010) and written expression (e.g., Graham et al., 2012). Teachers should know that students identified with weaknesses in EF—as is often the case, for example, for students with attentional disorders—may be at added risk in literacy. Students with any poor reader profile may have difficulties in EF, but problems in EF are especially likely to play a role in SRCD and MRD, profiles that involve comprehension difficulties. Intervention involving certain EF processes such as planning, monitoring, and organization—especially when done in relation to reading and writing, not in isolation—can benefit the literacy achievement of students with weaknesses in these areas (e.g., Cartwright, 2015; Vaughn et al., 2022). Such intervention should also address individual students' needs in word reading and/or language comprehension.

A Few Cautions

An essential point to remember about poor reader profiles is that although they are extremely useful educationally, they are descriptive, not at the level of causation, as shown in Table 1.2. The fact that a student has a profile of SWRD, with significant problems in PA and word decoding despite strong language comprehension, does not, by itself, mean the student has dyslexia. Like Ms. Bentley's student Drew, students with dyslexia do often have a profile of SWRD, but there are other reasons why a student could have this profile, including a core literacy curriculum that fails to adequately address foundational skills in reading. As another example, although some students with autism spectrum disorders evidence a profile of SRCD, with difficulties concentrated in language and reading comprehension rather than word reading (Norbury & Nation, 2011), many other causes may underlie a profile of SRCD, such as limited experiences with English vocabulary and academic language, as sometimes seen in English learners (Li et al., 2021).

Although poor reader profiles are very useful in initial planning of intervention, they do not eliminate the need for in-depth, ongoing assessment or grouping considerations beyond the profile. Two students with SWRD, for instance, might be functioning at very different decoding levels, with one needing instruction at the one-syllable level and the other needing instruction in decoding multisyllabic words. Grouping these two students would not be advisable. Likewise, two students with SRCD might have very different underlying comprehension needs and also not be suited for grouping together in instruction. Furthermore, individual poor reader profiles are not necessarily stable over time. A student with MRD might respond well to phonics intervention in the elementary grades, with his or her word-reading problems fully resolved but with lingering problems in language comprehension, yielding a profile of SRCD in the later grades.

Finally, poor reader profiles involve the use of cutoff points for deciding what is "average" or higher, and what is "below average," and an individual poor reader's profile might be unclear in a given test administration. Here is an example. All standardized tests specify a range for average scores, often 90 to 109 for standard scores. A poor reader who has language comprehension standard scores around 100, and real word reading of 75, has a profile of SWRD. In contrast, consider the poor reader whose language comprehension scores are in the low 90s, and whose word-reading scores are in the mid- to high 80s. Technically, the student's language comprehension is in average range and word reading is below average, but based on standardized test data, the profile is much less clear for this second student than that for the first.

Identification of any poor reader's profile should not rely solely on standardized test data taken at one point in time. In the situation just described, additional assessment data—from screening and progress monitoring assessments, informal assessments, and classroom performance—as well as information about a student's educational history can be especially valuable. Although the different poor reader profiles are not always stable over time, the profiles often do manifest in distinctive ways in a student's history. For example, students with SWRD typically show a history of difficulties in phonics skills in the early grades, whereas those with SRCD do not. Consideration of a student's educational history may therefore help clarify his or her poor reader profile. Chapter 3 examines these issues, with some specific examples of students.

The Value of Structured Literacy Interventions

Knowledge about poor reader profiles can help practitioners better understand poor readers' individual needs, an understanding critical to providing appropriately targeted interventions (Connor & Morrison, 2016; Connor et al., 2011). However, without interventions that are actually effective in improving poor readers' reading and writing, the value of profiles is limited. To help a wide range of poor readers, practitioners also need SL interventions. These interventions can benefit struggling readers with all three poor reader profiles, whether they are beginners or functioning at more advanced levels, and whether or not they have disabilities. *Structured Literacy* is an umbrella term for a variety of commercial programs and instructional approaches that share an emphasis on certain types of **content**, as well as specific **instructional features** (International Dyslexia Association, 2019, 2020; Spear-Swerling, 2018, 2022c).

The Content of SL: Key Areas of Language and Literacy

The content of SL involves key areas of language and literacy: PA, phonics, orthography, morphology, vocabulary, syntax, and discourse comprehension. Research has shown that these areas are critical in learning to read, spell, and write, as well as often implicated in reading difficulties (Carlisle, 2010; Clarke et al., 2014; Fletcher, Lyon,

Fuchs, & Barnes, 2019; Foorman et al., 2016; Moats, 2020; National Reading Panel [NRP], 2000; Oakhill et al., 2015; Seidenberg, 2017; Stanovich, 2000).

Table 1.3 displays these areas, with a brief description of each area and some examples. PA, in the first row of Table 1.3, involves sensitivity to and the ability to manipulate phonemes (individual sounds) in spoken words, such as being able to blend sounds into a whole word or segment a spoken word into its constituent sounds. PA is especially important to the early stages of learning to read because in order to learn to map printed letters to sounds—that is, to crack the alphabetic code—children first have to understand that spoken words comprise individual phonemes; in order to decode a printed word, they must not only know grapheme–phoneme (letter–sound)

TABLE 1.3. Content of Structured Literacy: Important Components of Language and Literacy

Component	Description	Sample expectations for students
Phonemic awareness	Sensitivity to phonemes (sounds) in spoken words and the ability to manipulate them	Blend individual sounds (phonemes) such as /s/, /u/, /n/ to form the word *sun*; segment *sun* into its individual sounds.
Phonics	Knowledge of phoneme–grapheme/grapheme–phoneme correspondences and the ability to use that knowledge in reading and spelling unfamiliar words	Relate the letter *m* to the sound /m/ and the sound /m/ to the letter *m*; use this knowledge in reading and spelling words such as *am*, *mat*, or *men*.
Orthography	Knowledge of common letter sequences and spelling patterns in English	Recognize that words with a vowel–consonant-*e* pattern (e.g., *hope*, *shake*) usually have a first vowel that is long and an *e* that is silent; apply common spelling generalizations such as the "floss" rule to spell words such as *pill*, *mess*, and *stuff*.
Morphology	Knowledge about meaningful word parts (e.g., roots and affixes) and the ability to use that knowledge in reading, spelling, and understanding words	Recognize common roots such as *astro*, *ject*, and *psych*, including their meanings and spellings; read, spell, and understand words with shared roots from semantically related word families (e.g., *astronomy*, *astronomer*, *astrophysics*).
Vocabulary	Knowledge of word meanings in both listening and reading	Understand the meaning of grade-level words, including academic vocabulary.
Syntax	Knowledge about sentence structure	Understand, in both listening and reading, grammatically complex sentences, such as those with center-embedded clauses or passive voice, as expected for grade level.
Discourse comprehension	Listening and reading comprehension beyond the sentence level (e.g., paragraphs, stories, conversations); depends in part on background knowledge	Understand narratives and informational text while either listening or reading, including having adequate background knowledge to understand grade-level texts.

correspondences, but also blend the sounds once they have pronounced them. Likewise, to spell a word, they must segment a spoken word into its individual sounds before they can pair the appropriate grapheme with each sound.

Phonics, when used to refer to a component of reading rather than to an approach to instruction, means knowledge of grapheme–phoneme and phoneme–grapheme correspondences (e.g., the phoneme /s/ usually corresponds to the letters *s*, *c*, or *ss*), as well as the ability to apply that knowledge in reading or spelling unfamiliar words. Typical readers learn phonics skills mainly in the primary grades, although further developments in word reading, such as those involving morphology and etymology (word origins), continue beyond the primary grades.

Orthography involves knowledge about common letter sequences and spelling patterns in English. English has many regularities and recurrent patterns, but most English words cannot be decoded letter by letter. Instead, students must recognize common letter patterns—such as those involving common vowel patterns (e.g., *igh*), vowel–consonant-*e* syllables (e.g., *ride*, *broke*), and consonant-*le* syllables (e.g., the -*dle* in *candle*) —and be able to use that knowledge to read and spell words.

Morphology involves knowledge about meaningful word parts, such as roots, prefixes, and suffixes. English represents morphemes as well as phonemes in written words, so knowledge about morphology is valuable in multiple ways, including in reading, spelling, and understanding words. For example, if a student recognizes the root *psych,* as well as how to read and spell it, this knowledge can help the student read and spell semantically related words such as *psychology, psychologist, psychiatrist, psychiatric, psyche*, and so on. Furthermore, if the student knows that this word part means "mind," this knowledge can help in inferring the meanings of semantically related words. Morphology is important even in the earliest stages of reading, when children have to recognize, for instance, that dogs is not spelled *dogz* even though its final sound is /z/ because *dogs* is a plural, and to spell plurals, one uses -*s* or -*es*. Morphology becomes even more important at advanced stages of reading, when students have to read, spell, and understand an increasing volume of multisyllabic words, such as words with Greek and Latin roots (Carlisle, 2010).

Vocabulary refers to knowledge of word meanings, both in listening and in reading. Vocabulary directly influences reading comprehension because if there are many individual words in a text whose meanings a student does not know, this will inevitably affect the student's comprehension of that text. Vocabulary plays a role at all stages of reading but becomes especially important as students advance beyond the primary grades and the vocabulary used in grade-level reading materials becomes much more sophisticated (Chall, 1983).

Syntax is the area of language involving sentence structure. For example, a sentence with a center-embedded clause, such as *The cat that jumped off the table and scratched the boy ran under the bed*, may be difficult for typical young children and older students with syntactic weaknesses to understand; they may think that it is the boy, not the cat, that ran under the bed because of the juxtaposition of *boy* and *ran* in the sentence. Like vocabulary, syntax has a direct influence on students' reading comprehension, and syntactic demands in texts increase across grades. The earliest texts used in school tend to contain short, simple sentences, whereas more advanced texts contain a higher proportion of syntactically complex sentences.

Finally, *discourse comprehension* involves the understanding of language beyond the sentence level, with a direct impact on reading comprehension, and with escalating demands for students beyond the primary grades. Among other skills, students need to understand how different types of texts—such as narratives and a range of informational text structures—are organized (Oakhill et al., 2015). They must recognize in reading, and be able to use in their writing, common cohesive ties such as *for example*, *in summary*, and *in contrast*, as well as resolve anaphoric references such as pronouns (e.g., when a text says *she*, to whom is it referring?).

Background knowledge is particularly important to discourse and reading comprehension (Oakhill et al., 2015). As the opening story about Ms. Bentley's students illustrates, when students lack background knowledge for a text, comprehension will be difficult. Furthermore, background knowledge plays a role in inferencing (Elleman, 2017), that is, understanding what is not explicitly stated to achieve full comprehension of a text. For example, suppose ninth-grade students are reading a news article about Volodymyr Zelensky of Ukraine. If the students do not have background knowledge about Winston Churchill and the Battle of Britain, they will likely have trouble inferring the meaning of a phrase such as *Zelensky was seen as an almost Churchillian figure*, or to understand that the phrase is a compliment.

The Instructional Features of SL

The instructional features of SL approaches are displayed in Table 1.4. Two of these features involve instruction that is **explicit and systematic**. *Explicit* means that key concepts and skills—such as common grapheme–phoneme correspondences, important spelling generalizations, essential vocabulary and background knowledge for understanding a text, and common text structures—are directly taught by the teacher. Teachers model and clearly explain new concepts and skills, with multiple, well-chosen examples. *Systematic* means that important concepts and skills are taught in a logical sequence, with simpler concepts and skills taught before more complex ones. Another feature of SL, related to systematic teaching, involves **attention to prerequisite skills in instruction**. For instance, students are not expected to decode or spell complex multisyllabic words if they have not yet mastered prerequisite skills such as decoding and spelling simpler word patterns; they are not expected to understand syntactically complex sentences if they cannot yet comprehend simpler sentences.

SL approaches involve the provision of **targeted, unambiguous, prompt feedback** to students' responses, with affirmative feedback when students respond correctly, and feedback to errors that is clear, concise, and designed to help the student improve. For example, during students' oral reading of text, teachers do not ignore word-reading errors, but provide scaffolding and cues—such as pointing to part of a word that was misread—to help students read words correctly.

In SL approaches, teachers' instructional choices are **planned and purposeful**. These careful choices include instructional examples, texts, and tasks. For instance,

TABLE 1.4. Features of Structured Literacy

Feature	What it means	Example(s)
Explicit teaching	Key skills are directly taught, modeled, and clearly explained by the teacher	Teacher clearly models and explains how to segment a simple word into phonemes; how to apply a comprehension strategy, such as summarization
Systematic teaching	Instruction follows a planned, logical sequence, simple to complex	Children learn how to spell simple consonant–vowel–consonant words before spelling short vowel words with consonant blends; how to write correct sentences before writing paragraphs
Attention to prerequisite skills	Instruction considers prior skills needed to complete or understand a more advanced task	In teaching the meaning of a new vocabulary word, teacher uses clear definitions with words children will know
Targeted, unambiguous, prompt feedback	Teacher provides timely feedback to children's mistakes that helps children correct errors and avoid similar mistakes in the future	Teacher asks questions during children's text reading, with prompt clarification of misunderstandings as needed
Planned, purposeful choices of examples, tasks, and texts	Examples of words, instructional tasks, and texts for reading/writing are carefully chosen to fit children's current skills and avoid confusion	Phonics activities avoid the use of phonetically irregular words; children with limited decoding skills read phonetically controlled (decodable) texts
Synthetic-phonics approach at grapheme–phoneme level for initial phonics and spelling instruction	Initial approach emphasizes grapheme–phoneme correspondences and blending rather than larger units (e.g., whole words, onset–rime)	Children learn to decode a word, such as *shack*, by learning phonemes associated with the graphemes *sh, a,* and *ck,* and how to blend the phonemes into the correct word
Consistent application of skills and teaching for transfer	Children are expected to apply skills they have learned to varied and increasingly complex tasks, with tasks chosen to facilitate application of those skills	During oral reading of text, teacher draws children's attention to decoding errors and has child correct them; in writing activities, children are expected to spell previously learned words correctly
Data-based decision making	Assessments are used on a continuing basis to target interventions, monitor progress, and make needed adjustments	Assessments help a teacher target the specific comprehension weaknesses of a poor comprehender

Note. From Spear-Swerling (2022b). Copyright © 2022 The Guilford Press. Reprinted by permission.

teachers working with poor readers in the early stages of decoding and spelling present words in a carefully structured sequence, typically facilitated by a scope and sequence that establishes an order for teaching specific skills, from simple to complex. Specific instructional sequences can vary, and there is not one ideal scope and sequence; however, any sequence used in SL filters out potentially confusing words that do not fit the patterns students have learned. These words are eventually taught, but only after students have a command of simpler word types. Also, students in these early stages of word reading are placed for instruction in decodable texts, texts controlled to the specific word patterns that students have learned, so that students have ample opportunities to practice their developing decoding skills. Later, once students have learned a variety of word patterns, they do not need decodables, but in intervention, they still generally read texts that are at their instructional levels—not too difficult, and not too easy.

Texts used in SL approaches also are purposefully chosen with regard to comprehension, such as texts tapping vocabulary or background knowledge that students know or have been taught. As another example, if students are learning how to summarize a text, teachers begin with texts that lend themselves to summarization, rather than choosing a text that does not. The aim is to provide students ample opportunities to understand and apply what they are learning, while at the same time avoiding undue confusion, such as confusion caused by unintentionally misleading examples or by overwhelming students with too many new skills at once. These kinds of planned, purposeful choices can improve poor readers' chances of success and help increase progress (Fletcher et al., 2019).

In addition to teaching phonics skills explicitly and systematically, SL approaches generally use a particular approach to initial phonics instruction: **a synthetic-phonics approach at the grapheme–phoneme level**, for both decoding and spelling. In this approach, beginning readers learn grapheme–phoneme (and phoneme–grapheme) correspondences, as well as how to blend and segment phonemes. Teaching of PA skills is integrated with phonics instruction (see, e.g., Al Otaiba, Allor, & Stewart, 2022). Synthetic phonics at the grapheme–phoneme level is not synonymous with decoding all words in a letter-by-letter fashion; even early on, children must learn common letter patterns for phonemes such as /sh/, /ch/, and /th/.

The point, however, is that initial instruction is at the phoneme level, which contrasts with other phonics approaches, such as *analytic phonics* (e.g., teaching word families), in which students learn highly patterned words but are expected to infer common phonics relationships, or onset–rime approaches, in which initial instruction emphasizes common onsets (i.e., any consonants in a syllable that precede the vowel, such as the *sh* in *shop*) and rimes (the rest of the syllable from the vowel onward, e.g., the *-op* in *shop*). Regardless of the phonics approach that is employed, children must eventually learn to attend to larger units within words, such as common morphemes. Table 1.5 contrasts examples of how children are taught to decode words using synthetic phonics at the grapheme–phoneme level with other phonics approaches to the same words.

TABLE 1.5. Some Different Approaches to Phonics Instruction

Initial phonics approach	Description	Sample word: *vat*	Sample word: *stick*
Word families (analytic phonics approach)	Teacher presents highly patterned words for children to learn; children are expected to infer the phonics pattern, as well as apply it to reading and spelling unfamiliar words	Child learns the family of words *sat, rat, cat, mat,* and so forth, and infers the pronunciation of *vat*	Child learns the family of words *sick, pick, chick, thick,* etc., and infers the pronunciation of *stick*
Onset–rime	Teacher teaches sounds for common onsets (e.g., single consonants, blends, consonant digraphs) and common rimes (-*at, -it, -ack, -ick, -ake,* etc.), as well as how to blend and segment onsets and rimes	Child learns that the onset *v* corresponds to /v/ and how to pronounce the rime -*at,* then blends *v-at, vat*	Child learns how to pronounce the onset *st-* and the rime -*ick,* then blends *st-ick, stick*
Synthetic-phonics, initial grapheme–phoneme level	Teacher teaches common grapheme–phoneme correspondences, as well as how to blend and segment phonemes	Child learns that *v* corresponds to /v/, *a* to /a/, and *t* to /t/, then blends *v-a-t, vat*	Child learns that *s* corresponds to /s/, *t* to /t/, *i* to /i/, and -*ck* to /k/, then blends *s-t-i-ck, stick*

Yet another feature of SL approaches involves **consistent application of skills and teaching for transfer** (Wanzek, Al Otaiba, & McMaster, 2020). Students are expected to apply previously taught skills to subsequent, increasingly complex texts and tasks. Texts and tasks are carefully chosen so as to help promote transfer. This aspect of SL means that review of previously taught skills is built into instruction in a comprehensive way, although some review is also always part of SL lessons.

Finally, SL approaches involve **data-based decision making**—in particular, the use of appropriate assessments to inform intervention. As shown by the example of Ms. Bentley's three fifth graders, appropriate assessments are a critical first step in planning interventions. Once intervention has been designed, other assessments are vital to monitoring students' progress and to adjusting interventions as needed. Chapter 3 discusses assessment in detail.

Research Support for SL Approaches

As previously noted, the content of SL—key components of language and literacy—is very well supported by research from the past several decades, which shows that these areas play important roles in literacy development and are often implicated in literacy difficulties. Research also supports the instructional features of SL, which are highly consistent with research on effective methods of intervention for a variety of struggling readers, including those with disabilities, as well as poor and at-risk readers in general (Archer & Hughes, 2011; Cardenas-Hagan, 2020; Fletcher et al., 2019; Gersten et al., 2008; NRP, 2000; Vaughn et al., 2022; Wanzek et al., 2020).

With regard to initial approaches to phonics instruction, the report of the NRP (2000) found clear benefits to explicit, systematic phonics instruction as compared to no phonics teaching or to incidental teaching of phonics, but could not differentiate among the phonics approaches illustrated in Table 1.5. To be sure, any explicit, systematic phonics approach is far preferable to no phonics teaching. However, post-NRP research suggests a significant advantage of initial synthetic-phonics approaches at the grapheme–phoneme level (Brady, 2011, 2020; Christensen & Bowey, 2005; Sargiani, Ehri, & Maluf, 2022) over other phonics approaches. This advantage is seen especially in relation to reading and spelling more advanced words, as well as students' abilities to transfer their skills to unfamiliar words—and learning to read unfamiliar words is, after all, the main point of phonics teaching. Moreover, this approach enables teachers to integrate PA with phonics instruction rather than teaching PA separately (Johnston & Watson, 2004). Also, other approaches to phonics instruction, such as onset–rime, ultimately require a transfer to a phoneme-level approach because many words in English do not readily lend themselves to onset–rime decoding, such as long words. An initial synthetic-phonics approach at the grapheme–phoneme level avoids the need to make this transfer.

SL approaches are sometimes wrongly viewed as involving only teaching of phonics, or as only appropriate for students with phonics needs. However, SL approaches are effective for teaching higher-level literacy skills, as well as foundational skills (Vaughn et al., 2022), and these approaches can benefit students with a variety of reading profiles. For example, Ms. Bentley's student Drew, who had SWRD, could benefit from SL interventions for reading long words (Kearns, Lyon, & Kelley, 2022). Marcus, who had SRCD, could benefit from SL interventions for vocabulary, oral language comprehension, and reading comprehension (Coyne & Loftus-Rattan, 2022; Stevens & Austin, 2022; Zipoli & Merritt, 2022). Eli, who had MRD, could benefit from SL interventions involving all of these areas. Targeting individual poor readers' needs correctly in intervention is critical to effectiveness (Connor & Morrison, 2016); with appropriate targeting, SL interventions can help a broad range of struggling readers.

What Do Non-SL Practices Look Like?

Although SL is an umbrella term, certain popular core general education practices and interventions clearly do not fall under the SL umbrella. Some of these non-SL practices are more common with children at beginning levels of reading, especially non-SL practices involving teaching of foundational skills, whereas others are commonly found with students at relatively advanced levels of reading. Table 1.6 contrasts SL practices with examples of non-SL practices for students at early and more advanced stages of reading.

TABLE 1.6. Some SL and Non-SL Practices for Beginning and More Advanced Readers

Stage	SL practices	Non-SL practices
Beginning readers	• Basic phonics skills taught explicitly and systematically, using initial synthetic-phonics, grapheme–phoneme level approach • Use of a scope and sequence for teaching foundational skills to help ensure prerequisite skills for decoding and spelling are addressed • Beginning decoders usually read decodable texts • In text reading, students are encouraged to look carefully at words and apply decoding skills, *then* check to ensure that what has been read makes sense • Spelling generalizations, such as the "floss" rule, are explicitly taught and practiced	• Basic phonics skills usually taught, but often not systematically, and often with a larger-unit approach (e.g., word families or onset–rime) • Instruction in foundational skills may not use a scope and sequence, so prerequisite skills are not always addressed • Beginners often read predictable texts • In text reading, students may be encouraged to use picture or sentence context rather than looking carefully at words to decode • Application of basic phoneme–grapheme correspondences in spelling usually taught, but spelling generalizations, such as the "floss" rule, often not explicitly taught or practiced
More advanced readers	• Skills for decoding long words, such as use of morphology, taught explicitly and systematically • Advanced spelling skills, such as spelling of Latin- or Greek-derived morphemes, taught explicitly and systematically • Students read texts at or near their instructional levels • Important prerequisite skills for understanding a text, such as vocabulary and background knowledge, addressed in instruction • Instructional strategies to help students understand challenging syntax are used • Different passage structures for informational texts are explicitly taught • Explicit teaching about cohesive ties (e.g., cause–effect signal words such as *because, consequently, as a result*) is provided	• Teaching of decoding beyond basic phonics skills sometimes not addressed • Advanced spelling skills often not taught; focus may be on memorizing specific words, without attention to morphology or other useful patterns in words • Poor readers may be expected to read grade-level texts that are much too difficult for them • Important prerequisite skills for understanding a text, such as vocabulary and background knowledge, may not be addressed • Syntax often is not addressed in instruction • Differences between narratives and informational texts are usually taught, but individual informational passage structures (e.g., compare–contrast, problem–solution), as well as cohesive ties, may not be explicitly taught

For beginning readers, a highly influential non-SL approach involves the three cueing systems model (Clay, 1994; Goodman, 1976; for a discussion of the influence of this model in education, see also Hanford, 2019). The three cueing systems model maintains that good readers do not attend carefully to all the letters in a word to decode, but rather make use of partial letter cues—such as the first and last letter of words—along with meaning and sentence structure to read unfamiliar words. Despite the fact that this model is not consistent with research on how beginners progress well in reading (Foorman et al., 2016; Moats, 2017; Seidenberg, 2017; Stanovich, 2000), its popularity in education has led to many problematic practices, especially for poor and at-risk readers. These practices include teacher feedback that encourages guessing rather than looking carefully at words to decode, as well as the use of predictable texts in beginning reading. Predictable texts are written and structured to encourage guessing based on pictures and sentence context rather than consistent application of decoding skills. Table 1.7 contrasts examples of decodable and predictable texts.

At more advanced reading levels, SL approaches address skills for decoding and spelling long, complex words, such as morphology, useful generalizations, and orthographic patterns. However, in non-SL approaches, these skills often receive little attention (Moats, 2017, 2020). Students at advanced levels generally do not require decodables, but in SL approaches, they would be placed in texts at or near their instructional levels, whereas in non-SL approaches, they may be reading texts that are far too difficult

TABLE 1.7. Examples of Decodable Text and Predictable Text

Decodable text	Predictable text
Ben has a tan cat. The cat is Max. [picture of smiling boy with cat]	Good morning! It's time to have breakfast. What does Nicholas want to eat? [picture of smiling boy at table]
Ben has a lot of fun with Max. [picture of Ben and Max playing]	He can eat oatmeal. [picture of bowl of oatmeal]
Max likes to sit on a red rug in the den. [picture of Max on the rug]	He can eat waffles. [picture of waffles on a plate]
A big bug is on the rug near Max. [picture of bug]	He can eat bacon. [picture of bacon on a plate]
Max sees the bug run by him. [picture of Max looking startled]	He can eat scrambled eggs. [picture of scrambled eggs on a plate]
CVC words: *Ben, has, tan, cat, is, Max, lot, fun, sit, on, red, rug, in, den, big, bug, run, him* High-frequency words (not CVC): *a, the, of, with, likes, to, near, sees, by* Other words: (no other words)	CVC word: *can* High-frequency words (not CVC): *good, morning, it's, time, to, have, breakfast, what, does, want, eat, he* Other words: *Nicholas, oatmeal, waffles, bacon, scrambled, eggs*

Note. From Spear-Swerling (2022b). Copyright © 2022 The Guilford Press. Reprinted by permission.

for them, to the point that success is not possible even with good teacher scaffolding and preteaching. Non-SL approaches also may ignore important prerequisite skills for understanding a text, such as teaching of key vocabulary and background knowledge (Wexler, 2019), and syntax is rarely addressed in these approaches.

Like many teachers, Ms. Bentley had been prepared in non-SL rather than SL approaches. Her preparation had actively discouraged her from using explicit, systematic teaching, as had the core general education practices in use at her school. Furthermore, she was expected to address grade-level standards without regard to whether students had mastered prerequisite skills for those standards, as well as to have students read texts that were far too difficult for them. These issues were especially acute with her most challenging students—Drew, Marcus, and Eli—because of the extent of the students' difficulties and problems with grouping them together. Knowledge about poor reader profiles, combined with the use of appropriate SL interventions, could enable all of these students, and many others, to be much more successful in reading.

SUMMING UP: The Value of SL for Different Poor Reader Profiles

Here are the most important points from this chapter:

- Two key ideas can enable practitioners to improve their effectiveness in teaching struggling readers: common poor reader profiles, which describe common patterns of reading difficulties, and SL interventions.

- Three common poor reader profiles, based in the SVR, are SWRD, SRCD, and MRD.

- Knowledge about the profiles is critical to targeting and designing interventions appropriately.

- SL approaches involve specific content—important areas of language and literacy—as well as certain features of instruction that are highly effective for poor and at-risk readers.

- Features of SL include explicit, systematic instruction; attention to prerequisite skills; prompt, targeted feedback; the use of a synthetic-phonics approach at the grapheme–phoneme level in initial phonics instruction; planned, purposeful instructional choices; teaching for transfer; and data-based decision making.

- SL interventions can benefit all profiles of poor reading, whether they involve weaknesses in foundational skills or in higher-level components of literacy.

APPLIED EXERCISES

Exercise 1

Shari is a beginning fourth grader who was identified with reading problems in grade 2. She has been receiving SL interventions for phonics and reading fluency for about the past year and a half, and she has made good progress, although she still needs some additional intervention involving long words. Recently, however, Shari has started evidencing some difficulties with reading comprehension, even when she is reading texts at her instructional level, texts that she can decode fluently. Shari's teachers are puzzled by the emergence of this new problem with comprehension. What poor reader profile does Shari appear to have, and how could it explain her emerging reading comprehension difficulties? What kinds of additional assessments could confirm it and help inform her intervention?

Answer

Shari appears to have a profile of MRD, involving weaknesses in both word reading and language comprehension. In the early grades, Shari's difficulties with word reading might have been more obvious than her language comprehension weaknesses, especially if those weaknesses are relatively mild, because the texts Shari could read did not place heavy demands on comprehension. However, Shari's decoding has improved to the point that she now can read more challenging texts that place greater demands on her comprehension. Further assessment of Shari's oral language comprehension, especially her oral vocabulary knowledge and broad listening comprehension, with more in-depth assessment of language (e.g., syntax) as warranted, could help confirm whether Shari has a profile of MRD. These assessments also could be very helpful in adjusting Shari's intervention to include additional areas of comprehension in which Shari is weak.

Exercise 2

A ninth-grade poor reader with a profile of SRCD has difficulties with higher-level EF involving planning, monitoring, and organizational processes. How might these kinds of difficulties affect the student's reading comprehension and written expression? How could SL interventions improve the student's performance in these areas?

Answer

In reading, the student might have weaknesses in monitoring comprehension, as well as identifying the gist of a text and summarizing it. In written expression, planning and organizing a piece of writing, as well as monitoring processes such as identifying errors for editing and revision, could be weaknesses. Formal and informal assessments could help to determine whether these areas are in fact problematic. If so, addressing these difficulties through explicit, systematic teaching of comprehension monitoring, summarization, and important writing processes, along with prompt, targeted feedback and other features of SL, could greatly benefit this student.

Exercise 3

What type of initial phonics teaching is usually emphasized in SL approaches? How is this approach different from other initial phonics approaches, and what are its advantages? Explain how a beginning reader would learn to decode a word such as *smash* in SL approaches.

Answer

SL approaches typically emphasize a synthetic-phonics approach at the grapheme–phoneme level in initial phonics instruction. To decode a word like *smash*, children would be taught grapheme–phoneme correspondences for *s*, *m*, *a*, and *sh*, and how to blend the phonemes associated with those graphemes. Other phonics approaches involve larger units for initial instruction, such as whole words or onsets and rimes. Although the use of synthetic phonics at the grapheme–phoneme level places somewhat greater demands on children's phoneme blending skills than do other initial phonics approaches, it has many advantages: It appears to be more effective, especially in developing skills for reading advanced words and unfamiliar words; PA instruction can be integrated with phonics instruction; it is applicable to a wider range of words right from the start rather than being limited to words with common rimes or word families; and it avoids the need eventually to transfer from a larger-unit phonics approach to a grapheme–phoneme level.

CHAPTER 2

The Structure of Language

Dr. Tameka Jackson, a professor of reading, teaches in a graduate-level university program. Most of her students are inservice teachers pursuing master's degrees in reading, special education, or elementary education. Last year, her department began offering a series of courses on SL, and Dr. Jackson is now teaching a practicum in which the master's candidates have to tutor poor readers using SL interventions. Unfortunately, despite their inservice teaching experience, Dr. Jackson has found that many of her master's candidates are having significant problems implementing SL in their teaching.

One common problem has to do with making planned, purposeful instructional choices. In phonics activities, some teacher candidates choose inappropriate examples of words, such as the candidate Dr. Jackson observed yesterday, who chose the word *charm* as an example of a short-vowel, closed syllable word. However, *charm* is a vowel-*r* word; it does not have a short vowel. Today, a different candidate chose a book with especially challenging syntax for a poor reader with significant syntactic weaknesses to read.

Provision of targeted feedback is another difficulty. Some candidates encourage poor decoders to "sound out" words inappropriately, including one candidate who encouraged a child to blend the -*ng* in *wing* as a combination of the sounds /n/ and /g/. However, -*ng* represents one sound, a digraph not a blend (Moats, 2020). On other occasions, candidates overlook opportunities for useful scaffolding and feedback, such as neglecting to draw poor comprehenders' attention to important signal words in a text.

Interpretation of assessments is yet another problem. When a ninth-grade poor reader misspelled the word *competition* as *compitition* in a spelling assessment, his tutor attributed this error to lack of knowledge about short /e/ and short /i/, and she planned her lesson accordingly. But the second vowel sound in *competition* is a schwa, a sound that can be represented by a variety of vowels, including the letter *i*. What would be more helpful to the student is not instruction in basic phoneme–grapheme relationships, which he already knows, but rather teaching about morphology (e.g., the root word of *competition* is *compete*).

In all of these instances, the students were perplexed, or at least not helped, by their tutors' unintentionally confusing instruction.

Research on Teacher Knowledge about Language Structure

All of these difficulties reflect limitations in teacher candidates' knowledge about language structure. Does Dr. Jackson have an unusually weak group of candidates, educators incapable of teaching with SL approaches? Not at all. In the absence of explicit instruction about language structure, these kinds of problems are common even in experienced teachers, including some reading specialists and special educators (Brady et al., 2009; Moats, 1994; Porter, Odegard, McMahan, & Farris, 2021; Spear-Swerling & Cheesman, 2012).

Contrary to what is sometimes believed, an understanding of language structure is not an automatic consequence of proficient adult reading. For example, even teacher candidates with strong word attack skills can lack knowledge about English word structure (Spear-Swerling & Brucker, 2006); in fact, literate adults' knowledge of word spellings creates confusions for them in analyzing the phonemic structure of words (Scarborough, Ehri, Olson, & Fowler, 1998). Information about language structure is often overlooked in teacher preparation, at least partly because some teacher educators themselves lack this knowledge (Joshi et al., 2009). However, Dr. Jackson was knowledgeable about language structure, which enabled her to recognize that this area needed increased attention in course instruction.

Encouragingly, research suggests that when teachers are explicitly taught language structure, they learn it (Brady et al., 2009; Spear-Swerling, 2009). Furthermore, improvements in teacher knowledge can contribute to better reading progress in students (Spear-Swerling & Brucker, 2004), whereas a lack of teacher knowledge can result in poor reading progress even when a research-based intervention is used (Piasta, Connor, Fishman, & Morrison, 2009). In other words, teacher knowledge and effective interventions are *both* important; the use of SL approaches does not eliminate the need for knowledgeable teachers.

All teachers of reading should have a strong grasp of language structure, and for teachers to implement SL approaches effectively, knowledge about the structure of language is essential—hence this chapter, which provides a foundation for subsequent chapters on assessment and intervention. Knowledge of language structure at multiple levels—words, sentences, discourse—is critical to meeting the needs of poor readers with different profiles, so the chapter addresses each of these levels. Opportunities to practice analyzing language structure are important to learning this content, so the organization of the chapter departs slightly from that of other chapters, with practice exercises interspersed in the text and answers to those exercises at the end, in lieu of the usual application exercises. In addition, a full Teacher Knowledge Survey that assesses all of the content explained in this chapter, with an answer key, is available as an online supplement to this book (see the box at the end of the table of contents). Still, the discussion of individual topics is necessarily brief, and some important topics are omitted here, such as spelling generalizations. For in-depth coverage of language structure at all levels, including spelling, see Moats (2020). Other helpful resources on language structure include Hennessey (2021), Henry (2010), and Oakhill and colleagues (2015).

First, **an important distinction** involves what teachers need to know and what students need to know. All of the content of this chapter is important for SL teachers to know. Furthermore, some of the content also is important to teach to students, such as common grapheme–phoneme correspondences and common morphemes at the word level, or text structure at the discourse level. However, not everything discussed here is necessary or even desirable to teach students. For instance, teachers need to recognize irregularities in words, so that they can choose appropriate examples of words for instruction, analyze students' errors correctly, and provide helpful feedback to errors. Students do not necessarily need to analyze or explain irregularities in words; they just need to be able to read and spell the words. Likewise, linguistic terms such as *consonant digraph* or *center-embedded syntax* are important for teachers to understand because of their implications for assessment and instruction, but students do not necessarily need to know or be able to define these terms.

Different SL approaches vary in the extent to which they teach linguistic terminology and concepts to students, and having a shared vocabulary of some terms can be useful. The key point is that SL instruction should emphasize actual reading, spelling, and writing tasks, not tasks peripheral to reading (Fletcher et al., 2019). For example, if syllable types are taught to students, the focus should be on having the students apply knowledge about syllable types to read unfamiliar words, not recite definitions of syllable types.

Word-Level Language Structure

Some Basic Terminology

Let's begin with a review of some basic terms relevant to understanding English language structure at the word level.

A **phoneme** is the smallest unit of sound in a language, with sounds represented using forward slashes; /s/ refers to the sound heard at the beginning of the word *sun*, not to the name of the letter *s*. *Sun* has two additional phonemes, short /u/ and /n/. The number of phonemes is not necessarily the same as the number of letters in a word; *fish* has three phonemes, /f/, short /i/, and /sh/, but four letters. Also, both *sun* and *fish* are transparent words, words whose spellings make their underlying phonemic structure apparent. Other words are less transparent, such as *six*, which might seem to have three phonemes but actually has four: /s/, short /i/, /k/, and /s/.

A **grapheme** is the letter or letter pattern corresponding to a phoneme. For instance, the most common grapheme for /f/ is the letter *f*, but /f/ can also be represented by other letter patterns, including *ff* (*staff*, *puff*) and *ph* (*phone*). Vowel phonemes in particular can be associated with multiple graphemes. The sound for long /a/ can be represented by *a* (*table*), *ai* (*rain*), *ay* (*play*), *a*-consonant-*e* (*take*, *made*, *flame*), and *ei* (*veil*), among others. This characteristic of English can make learning to spell very challenging, especially for poor readers.

A **morpheme** is the smallest unit of meaning in a language, which includes not only free morphemes, individual words that can stand alone (e.g., *wood*, *fast*, *sun*, *look*, *wise*, *read*), but also bound morphemes, that is, meaning units that are always a part of a longer word (e.g., *-en* in *wooden*, *-er* in *faster*, *-y* in *sunny*, *-ed* and *-ing* in *looked* and *looking*, *un-* in *unwise*, *re-* in *reread*). The *-ed* in *looked* conveys meaning because it indicates that the looking happened in the past, and the *-y* in *sunny* changes the word from a noun to an adjective, indicating a describing word related to *sun*. Just as the number of phonemes in a word is not necessarily equal to the number of letters, the number of morphemes is not necessarily the same as the number of syllables; *breakable* has three syllables but two morphemes, the base word *break* and the suffix *-able*, which makes it an adjective.

Words can be transparent in relation to their morphemic as well as phonemic structure. The examples just provided involve transparent words, but other words are less transparent, such as *kept*. *Kept* is an irregular past tense of *keep* and involves two morphemes, the base word *keep* and the past tense ending, here *-t* instead of *-ed*, with spelling changes to the base word. As students advance in reading, they must be able to recognize morphemes common in multisyllabic words, such as Greek- and Latin-derived roots and affixes (e.g., roots, prefixes, and suffixes in words such as *astronomy*, *prediction*, *auditory*, *manufacture*, *psychologist*). To be a morpheme, a letter pattern must convey the appropriate meaning in the context of the word. The *car* in *carpool* is a morpheme because a *carpool* involves a pool of cars. However, the *car* in *carpet* is not a morpheme because a carpet is not a car for your pet or a pet for your car.

Vowel letters are *a, e, i, o, u*, and sometimes *y*. **Consonant letters** are any letter that is not a vowel, for example, *b, c, d, f, g, h, j, k*, and so on. **Y is a consonant when it is the first letter of a syllable** (e.g., *yellow, yes, yard, backyard*, both *y*'s in *yoyo*), where it has the sound /y/ as heard in these words. **Everywhere else, *y* is a vowel** (e.g., *type, fly, gym, tryst, sunny, windy*), where it has one of three sounds: short /i/ as in *gym*, long /i/ as in *type*, or long /e/ when it is an ending, as in *sunny*.

Consonant digraphs are consonant combinations in which the letter pattern takes a new sound, not the sound of the individual letters comprising it. For example, the consonant digraph *sh*, as in *shop*, does not represent a combination of the phonemes /s/ and /h/, but rather relates to an entirely different phoneme, /sh/. Common digraphs include not only *sh* but also *ch* (*chip, chat*), *th* (unvoiced as in *bath*, and voiced as in *then*), *-ck* (*stick, rock*), and *ph* (*graph, phone*).

Consonant blends are consonant combinations in which the letter pattern retains the sound of its constituent letters—such as *sp* (*spend, spill, grasp*); *sl* (*slip, slant*); *str* (*stress, strap*); *fl* (*flop, fling*); *br* (*bring, brew*); *nd* (*land, end*); *mp* (*lamp, imp*); and many, many others. Students do not have to memorize sounds for individual blends as they must with digraphs. Rather, they can pronounce the sounds associated with each letter and blend them together.

A **schwa sound** is an unaccented vowel sound, similar to a brief short /u/ or short /i/, often found in the unaccented syllables of long words. Examples of schwas include the phonemes associated with the *e* in *carpet*, the *a* in *along*, the second syllable of *candle*, and the *o* in *bishop*. Schwas can cause difficulties for students in blending the syllables of multisyllabic words they are trying to decode, as will be discussed later in this chapter.

In spelling, schwa sounds can be represented by many possible vowel spellings. Therefore, students often must have some familiarity with the printed word in order to know how to spell that part of the word. For instance, the schwa sound in the second syllable of *bishop* could be spelled with an *i*, *e*, or *u* rather than an *o* (e.g., *biship*, *bishep*, *bishup*). In this case, the student cannot hear that the second vowel sound is spelled with an *o*, nor is there a phonics rule to tell the correct letter to use; the student simply has to have some familiarity with the printed word to know the correct spelling of this part of the word. For some words, such as the *competition* example given at the outset of this chapter, morphology can also be very useful in facilitating correct spelling of a word.

Common Grapheme–Phoneme Correspondences

Common grapheme–phoneme relationships in English are shown in Figure 2.1, with a sample word illustrating each correspondence. The figure lists only the most common correspondences for one-syllable words. Many of these correspondences are taught to typical readers in grades K–2, and most or all would be explicitly taught as part of SL approaches, including to poor decoders beyond grade 2 who do not know them.

Here are a few important points to note about Figure 2.1. First, some graphemes are associated with more than one phoneme. Sometimes a rule can help to determine the correct phoneme associated with the letter or letter pattern in a given word, as explained below for the letters *c* and *g*. Often, however, there is no consistent rule, and the student has to try alternative pronunciations to see which one produces a recognizable word. For instance, *ow* can be associated with /ow/, as in *cow*, or long /o/, as in *crow*. Suppose that beginning readers are trying to decode the unknown word *growl*. In SL approaches, they would be taught to try both pronunciations—long /o/, to rhyme with *bowl*, or /ow/, to rhyme with *howl*, the correct pronunciation. Students need to be sufficiently familiar with the spoken word to recognize the correct choice when they produce it, and they also need to be flexible in trying alternative pronunciations of a word.

Figure 2.1 groups the letter pattern *qu* with consonant digraphs because it is often taught at the same time as those patterns. But *qu* is best viewed as an oddity (Moats, 2020), not a digraph, because it is associated with the pronunciation /kw/ rather than with a single sound. The most important thing for students is simply to know the grapheme–phoneme relationship and to be able to apply it in reading and spelling words.

Conversely, the letter pattern *-ng*, as in *bring*, *sang*, *lung*, and so on, is a digraph, but in SL approaches, it is often taught as a combined letter pattern with the short vowels *ang*, *ing*, *ong*, *ung*. (The pattern *-eng* is usually omitted because of its rarity in one-syllable words.) These patterns sometimes are termed "welded" sounds (e.g., Wilson, 2018). Similarly, the pattern *-nk*, as in *sank*, *sink*, *wonk*, and *dunk*, which involves a blend of the digraph /ng/ and the phoneme /k/ but is spelled *-nk*, is usually taught as a combined pattern with each short vowel: *ank*, *ink*, *onk*, *unk*. The rationale

Single Letters

Single Consonants

b (/b/, *ball*)   c (/k/, *cat*, OR /s/, *cent*)
d (/d/, *dog*)   g (/g/, *go*, OR /j/, *giant*)
f (/f/, *farm*)   s (/s/, *sun*, OR /z/, *nose*)
h (/h/, *hot*)
j (/j/, *jet*)   Vowels (short and long
k (/k/, *king*)   [says name]*)
l (/l/, *lip*)
m (/m/, *mat*)   a (short /a/, *apple*; long /a/, *ape*)
n (/n/, *nut*)   e (short /e/, *egg*; long /e/, *eel*)
p (/p/, *pin*)   i (short /i/, *igloo*; long /i/, *ice*)
r (/r/, *rose*)   o (short /o/, *octopus*; long /o/,
t (/t/, *ten*)   *open*)
v (/v/, *van*)   u (short /u/, *umbrella*; long /u/,
w (/w/, *wig*)   *use*)
x (/ks/, *fox*)   y (same as short/long *i*, *gym*,
y (/y/, *yes*)   *type*)
z (/z/, *zip*)

Some Common Letter Patterns

Consonant Digraphs	Vowel Teams
sh (/sh/, *ship*)	ai (long *a*, *rain*)
ch (/ch/, *chop*)	ay (long *a*, *play*)
th (/th/, *them* OR	aw (/aw/, *draw*)
thick)**	ee (long *e*, *see*)
ck (/k/, *rock*)	ea (long *e*, *eat*;
qu (/kw/, *queen*)	short *e*, *bread*; OR
	long *a*, *steak*)
	ie (long *i*, *pie* OR
Vowel r	long *e*, *piece*)
ar (/ar/, *bark*)	igh (long *i*, *light*)
er (/er/, *her*)	oa (long *o*, *boat*)
ir (/er/, *bird*)	oy, oi (both /oy/, *boy*, *spoil*)
ur (/er/, *turn*)	oo (/oo/ as in *boot* OR /oo/
or (/or/, *fork*)	as in *foot*)
	ow (/ow/ as in *cow* OR long
	o, *snow*)
	ew, ue (both /oo/, *grew*, *true*)

Welded***	Common Suffixes
ang (/ang/, *sang*)	-es (/iz/, *dishes*)
ing (/ing/, *bring*)	-ing (/ing/, *jumping*)
ong (/ong/, *long*)	-ed (/id/, /d/, OR /t/, *ended*,
ung (/ung/, *lung*)	*fanned*, *jumped*)
	-y (long *e* as in *funny*)
	-ly (/le/, *sadly*)

*Long vowel sounds are the same as the letter name, except that long /u/ can correspond to two sounds: not only its name, /yoo/ as in *use*, but also /oo/ as in *tube*.

**The letter pattern *th* corresponds to two phonemes: voiced /th/, the sound heard in *them*, made with the vocal cords as well as the lips and tongue; and unvoiced /th/, the sound heard in *thick*, made similarly to voiced /th/ in relation to the lips and tongue, but without use of the vocal cords.

***These welded sounds (e.g., Wilson, 2018) involve more than one phoneme but are often taught as a single unit because of the challenges for many children in blending the vowel with the consonant digraph, *-ng* (/ng/), that follows it. Although not shown in the figure, *-ank* (as in *sank*), *-ink* (as in *think*), *-onk* (as in *bonk*), and *-unk* (as in *dunk*) are often also taught as units for similar reasons. (Because they are rare in one-syllable words, *-eng* and *-enk* are frequently omitted.)

FIGURE 2.1. Some common grapheme–phoneme correspondences in English.

for teaching these larger letter patterns is that it is often difficult for students to blend the short vowel with the /ng/ or the /ng/ plus /k/. Importantly, the *-ng* pattern does *not* represent a blend of the phonemes /n/ and /g/, as Dr. Jackson's master's candidate was teaching it, but rather is one sound, produced in the back of the throat (Moats, 2020). Likewise, *-nk* is not a blend of the phonemes /n/ and /k/.

PRACTICE EXERCISE: *Phoneme Counting and Morpheme Counting*

Before proceeding further, a practice exercise involving phonemes and morphemes, shown in Figure 2.2, may be helpful for readers to check their understanding. See the end of the chapter for answers to all practice exercises.

Part 1. Phoneme counting. Specify the number of phonemes in each of the following words. Then specify the *first* and *last* phoneme in each word. If a word seems difficult, try pronouncing it in front of a mirror to help you detect individual phonemes.

Example: cash—three phonemes; first = /k/, last = /s/

1.	flop	8.	thigh
2.	cheat	9.	tube
3.	time	10.	fuse
4.	pay	11.	bring
5.	groan	12.	brink
6.	inch	13.	ox
7.	splint	14.	poodle

Part 2. Morpheme counting. Specify the number of morphemes in each of the following words. Then specify the *first* and *last* morpheme in each word.

Example: brushed—two morphemes, *brush* + *-ed*; first = *brush*, last = *-ed*

1.	taller	8.	interplanetary
2.	unlikely	9.	tastiest
3.	rereading	10.	bent
4.	untruthfulness	11.	target
5.	watercolors	12.	disruptive
6.	softener	13.	astronomers
7.	bedroom	14.	butter

FIGURE 2.2. Practice Exercise: Counting phonemes and morphemes.

Readers may find the second column of items in both the phoneme counting and morpheme counting exercise more difficult than the first column. This is because the items in the first column are more transparent than the items in the second column.

Syllable Types

One especially challenging aspect of English for beginning readers involves its variability in grapheme–phoneme relationships for vowels. Unlike more transparent languages such as Spanish, in which a vowel letter usually has a consistent sound across words (e.g., the Spanish vowel *a* in *taco*, *tamale*, *habla*, and *adios*), in English, the phonemes associated with a particular vowel letter vary depending on the position of the vowel in the word and the other letters surrounding it. Syllable types can be a helpful way for students to determine the vowel sound of an unfamiliar one-syllable word. They are frequently, though not universally, taught as part of SL approaches. Table 2.1 lists the most commonly taught syllable types for one-syllable words, along with a concise definition of each syllable type, its vowel sound, some sample words, and some additional comments about each syllable type.

As shown, commonly taught syllable types are **closed, silent *e*, open, vowel *r* (VR), vowel team (VT),** and **consonant -*le* (-*cle*).** Closed syllables have a short vowel, whereas silent e and open syllables each have long vowels. Consonant-*le* syllables have a schwa sound.

TABLE 2.1. Syllable Types Chart

Syllable type (synonyms)	Definition	Vowel sound	Examples	Comments
Closed	Has only one vowel and ends in a consonant	Short	*mat, blast, scratch; in, stick, flip; hot, crop, pond; pet, end, deck; slush, up, rust*	This syllable type is usually the first one taught to children; syllables that fit the definition of closed but do not have a short vowel (e.g., VR) must be filtered out at this early stage.
Silent *e* (SE; magic *e*)	Has a -VC*e* pattern (one vowel, followed by one consonant, followed by a silent *e* that ends the syllable)	Long	*ate, take, flame; ice, stride, fine; note, choke, throne; theme, eke; rude, flute, use*	Words with a -VVC*e* pattern (e.g., *cruise*) or -VCC*e* pattern (e.g., *chance*) are not classified as silent *e* and do not have a long vowel sound.
Open	Has only one vowel that is the last letter of the syllable	Long	*hi, go, so, she, he, me, flu, fly, by, try*	This syllable type becomes especially useful as children progress to two-syllable words. For example, the *bu* in *bugle*, *na* in *nation*, and *ra* in *raven* are all open syllables.
Vowel team (VT)	Contains a VT (e.g., *ay, ai, aw, igh, ow, oo, ee, ew*)	Takes sound of VT unit	*aim, stay, draw; night, tie; foot, own, throat; seal, sheep, flew; true, Sue*	If a VT is associated with more than one sound (e.g., *ow, ie*), students must try each sound to see which one produces a recognizable word.
Vowel *r* (VR; bossy *r*, *r*-controlled)	Has only one vowel, followed immediately by the letter *r*	Takes sound of VR unit	*art, farm, hard; fork, short, born; stir, irk, first; herd, term; churn, lurk, hurt*	Words with a -*vre* pattern (e.g., *share, fire, cure*) or VT + *r* (e.g., *fear, cheer, board*) should not be included in this category and can often be decoded by children as SE or VT, respectively.
Consonant-*le*	Has a consonant-*le* pattern (a consonant, followed by an *l*, followed by an *e*, which ends the syllable)	Schwa	The -*ble* in *fable*; the -*zle* in *drizzle*; the -*tle* in *turtle*; the -*fle* in *rifle*	These syllables are always part of a longer word and are never accented; they are usually the last syllable type that is taught.

For VR and VT syllables, children need to be taught the VR and VT letter patterns, such as those shown in the right-hand columns of Figure 2.1, as well as their corresponding sounds. To identify the syllable type, students simply look for these patterns in words, then apply the sounds to read the words. Words with VR patterns—such as *ar*, *er*, *ir*, *ur*, *or*—do not have a short sound as in a closed syllable, but rather the sound of the VR pattern; therefore, teachers must filter out these words from phonics activities involving closed syllables until students reach the point in an instructional sequence where they can differentiate VR from closed.

Several common vowel patterns do not involve two or more vowels but can still be taught in a similar manner to VT syllables. These patterns include *all* (as in *fall*, *tall*, *ball*); *alt* (as in *salt*, *halt*, *malt*); *ind* (as in *find*, *mind*, *bind*); and *old* (as in *bold*, *cold*, *mold*). Students can learn sounds for these letter patterns just as they learn VT and VR patterns, then learn to recognize and read them in words.

In determining syllable types, if a word has *qu* in it, do not count the *u* that is part of this pattern as a vowel because the *u* does not function as a vowel in this context. The word *quit*, for instance, has only one vowel, *i*; the *u* does not count because it is part of the *qu* pattern. *Quit* also ends in a consonant, so it is a closed syllable, and the *i* has a short sound. Likewise, the word *quite* has a -VCe (not a -VVCe) pattern, making it a silent e syllable, with a long /i/.

A Generalization for the Letters *C* and *G*

A helpful rule exists for determining the correct sound for *c* (/k/ or /s/) and for *g* (/g/ or /j/). These sets of sounds are often termed "hard" and "soft," but students do not necessarily have to know this terminology; they just need to know which sound to try first for each letter. The generalization is that when the letter *c* (or *g*) is followed by the letters *e*, *i*, or *y*, it is pronounced /s/ (or /j/ in the case of *g*). Otherwise, it is pronounced /k/ (or /g/ for *g*). For *c*, examples of words with the pronunciation /s/ are *cent*, *cell*, *city*, *cyst*, *place*, and *icy*. Examples in which *c* takes the /k/ sound, because the letter *c* is not followed by *e*, *i*, or *y*, include *cup*, *cool*, *cab*, *clip*, and *crumb*. For *g*, comparable examples for the /j/ pronunciation are *gem*, *giant*, *gel*, *page*, and *gym*; and for the sound /g/, examples of words are *gap*, *gull*, *go*, *glib*, and *grasp*.

There are a number of common exceptions to the rule for *g-* words such as *gift* and *get*, in which the *g* is followed by an *e*, *i*, or *y*, and therefore should be associated with /j/ but is not. However, the rule is still useful for many words. This is especially true as students advance to silent-*e* words (e.g., words such as *ice*, *twice*, *rice*, *pace*, *place*, *race*, *age*, *page*, *stage*, *rage*, *cage*, *huge*) and beyond, to long words.

PRACTICE EXERCISE: *Syllable Types and Words with C or G*

Figure 2.3 presents another practice exercise for readers to check their understanding. This exercise uses nonsense words because the goal is for readers to classify each word by using knowledge of syllable types, not by reading the words first. However, real

Part 1. Classify each of the nonsense words below by syllable type, using the syllable types shown in Table 2.1. For each item, also provide a sample real word with the same vowel sound.

Example 1: clisp—closed syllable; sample real words with the same vowel sound (short *i*): *lisp*, *wisp*, *clip*, *in*, *sit*

Example 2: shrow—vowel team; the vowel sound could be either /ow/ OR long /o/: sample real words are *cow*, *brow*, *growl*, *crowd*, OR *show*, *flow*, *grown*, *bowl*

1. flawn
2. garp
3. bime
4. -zle (end of a longer word)
5. thrink
6. sho
7. drace

8. cly (one-syllable word, not the end of a longer word)
9. quift
10. thork
11. cyll
12. gu
13. yeef
14. troin

Part 2. For each word above containing the letter *c* or *g* (#2, 7, 8, 11, and 12), tell the sound you would expect the letter to have (/s/ or /k/ for *c*, and /j/ or /g/ for *g*).

FIGURE 2.3. Practice Exercise: Syllable types and words with *c* or *g*.

words should generally be used with students, with an emphasis on real words that students do not already know how to read.

In the practice exercise, to check readers' knowledge of the vowel sound and pronunciation of each word, readers also are asked to give a sample real word with the same vowel sound as the nonsense word. For example, the nonsense word *glame* should be classified as a silent-*e* word, which then means it has a long vowel sound—long /a/ as in *tame*, *same*, *ape*, *cave*, *made*, and many other words. A second step of the exercise asks readers to determine, for words containing a *c* or *g*, which sound these letters will have, using the relevant rule given earlier.

Phonetically Irregular Words

Irregular words are words that are not pronounced as expected according to the usual grapheme–phoneme relationships or phonics generalizations that apply for most words. Teachers need to recognize irregular words because of their implications for assessment and instruction; for instance, they are not good examples to use in phonics activities, and they often require different feedback when students read them incorrectly. To determine whether a given word is irregular, try to read it using the common grapheme–phoneme relationships and phonics rules discussed in this chapter; if that does not yield the correct word, then classify it as irregular.

Examples of **phonetically irregular words** are as follows:

- *done* (a silent-*e* pattern, should be pronounced to rhyme with *bone*—but it is not pronounced as expected, so it is irregular)
- *two* (an open pattern, should be pronounced to rhyme with *go*; also, the *w* should not be silent but rather should be pronounced as in *twin*—so the word is irregular)

- *what* (a closed pattern, should be pronounced to rhyme with *cat*, but the vowel is not pronounced as expected, so the word is irregular)
- *girl* (the *g* should say /j/ not /g/ here, so the word is irregular)
- *people* (has a silent *o* in the middle of the word that is unexpected and not part of a vowel team or other common letter pattern; therefore, the word is irregular)

Examples of **phonetically regular words** include:

- *boy* (a vowel team word that is pronounced as expected based on typical grapheme–phoneme relationships—therefore, it is regular)
- *at* (a closed syllable with a short /a/ that is pronounced as expected, a regular word)
- *make* (a silent-*e* word, again regular, because it is pronounced as expected, with a long /a/ and silent *e*)
- *knife* and *write* (both silent-*e* syllables pronounced as expected; *kn* and *wr* are stable patterns expected to have a silent *k* and silent *w*, respectively, so the words are regular)
- *wood* (a vowel team syllable in which the *oo* vowel team has one of its two expected sounds [see Figure 2.1], so this is a regular word)

Irregular words are not synonymous with sight words. Sight words are common words that teachers often have children practice to the point of automaticity, to facilitate fluency of text reading. However, many common words are not phonetically irregular, as illustrated by the regular word examples *boy*, *at*, and *make* given earlier. Also, as the examples of irregular words show, many irregular words are only irregular in relation to part of the word, often the vowel. Therefore, phonics knowledge remains relevant for these words. For instance, all of the letters in *people* have their expected sounds, except for the silent *o*.

Language Structure for Long Words

To read long words, those of two or more syllables, strategies for breaking the words into manageable parts are necessary. Many teachers of struggling readers have seen students who can decode one-syllable words with reasonable accuracy, but who make wild guesses based on the first few letters of a long word because they do not have a good strategy for approaching the word. Difficulties reading long words despite adequate basic phonics skills are common in poor readers in the middle elementary and later grades (Hiebert, 2022; Kearns et al., 2022).

Generalizations for syllabicating long words are one helpful strategy for breaking a long word into manageable parts, especially for two-syllable words. Morphology also is very valuable in multiple ways. Other important considerations for reading long words include the need to be flexible (Kearns et al., 2022); dealing with accent patterns and schwa; and etymology. Each of these areas is addressed further below.

Generalizations for Syllabicating Two-Syllable Words

Generalizations for syllabicating two-syllable words involve looking for specific letter patterns in printed words, then dividing the word using the generalization and pronouncing each syllable. Here are five useful generalizations for syllabication.

1. **Look for compounds.** In a compound word (e.g., *bedroom*, *aircraft*, *football*), divide between the two smaller words: bed / room, air / craft, foot / ball.

2. **Divide immediately before -*cle*.** If a word ends in a -*cle* syllable (*bundle*, *staple*, *gargle*, *ruble*), divide immediately before the -*cle*, for example, bun / dle, sta / ple, gar / gle, ru / ble. To read these words correctly, the -*cle* syllable must be kept together as a unit, especially if the first syllable is open. For instance, *staple* divided after the *p* yields stap / le, with a short /a/, not the correct pronunciation of the word.

3. **Look for VCCV patterns.** If a two-syllable word has a vowel–consonant–consonant–vowel (VCCV) pattern, divide between the two consonants. Examples of VCCV words include *tennis*, *hornet*, *magnet*, and *garden*. These words are divided as follows: ten / nis, hor / net, mag / net, and gar / den. The two consonants in the VCCV pattern do not have to be the same letters. Also, if the two consonants in the VCCV pattern form a consonant digraph, as in *bishop*, *gopher*, and *rather*, treat the word as VCV, not VCCV—see #4 below.

4. **Look for VCV patterns.** If a two-syllable word has a vowel–consonant–vowel (VCV) pattern, with just one consonant between two vowels, divide first before the consonant, and see if that yields a pronunciation that is a real word; if not, try dividing after the consonant. Examples of VCV words include *comet*, *fever*, *humid*, and *second*. For instance, the VCV pattern in *comet* is *ome*. First, divide before the *m*: co / met. This yields an open syllable with a long *o* for the first syllable, pronounced like coh-met, not a real word. Next, try dividing after the *m*: com / et. Now the first syllable is closed, with a short vowel, which is the correct word. The other examples would be divided this way: fe / ver, hu / mid, sec / ond.

Words with a consonant digraph between two vowels—*bishop*, *gopher*, *rather*—are treated as VCV because they have just one consonant sound between two vowels, even though it takes two letters to form the consonant sound. Therefore, *bishop* would be divided as bish / op, not bis / hop. Divide gopher as go / pher, and rather as rath / er.

As is true for VT words in which the VT may have more than one sound, to read VCV words correctly, students have to be flexible in applying possible pronunciations of the word, and they need to have some oral familiarity with the word to recognize the correct pronunciation.

5. **Divide immediately after a prefix and before a suffix.** Letters in affixes are generally kept together as a unit. So two-syllable words with affixes, such as *dislike*, *statement*, *predict*, and *lotion*, would be divided this way: dis / like, state / ment, pre / dict, lo / tion.

Although these generalizations can apply to words of three or more syllables as well as two-syllable words, syllable division in very long words is often fluid and ambiguous. For many of these words, morphology may be more helpful than syllabication strategies.

Morphology and Long Words

Knowledge about morphology is valuable not only for reading words but also for spelling and understanding them. Roots and affixes involving long words of Latin and Greek derivation are particularly common in an academic context. For example, many words of Greek derivation occur in science and math (e.g., *hemisphere, chemistry, psychology*). Latin-derived words have a root word, one that cannot stand alone, with one or more affixes. Examples of such words include *disrupt* (dis + rupt); *inscription* (in + script + ion); *incredibly* (in + cred + ible + y); *submergence* (sub + merge + ence); and many others. Morphemes from Greek-derived words do not necessarily have clear roles as roots or affixes (Moats, 2020) but still carry meaning and recur across many semantically related words (e.g., the morpheme *tele*, which means from a distance, in *telephone, telegraph, television, telecommunications, telecast*, and so on).

As the examples illustrate, although there may be some spelling changes when roots and affixes are combined, the spellings of affixes and roots are relatively stable across related words. Therefore, in spelling an unfamiliar word such as *telegraph*, a student who understands this stability and is familiar with the morpheme *tele* knows that the beginning of the word will likely be spelled *tele*, not *teli* or *tela* or *telu*. Because roots and affixes convey meaning (e.g., *rupt* means *break*, *cred* means *believe*, *sub* means *under*), learning about morphology also can help students understand a wide network of semantically related words. Table 2.2 provides a few examples of long words with common Latin- or Greek-derived morphemes, along with the meanings of the morphemes and examples of related words or words with shared roots (e.g., *dict*, *rupt*). For much more detail about common morphemes in Latin- and Greek-derived words, see Moats (2020) and Henry (2010).

Some letter patterns have distinctive sounds in Latin- or Greek-derived words. For instance, the *ch* in the Latin-derived words *chemistry, chorus*, and *chloroform* is associated with the phoneme /k/ rather than /ch/; in Greek-derived words, the initial *p* in the letter patterns *pn* or *ps* (e.g., *pneumonia, pneumatic, psychology, psyche*) is silent. When students are learning to read or spell these words, explicit teaching of these patterns in the context of specific words is helpful.

Accent Patterns, Schwa, and Increased Need for Flexibility

To read long words, students must not only read their individual parts but also put the parts back together to form a recognizable word. One aspect of English that complicates this task of synthesizing parts into a whole word is that English words put greater stress, or accent, on one syllable of a long word than other syllables, and the unaccented syllables often have a schwa sound. Furthermore, which syllable is stressed

TABLE 2.2. Examples of Words with Common Latin- or Greek-Derived Morphemes

Sample word (language)	Morphemes[a]	Examples of semantically related words and words with shared morphemes
mortality (Latin)	*mor, mort* (meaning = death) + *al* (suffix) + *ity* (suffix)	mortal, immortal, immortality, mortician, mortuary, postmortem, moribund
transportability (Latin)	*trans* (prefix, meaning = across) + *port* (meaning = carry) + *ability* (suffix)	transport, transportation, import, importation, export, exportation, porter, portable, importable, exportable
incredible (Latin)	*in* (prefix, meaning = not) + *cred* (meaning = belief) + *ible* (suffix)	credible, credibility, credulous, incredulous, incredulity, credit, creditor, discredit, discredited
interruption (Latin)	*inter* (prefix, meaning = between, among) + *rupt* (meaning = break) + *ion* (suffix)	interrupt, rupture, erupt, eruption, corrupt, corruption, corruptly, corruptible, incorruptible
predictable (Latin)	*pre* (prefix, meaning = before) + *dict* (meaning = say) + *able* (suffix)	predict, unpredictable, unpredictability, predictability, predictive, predictably, edict, dictation, contradict, contradictory
psychology (Greek)	*psych* (meaning = mind) + *ology* (meaning = the study of)	psychologist, psychological, psychiatrist, psychiatric, psyche, psychopath, neuropsychology, neuropsychological
thermal (Greek)	*therm* (meaning = heat) + *al* (suffix)	thermometer, thermostat, thermos, thermodynamics, geotherm, geothermal
biographer (Greek)	*bio* (meaning = life) + *graph* (meaning = write) + *er* (suffix)	biography, biographical, biology, biological, biologist, biome, neurobiology, biopsychology, biochemist, biodegradable, grapheme, graphology

[a]The suffixes shown here, called derivational suffixes, frequently change the part of speech of a word—for example, from a noun to an adjective or from an adjective to an adverb.

can be unpredictable. The same word can sound quite different depending on where the stress is placed.

Consider a word such as *canopy*. The stress is on the first syllable of this word, with the second syllable reduced to a schwa: CAN-up-ee. However, the word could just as plausibly be read with the accent on the second syllable: cuh-NOP-ee. There is no rule to tell readers who are unfamiliar with the printed word which syllable is stressed; readers must simply try different ways of reading the word to see which one produces a recognizable word. Even in semantically related words, sometimes there are shifts in accent patterns. In the word *invite*, the accent falls on the second syllable—in-VITE—but *invitation* is in-vuh-TA-shun, not in-VITE-uh-shun.

This situation is similar to the one discussed previously for VT words and VCV words, and highlights the need to be flexible in trying different pronunciations of long words. Students also must have some familiarity with the spoken word in order to recognize the correct version when they have produced it (Kearns et al., 2022), and they often must have some familiarity with the printed word in order to spell it correctly. To spell *invitation* correctly, morphology—knowledge that the root word is *invite*—can help in spelling the word. However, to spell the schwa vowel in *canopy*, students simply must be familiar with the printed word.

> **PRACTICE EXERCISE:** *Irregular Words and Knowledge about Long Words*
>
> Figure 2.4 involves another practice exercise for readers to check their understanding of phonetically irregular words as well as long words, with answers at the end of this chapter.

Etymology

Etymology refers to the history and origin of a word. In addition to Anglo-Saxon words, modern English has many words borrowed from other languages, not only Latin and Greek, but also Spanish, French, Italian, and other languages. Often, when a word has been borrowed from another language, the English word retains at least part of the spelling and pronunciation of the word in the original language. Therefore, understanding the etymology of a word can be very helpful to reading and spelling it,

---

Part 1. Identify which of the words below are phonetically irregular, based on the generalizations discussed in this chapter. There are six irregular words.

1. too	6. broad	11. blue
2. go	7. wrap	12. three
3. pretty	8. great	13. gone
4. only	9. pond	14. who
5. quest	10. friend	15. will

Part 2. Divide each of the following two-syllable words using one of the five syllable division rules. Indicate which rule applies to the word.

Example: *mutton*, mut / ton, VCCV

1. preview	6. spotlight
2. cupcake	7. travel
3. Bible	8. igloo
4. wither	9. noodle
5. capture	10. arise

Part 3. Divide each of the following multisyllabic words using morphology. Decide where the accent falls, and locate any schwa vowels.

Example: *portable*, port / able; accent—first syllable; schwa vowels—second and third syllables

1. indestructible
2. postmortem
3. biographical
4. geothermal
5. reactive

FIGURE 2.4. Practice Exercise: Irregular words and knowledge about long words.

which is why in spelling competitions, contestants often ask for the language of origin of words.

For example, in common one-syllable words, usually of Anglo-Saxon origin, the letter pattern *qu* typically is associated with the sound /kw/, as in *quick, queen,* and *quit.* However, consider *qu* when it is part of an *-ique* pattern in a long word: *antique, boutique, mystique, Monique.* Here, the pattern is not associated with /kw/, but rather with /eek/, because these are all words of French origin. As another example, in words of Spanish origin, when two vowels come together, each vowel is typically heard, so words such as *fiesta, siesta,* and *sierra* are not pronounced feesta, seesta, and seera, as they might be in English; they retain part of their Spanish pronunciation.

Readers do not need to know letter sounds in all languages in order to read well in English. However, it is useful for students to understand the relevance of etymology, especially at more advanced stages of word reading. If teachers draw students' attention to word origins and explain why certain words are pronounced or spelled in unusual ways—not as they would be in English—that knowledge can assist students in learning to read and spell those words. Knowledge about etymology can help build students' vocabularies as well.

Sentence Structure (Syntax)

Sentence structure is an important building block of literacy (Hennessey, 2021). Syntactic weaknesses can directly affect students' listening and reading comprehension, as well as their ability to produce correct sentences. Here is a brief overview of different sentence structures in English, followed by examples of potentially challenging syntax in reading and common sentence structure errors in students' writing.

Different Types of Sentences

First, let's review some key terms: an **independent clause** is a group of words with a subject and a verb, one that conveys a complete thought and can stand alone (e.g., *Mary went to the store*). A **dependent clause** also has a subject and a verb but cannot stand alone (e.g., *Because she needed milk*). Within sentences, clauses are often connected by different types of conjunctions, including coordinating conjunctions and subordinating conjunctions. The most common **coordinating conjunctions**, which link independent clauses, can be remembered with the mnemonic FANBOYS: *for, and, nor, but, or, yet,* and *so.* **Subordinating conjunctions** link a dependent clause to an independent clause, adding information—for instance, about time, place, or cause and effect—to the main idea of a sentence. Subordinating conjunctions are numerous, but some frequently used ones include *because, although, as, that, which, who, if, when, whenever, unless, since, until, where, wherever, whereas, before,* and *after.*

Table 2.3 lists four sentence types, with some examples of each. As illustrated, simple sentences have one independent clause. Compound sentences have two or more independent clauses connected by a coordinating conjunction. Complex sentences have

TABLE 2.3. Four Sentence Types

Sentence type	Description	Examples[a]
Simple	Has one independent clause	<u>Lola loves to eat pancakes with syrup.</u> <u>John and Mary traveled to England.</u> <u>The red sports car sped down the highway.</u>
Compound	Has two or more independent clauses, connected by a coordinating conjunction (e.g., *but, or, and, so, yet*)	<u>Lola loves to eat pancakes with syrup,</u> but <u>she hates broccoli.</u> <u>Mrs. Murphy grows all kinds of vegetables,</u> and <u>she is an excellent gardener.</u>
Complex	Has an independent clause and at least one dependent clause, with a subordinating conjunction	*After the sun set,* <u>the enemy forces began massing at the border.</u> <u>Mr. O'Donnell gave the students a poor grade</u> *because they did not follow the directions for the assignment.*
Compound–complex	Has two or more independent clauses and at least one dependent clause, with both a coordinating and subordinating conjunction	*As I am a vegetarian,* <u>I couldn't find anything to eat at the luncheon,</u> so <u>I went home early.</u> <u>The lifeguard,</u> *who had been briefly distracted by a fight on the beach,* <u>sprang to attention</u> *when he saw the struggling swimmer,* and <u>he jumped into the water.</u>

[a]Independent clauses are <u>underlined</u>, with dependent clauses in *italics*.

an independent clause with at least one dependent clause and a subordinating conjunction. Compound–complex sentences are a combination of the last two sentence types, with two or more independent clauses and at least one dependent clause.

Sentences That Are Potentially Confusing

Some sentences have structures that, while syntactically correct, are known to be potentially confusing (Oakhill et al., 2015; Zipoli & Merritt, 2022). Consider the difficulties that even many literate adults have in understanding a dense or lengthy legal document. Syntactic challenges are one reason that these documents tend to tax comprehension, at least for those of us who are not lawyers. Teachers who are aware of syntactically challenging sentences can better assess and address students' comprehension difficulties (Hennessey, 2021). Sentence types that may be challenging to comprehend include the following:

• **Sentences with double negatives:** Double negatives abound in legal documents, for example, *The renter may not terminate this lease under clause 15 unless the landlord has not fulfilled his or her obligations as listed under clause 11.* The double negatives *may not terminate* and *has not fulfilled* help make this sentence confusing to understand.

- **Sentences in passive voice:** An example of this kind of sentence is *The new nurse was led by the emergency physician to the hectic scene in the ambulance bay.* Because of small function words such as *by*, this sentence is more difficult to understand than one in active voice: *The emergency physician led the new nurse to the hectic scene in the ambulance bay.* The fact that the sentence is reversible—that is, the emergency physician could also be led to the ambulance bay by the new nurse—further increases the difficulty (Zipoli & Merritt, 2022).

- **Long sentences with multiple clauses and phrases:** Consider the sentence *Before leaving for school in the morning, Mary made oatmeal for breakfast, then washed all the dishes, putting the plates back in the cabinet in the kitchen and the silverware in the drawer next to the sink.* This kind of sentence makes especially heavy processing demands on working memory, worsened if a student also struggles with reading words.

- **Sentences with center-embedded syntax that separate the subject from the main verb with multiple clauses or phrases:** An example of this kind of sentence is *The IT specialist who had worked in the physics department for years with his girlfriend Monica was arrested for hacking.* In this sentence, Monica, rather than her boyfriend, might be misunderstood as the hacker because of the center-embedded dependent clause (*who had worked in the physics department for years with his girlfriend Monica*), which separates the main noun (*IT specialist*) from its verb (*was arrested*).

- **Sentences with anaphoric references (e.g., pronouns such as *he, she, it*) in which the pronoun comes before the noun it refers to, or in which the pronoun is separated from the noun by multiple clauses or phrases:** Consider this sentence: *Long before her death in the Andes last year in a catastrophic plane crash, Aunt Gertrude revised her will to exclude her greedy niece Thelma from inheriting her assets.* Sentences like this one require the reader to keep reading past the pronoun, in this case *her*, to figure out to which person *her* refers.

- **Sentences with antiquated or unusual syntax:** These sentences are common in classic literature and poetry, such as the following lines from Shakespeare's Sonnet 18: *Sometime too hot the eye of heaven shines / And often is his gold complexion dimm'd / And every fair from fair sometime declines / By chance or nature's changing course untrimm'd. . . .* In addition to the vocabulary and figurative language challenges of this kind of text, the syntactic demands are often difficult for many students.

Common Sentence Errors in Written Expression

Three types of sentence problems are common in students' writing. **Sentence fragments,** or incomplete sentences, usually involve a dependent clause standing alone, such as *Unless the check arrives in the mail sometime soon*, or *Because I really don't like to eat fish.* **Run-on sentences** involve two or more sentences run together without the appropriate conjunction or the correct punctuation: *Ronald was late for class again his professor was very annoyed*. A third type of problem involves **lack of varied sentences** in a student's writing. Students may write grammatically correct sentences, but ones that are all simple sentences, for example. Conversely, the use of many long, complex sentences makes writing less readable. Good writing usually involves varied sentences and also tries to avoid many of the potentially confusing sentence types discussed in the previous section.

PRACTICE EXERCISE: *Syntax*

Readers can check their understanding of this section using Figure 2.5, a practice exercise involving syntax.

Part 1. Identify each of the following sentences as syntactically correct or incorrect. If a sentence is correct, classify it as simple, compound, complex, or compound–complex. If a sentence is incorrect, classify it as either a run-on or sentence fragment, and provide an example of how it could be corrected. (There will always be multiple possible ways to correct the incorrect sentences.)

1. Although, he didn't think it was a good idea to keep the gas can so close to the grill.
2. Mr. Smith is a wonderful cook, and recently he made a delicious eggplant stew because his wife is a vegetarian.
3. Lisa loved all kinds of animals, so she had six pets, including a dog, three cats, a hamster, and a rabbit.
4. Richard does not enjoy reading books with depressing or overly serious themes.
5. Because John was running late, and because it was essential for him to get to work on time, he exceeded the speed limit.
6. Because John was running late, and because it was essential for him to get to work on time, he exceeded the speed limit, so he ended up with a traffic ticket.
7. The old mansion needed a lot of work, it still sold for a high price.
8. The Category 5 hurricane came barreling toward the coast, but fortunately, it veered back to sea unexpectedly.
9. The nurses went on strike because they were especially concerned about the low staff-to-patient ratios at the hospital.
10. Jack, Len, and Danny have been close friends ever since elementary school.
11. You can read at bedtime for half an hour, or you can turn out the light.
12. Mr. and Mrs. Johnson have a very old oak tree in their backyard.

Part 2. Identify which of the following sentences could be syntactically challenging to comprehend based on the categories of potentially difficult syntax discussed in the chapter. Briefly explain what is challenging about the sentence.

a. At the hardware store Mr. Bloom purchased a can of paint, three brushes, some tape, and a large box of thumbtacks.
b. When the police officers saw the robber, they chased him into an alley behind the new bookstore.
c. Despite all of their arguments over the years about their differing political views, Ted and Lucy remained friends well into old age.
d. Louie really doesn't like tear-jerker movies, but this past weekend he went to see one just to make his girlfriend happy.

FIGURE 2.5. Practice Exercises: Syntax.

Discourse Structure

This section focuses on the structure of written texts beyond the sentence level, such as narratives, textbooks, articles, and other types of reading material common in schools. One broad distinction involving text structure, with which many teachers are familiar, is between **narrative** and **informational** (sometimes termed "expository") texts.

Structural Differences in Narrative and Informational Texts

Besides the obvious differences in their content, these two types of texts also have important differences in their structure and the types of vocabulary they tend to use. Table 2.4 compares some differing characteristics of narrative and informational texts.

One important structural difference in these texts involves their overall organization. Most narratives have a setting, characters, and a plot. Often, there is an initiating event that kicks off the story—a character falls ill, commits a crime, or finds out a secret, for example. Inferring and understanding the characters' internal feelings and motivations is usually important to comprehension of narratives. Some evidence also suggests that narratives are more effective than informational texts in promoting empathy and theory of mind (Kozak & Martin-Chang, 2019; Mar & Rain, 2015).

In contrast, informational texts can include a range of organizational structures—such as description, sequence, cause and effect, compare and contrast, problem and

TABLE 2.4. Different Characteristics of Narrative and Informational Texts

Characteristic	Narrative texts	Informational texts
Content	Fiction—tells a story	Nonfiction—conveys information, an opinion, or an argument
Overall organization	Usually has a setting, characters, and a plot line, often driven by an initiating event; understanding characters' internal feelings and motivations often is important to comprehension	Not typically organized around characters and a plot; can contain a variety of structures (e.g., description, sequence, cause–effect, compare–contrast, problem–solution)
Use of headings and subheadings	Not generally used in a narrative; even chapter titles are often not essential to comprehension	Headings and subheadings often used and may be important to comprehension in highlighting key points
Use of informational aids such as graphs, figures, tables, maps	Not generally used in a narrative	These kinds of aids often are used and provide information that is important to comprehension
Type of vocabulary	Often, there is rich vocabulary (e.g., *fierce, flourishing, marveled*) that cuts across domains and is not specialized to one particular domain	May have rich vocabulary, but also often has specialized content vocabulary (e.g., in an earth science text, words such as *igneous, sedimentary, metamorphic*)

solution—usually combining more than one of these structures across passages within the text (Oakhill et al., 2015). Individual passages may not always fit neatly into a particular structure. However, most informational texts do not have a setting, characters, and a plot line, and understanding characters' internal feelings or motivations is not generally central to comprehending them.

Two other important structural differences between narrative and informational texts involves their use of headings and subheadings, and their inclusion of informational aids such as tables, graphs, charts, maps, figures, and glossaries. In a narrative text, these characteristics are typically absent. In fiction chapter books, individual chapters frequently have titles, but the titles rarely carry information critical to understanding the narrative; in fact, often they can be completely ignored, with little impact on comprehension. In contrast, in informational texts, headings and subheadings tend to highlight the most important ideas from a text, and ignoring them could impair comprehension. Likewise, tables, graphs, glossaries, and other informational aids are valuable in supplementing or enhancing what the text itself has to say.

Narratives and informational texts both are important sources of vocabulary, but they use somewhat different types of vocabulary. Narratives can be an excellent source of rich vocabulary that is not specific to a particular domain, what is sometimes termed Tier 2 vocabulary (Beck, McKeown, & Kucan, 2002). Tier 2 vocabulary is especially useful for general vocabulary building because the words are likely to be unfamiliar to many children and can be generalized to a wide range of texts (Coyne & Loftus-Rattan, 2022). Informational texts can contain this kind of vocabulary, too, but unlike narratives, informational texts also often include specialized, Tier 3 vocabulary (Beck et al., 2002)—words specific to a particular domain, such as a field of science, history, mathematics, art, music, and so on, which are important to students' content learning. For example, words such as *galaxy*, *asteroid*, and *orbit* are more likely to be found in a science text about the solar system than in a narrative. Furthermore, if they are new vocabulary words, they might be emboldened to indicate their importance—not a feature found in narratives.

These are not hard-and-fast distinctions, and some texts are exceptions to them or combine features of both text types. *The Magic School Bus on the Ocean Floor* (Cole, 1992), and the other books in this popular children's series, uses a narrative frame story about an endearing fictional teacher named Mrs. Frizzle, but also conveys accurate information about a range of science topics, combining aspects of both types of texts. As another example, a biography of a famous historical figure, while nonfiction in its content, might have many features of a narrative text, including characters and a plot line. Understanding characters' internal motivations also could be important to understanding this type of text.

Cohesive Ties

Cohesive ties are words or phrases indicating linkages between parts of a text (Oakhill et al., 2015). Two important kinds of cohesive ties are anaphora and connectives, sometimes called signal words.

Anaphoric references have already been briefly discussed in relation to the use of pronouns within a sentence. Pronouns may also be used to link one sentence to others, as when a female character is introduced in a narrative and then words such as *she* and *her* are used repeatedly to refer back to that character. Pronouns may also refer back to inanimate objects, concepts, events, or other antecedents in a sentence or text, such as the pronoun *one* in the following sentence: *Separation of church and state is a founding principle of our democracy, one that is vital to maintain.* Pronouns include demonstrative pronouns (e.g., *these, those*), as well as possessive pronouns such as *her, his, their,* and *our.* In written texts, a referent and its pronoun may be widely separated by multiple sentences, placing heavy demands on the reader's working memory and making attention to these words important (Moats, 2020).

Another type of anaphoric reference involves ellipses, the omission of words or phrases to avoid repetition when the antecedent is clear from context. Consider the following sentences: *Laurie and Amanda went to the prom. Lisa and Jane did, too.* The second sentence has an ellipsis because it does not restate the phrase *went to the prom*; this phrase is understood based on the preceding sentence.

Connectives, or signal words, are words or phrases that signal certain relationships between different parts of a sentence or a text. Words such as *because, consequently,* and *as a result* typically signal a cause-and-effect relationship: *Because Nora was exhausted from her difficult day at work, she decided to skip the party.* Other words—such as *at first, next, then,* or *first, second, third*—signal a sequence of events, ideas, or steps. Signal words such as *likewise, similarly,* or *moreover* indicate an idea that is consistent with or continues a previous point in a text, whereas other words—*to the contrary, but, however, in contrast*—signal a contrasting or contradictory point. Yet other groups of signal words indicate an example or a summary of previous points in a text. Although signal words are found in both narrative and informational texts, certain groups of signal words tend to correlate to specific informational passage structures, such as cause–effect, descriptive, or problem–solution structures.

Attention to signal words as well as overall text and passage structure in reading can facilitate comprehension; correct use of these features in writing can make a text clearer and more cohesive (Graham et al., 2016; Hennessey, 2021; Oakhill et al., 2015). Table 2.5 displays examples of groups of signal words, the relationships signaled, their associations with different informational passage structures, and some specific text examples for each group of words.

TABLE 2.5. Examples of Different Groups of Signal Words and Their Association with Various Passage Structures

Group of signal words	Relationship or linkage signaled	Passage structure association	Sample text
because, therefore, so, consequently, as a result, reason why	Cause and effect	Cause–effect: passage discusses cause and effect relationship(s)	During World War II, codebreakers were vital to the war effort, but most men were serving in the armed forces. Because of the limited availability of men, many women were hired to be codebreakers. Consequently, women played a key role in turning the tide of the war.
first, second, third . . . next, then, last, finally	Sequence	Sequence: passage provides a sequence of steps or events, usually chronological	Without a car, the trip to the excavation site in Pleasantville is complicated. First, you have to fly or take a train to Center City. Then, a bus takes you from Center City to Pleasantville. Last, you need a taxi or Uber to get from the bus station to the site itself.
for example, for instance, as an example, to illustrate, such as	Specific example of a previous statement	Descriptive: passage describes a topic, usually with examples	The circus dog had learned how to do all kinds of tricks. **For instance**, he could roll over, play dead, and retrieve things. He could even do more sophisticated tricks **such as** take a bow and wave good-bye to an audience.
problem, question, challenge, solution, answer	Problem and solution	Problem–solution: passage describes a problem and possible solution(s)	Chronic insomnia is a huge **problem** for many people. Sometimes this problem can be **solved** simply by adopting good sleep hygiene practices. These practices include going to bed and getting up at the same time each day.
similar to, same as, different from, like/alike, unlike	Compare and contrast	Compare–contrast: passage explains how two things are similar and different	This latest version of the classic film is **similar to** the original in many ways. Both versions of the movie have **similar** plot lines, characters, and themes. One important **difference** is that, **unlike** the original movie, the setting of the newest version is in the future, not in the 1940s.
moreover, furthermore, also, in addition, likewise, similarly	Similar, continuing point to a previous one	Found in a variety of passage structures	Millions of people in Europe have been impacted by the extreme heat this week. Dozens of people have died. **Furthermore**, the heat wave is expected to last for another 2 or 3 days.
however, but, nonetheless, nevertheless, to the contrary	Contrasting, contradictory point to a previous one	Found in a variety of passage structures	Millions of people in Europe have been impacted by the extreme heat this week. **However**, the heat wave is expected to end tonight. That will be a huge relief.
in summary, to sum up, overall, on the whole	Summary of previous points	Found in a variety of passage structures	**To sum up**, the most important thing to remember is that, if you suffer from insomnia, there is a lot you can do to alleviate the problem. Adopt good sleep hygiene practices. Avoid looking at screens too closely near bedtime. Don't drink coffee after noon. And see a sleep specialist if the problem persists.

Excerpt from the website of United Nations Climate Action, *What Is Climate Change?* (*www.un.org/en/climatechange/what-is-climate-change*)

Climate change refers to long-term shifts in temperatures and weather patterns. These shifts may be natural, such as through variations in the solar cycle. But since the 1800s, human activities have been the main driver of climate change, primarily due to burning fossil fuels like coal, oil and gas.

Burning fossil fuels generates greenhouse gas emissions that act like a blanket wrapped around the Earth, trapping the sun's heat and raising temperatures . . .

Many people think climate change mainly means warmer temperatures. But temperature rise is only the beginning of the story. Because the Earth is a system, where everything is connected, changes in one area can influence changes in all others.

The consequences of climate change now include, among others, intense droughts, water scarcity, severe fires, rising sea levels, flooding, melting polar ice, catastrophic storms and declining biodiversity . . .

Adapting to climate consequences protects people, homes, businesses, livelihoods, infrastructure and natural ecosystems. It covers current impacts and those likely in the future. Adaptation will be required everywhere, but must be prioritized now for the most vulnerable people with the fewest resources to cope with climate hazards . . .

Climate action requires significant financial investments by governments and businesses. But climate inaction is vastly more expensive. One critical step is for industrialized countries to fulfil their commitment to provide $100 billion a year to developing countries so they can adapt and move toward greener economies.

Exercise

Part 1. In the excerpt on climate change above from the United Nations Climate Action website, identify at least three examples of pronouns and the anaphoric referent of each pronoun.

Part 2. In the excerpt, identify four examples of signal words for cause and effect, and at least two examples of signal words for contrasting/contradictory points.

Part 3. How does the vocabulary in the excerpt exemplify the vocabulary of many informational texts? Specifically, what type of vocabulary is most prominent, Tier 2 or Tier 3? Give a brief explanation, along with several examples of words.

Part 4. What text structure is exemplified by the opening paragraphs of Figure 2.6 (i.e., "Climate change refers to . . . changes in one area can influence changes in all others")? Now read the passage shown in Chapter 9 in Figure 9.3. What is the text structure of this passage?

FIGURE 2.6. Practice Exercise: Discourse-level language structure.

PRACTICE EXERCISE

Figure 2.6 provides one final practice exercise, involving discourse-level language structure.

SUMMING UP: The Structure of Language

Here are key points from this chapter:

- Knowledge about the structure of language is essential to implement SL practices effectively.

- To implement SL interventions successfully with all three poor reader profiles, teachers need an understanding of language structure at word, sentence, and discourse levels.

- Important teacher knowledge about language structure at the word level includes an understanding of the phonemic and morphemic structure of words, common grapheme–phoneme/phoneme–grapheme relationships, syllable types, accent patterns and schwa, the need for flexibility in word reading, and phonetically irregular words.

- Important teacher knowledge related to sentence structure includes the ability to identify different sentence types, sentences with potentially confusing syntax, and common sentence errors in students' writing.

- Important teacher knowledge about discourse structure includes understanding key organizational differences between narrative and informational texts, the ability to identify common passage structures, and the ability to recognize anaphora and connectives (signal words).

ANSWERS TO PRACTICE EXERCISES

Phoneme Counting and Morpheme Counting (Figure 2.2)

(First/last are emboldened.)

Part 1: 1. four phonemes: **/f/**, /l/, short /o/, **/p/** 2. three phonemes: **/ch/**, long /e/, **/t/** 3. three phonemes: **/t/**, long /i/, **/m/** 4. two phonemes: **/p/**, **long /a/** 5. four phonemes: **/g/**, /r/, long /o/, **/n/** 6. three phonemes: **short /i/**, /n/, **/ch/** 7. six phonemes: **/s/**, /p/, /l/, short /i/, /n/, **/ch/** 8. two phonemes: **/th/**, **long /i/** 9. three phonemes: **/t/**, /oo/, **/b/** 10. four phonemes: **/f/**, /y/, /oo/, **/z/** 11. four phonemes: **/b/**, /r/, short /i/, **/ng/** 12. five phonemes: **/b/**, /r/, short /i/, /ng/, **/k/** 13. three phonemes: **short /o/**, /k/, **/s/** 14. five phonemes: **/p/**, /oo/, /d/, schwa vowel, **/l/**

Part 2: 1. two morphemes: **tall** + **-er** 2. three morphemes: **un** + like + **ly** 3. three morphemes: **re** + read + **ing** 4. four morphemes: **un** + truth + ful + **ness** 5. three morphemes: **water** + color + **s** 6. three morphemes: **soft** + en + **er** 7. two morphemes: **bed** + **room** 8. three morphemes: **inter** + planet + **ary** 9. three morphemes: **taste** + y + **est** 10. two morphemes: **ben[d]** + **ed [t]** (irregular past tense) 11. one morpheme: **target** (because *tar* and *get* do not have meaning in the context of this word) 12. three morphemes: **dis** + rupt + **ive** 13. four morphemes: **astr/astro** + onomy + er + **s** 14. one morpheme: **butter** (because here *but* is not a base word)

Syllable Types and Words with *C* or *G* (Figure 2.3)

(Sample words for vowel sounds are examples; many other answers are possible.)

Part 1: 1. VT, /aw/ as in lawn, fawn, saw 2. VR, /ar/ as in carp, card, far 3. silent e, long /i/ as in time, crime, ride 4. consonant-*le*, schwa vowel as in drizzle, puzzle, frazzle 5. closed syllable, short /i/ as in think, sing, sink 6. open syllable, long /o/ as in go, no, show 7. silent e, long /a/ as in face, grace, made 8. open syllable, long /i/ as in by, cry, hi 9. closed syllable, short /i/ as in shift, drift, hit (remember, the u in *qu* doesn't count as a vowel) 10. VR, /or/ as in fork, short, corn 11. closed syllable, short /i/ as in gym, tryst, him 12. open syllable, long /u/ as in flu, too, Sue 13. VT, long /e/ as in reef, tree, bee 14. VT, /oy/ as in coin, join, boy

Part 2: 2. /g/ 7. /s/ 8. /k/ 11. /s/ 12. /g/

Irregular Words and Knowledge about Long Words (Figure 2.4)

Part 1: The six irregular words are: *pretty* (the *e* should be short as in *Betty*); *only* (the *o* should be short as in *on*); *broad* (the *oa* should say long /o/ not /aw/); *friend* (the *ie* should say either long /i/ or long /e/ not short /e/); *gone* (should have a long /o/ as in *phone*); and *who* (should be pronounced /wo/ to rhyme with *go*, not /hoo/). Remember, words are not irregular simply because they have silent letters, as long as the silent letter is part of a stable pattern with a consistent pronunciation across most words (e.g., *kn, wr*).

Part 2: 1. pre / view (prefix) 2. cup / cake (compound) 3. Bi / ble (consonant-*le*) 4. with / er (VCV, exception to VCCV) 5. cap / ture (suffix) 6. spot / light (compound) 7. trav / el (VCV) 8. ig / loo (VCCV) 9. noo / dle (consonant-*le*) 10. a / rise (prefix)

Part 3: 1. in + de + struct + ible; accent on STRUCT; schwa vowels in second, fourth, and fifth syllables 2. post + mort + em; accent on MORT; schwa vowel in the third syllable 3. bio + graph + ic + al; accent on GRAPH; schwa vowels in the fourth and fifth syllables 4. geo + therm + al; accent on THERM; schwa vowel in the fourth (last) syllable 5. re + act + ive; accent on ACT; schwa vowel in the third syllable

Syntax (Figure 2.5)

Part 1: 1. sentence fragment, could be corrected to: *However, he didn't think it was a good idea . . .* and so forth 2. compound–complex 3. compound 4. simple 5. complex 6. compound–complex 7. run-on, could be corrected by inserting the word *but* or *yet* before *it* 8. compound 9. complex 10. simple 11. compound 12. simple

Part 2: c (pronoun, *their*, comes before anaphoric referent, *Ted and Lucy*)

Discourse-Level Language Structure (Figure 2.6)

Part 1: line 1, *long-term—these*; line 12, *Adapting to climate consequences—it* in line 13; last sentence, *industrialized countries—their*; last sentence, *developing countries—they*

Part 2: Cause–effect signal words are in line 3, *due to*; line 7, *because*; line 9, *consequences of*; and line 18, *so*. Signal words for contrasting/contradictory points are all four uses of *but* (line 2, line 6, line 14, and line 16).

Part 3: The most prominent type of vocabulary in this excerpt involves Tier 3 vocabulary, words from a specialized content domain, climate change. Examples of Tier 3 vocabulary in this text include *climate*, *fossil fuels*, *greenhouse gas*, *emissions*, *biodiversity*, *infrastructure*, *ecosystem*, and *greener economies*. These specialized words and terms are important for students to understand about the topic of climate change; they would not be featured in a typical narrative.

Part 4: Figure 2.6, cause–effect text structure; Figure 9.3, compare–contrast text structure.

CHAPTER 3

Assessment for Planning
Structured Literacy Interventions

Ben Harmolin, a K–12 school administrator, has been conducting a series of professional development sessions with the teachers in his district. The sessions have focused on background information about poor reader profiles, using assessments to identify individual poor readers' profiles, and translating assessment data into appropriate SL interventions. Teachers in Mr. Harmolin's district are generally quite experienced in giving and scoring a range of reading assessments. The concept of poor reader profiles—that reading problems can revolve around word reading, language comprehension, or both areas—is intuitively appealing to them because they have seen poor readers who exemplify these varied difficulties. They are keen to apply the profiles concept in educational practice. Nevertheless, many of the teachers are finding determination of individual students' profiles, as well as using profile information and additional assessments to design SL interventions, unexpectedly difficult. A wide array of assessment data exists for many poor readers, but organizing and interpreting those data in educationally useful ways is challenging.

The goals of this chapter are similar to those of Mr. Harmolin's PD: (1) to explain how to use appropriate assessment data to identify individual poor readers' profiles and (2) to use information about the profile, as well as other data, including diagnostic assessment, to design effective SL interventions. The chapter introduces an assessment map, a graphic organizer to assist with these goals, as well as detailed examples involving specific students.

The chapter assumes some foundational knowledge about assessment in reading, such as knowledge about technical adequacy of tests (e.g., reliability and validity); types of scores (e.g., standard scores); and the nature and purpose of different types of assessments, including individually administered standardized tests, curriculum-based measures (CBMs), and more informal techniques such as formative assessment. For further information about these areas, please see sources such as Farrall (2012) and Hougen and Smartt (2020).

Research on Reading Assessment

Assessment of important components of reading and language is fundamental to understanding individual students' reading difficulties (Farrall, 2012). Areas to assess are informed by the SVR (Gough & Tunmer, 1986; Hoover & Gough, 1990), discussed in Chapter 1, as well as Scarborough's rope model (2001), which shows components of oral language comprehension and word reading as many strands of a rope woven ever more tightly together over the course of reading development.

In the domain of word reading, an essential area to assess, especially in beginning readers or poor readers known to struggle with word reading, is phonemic awareness (PA). As noted in Chapter 1, PA involves sensitivity to sounds in spoken words and the ability to manipulate those sounds. PA plays a central role in beginners' ability to crack the alphabetic code, as well as to read and spell unfamiliar words (Brady, 2020; Stanovich, 2000). Oral tasks are used to assess PA, such as providing a spoken word that a child has to segment into individual phonemes, or the reverse, providing a set of phonemes that a child must blend into a whole spoken word.

Out-of-context assessment, presentation of words in a list or array, is necessary to accurately determine students' word-reading skills because poor readers often rely on context to compensate for weak word reading (Stanovich, 2000). Furthermore, assessment of word reading should include both real words and nonsense words. Nonsense words (e.g., *grick, blain*), sometimes called pseudowords, demonstrate students' ability to use the alphabetic code to read unfamiliar words, a vital skill in reading development. Real word reading should be assessed because of its intrinsic importance, and also because even with research-based phonics interventions, poor readers sometimes do not make the same gains in reading real words as nonsense words (Compton, Miller, Elleman, & Steacy, 2014). Assessment should consider not only accuracy of word reading but also automaticity (Kilpatrick, 2015)—that is, whether students recognize a word immediately and with ease—because automaticity of word reading is required for fluent reading of text. If students have to expend effort in reading words, this effort may drain mental resources for reading comprehension, even if words are being read accurately.

Most standardized test batteries for reading include a subtest assessing text reading fluency, that is, accuracy and rate of reading sentences or passages. Oral reading fluency (ORF) also may be assessed through CBMs, quick timed probes that correlate well with overall reading competence, especially at the elementary level (Brown-Chidsey & Steege, 2005; Hosp, Hosp, & Howell, 2007). ORF CBMs usually require a student to read a grade-appropriate passage orally for 1 minute, with a focus on two types of scores: (1) the student's accuracy of reading, measured as the percentage of words read correctly out of total number of words attempted in 1 minute and (2) the student's rate of reading, measured as words read correctly per minute. Accuracy and rate each provide important information in ORF assessment. For example, accurate text reading is a prerequisite for fluent reading and comprehension, and improvements in accuracy are valuable even if a student's rate of reading remains somewhat slow. Prosody—appropriate phrasing, expressiveness, and intonation of oral reading—is another key aspect of ORF and is often assessed through a rating scale (Hudson, Anderson, McGraw, Ray, & Wilhelm, 2022).

Timed silent reading measures may also be used to measure fluency. Silent reading assessments lend themselves to group administration, but they do not provide the full range of information about accuracy, rate, and prosody that ORF measures provide. Nevertheless, a silent reading fluency measure may be useful with some students, such as older students whose decoding is known to be accurate.

CBMs involving ORF have many advantages for initial screening when used as part of multistage screens (Fuchs, Fuchs, & Compton, 2012; Fuchs & Vaughn, 2012), as well as for progress monitoring. Among other benefits, they are quick and efficient to give, are sensitive to incremental progress, and can be readministered often (Brown-Chidsey & Steege, 2005). However, ORF CBMs may miss students whose reading difficulties revolve only around comprehension, those with a profile of specific reading comprehension difficulties (SRCD) (Clarke et al., 2014; Riedel, 2007; Scarborough, 2005); therefore, additional types of screening, such as oral language measures, are important to identify these students.

In the domain of oral language comprehension, a critical area to assess is vocabulary, which plays a central role in both oral language comprehension and reading comprehension (Beck et al., 2002; Pearson, Hiebert, & Kamil, 2007). For beginning or poor readers, an oral vocabulary measure should be used because limitations in decoding may impair these students' performance on a vocabulary measure that requires reading. At a minimum, assessment also should include a broad measure of oral language comprehension, one that involves sentences or passages to which the student must listen. Two common tasks used in these measures are a question-and-answer (QA) task, in which the examiner asks comprehension questions about the material to which the student has listened, or a cloze task, which requires filling in a blank in a sentence that has been read aloud. In a cloze task, the examiner might read a sentence such as *A boy was running down the* _____, and the student must provide a word that makes sense in the blank, such as *road*, *street*, *sidewalk*, or *path*. Further assessment of specific components of oral language can also be helpful, such as measures involving syntax or pragmatic language, especially for students whose reading difficulties are based partly or entirely in language comprehension.

Finally, reading comprehension assessment is a key area, one that has received considerable attention from researchers (e.g., Barquero & Cutting, 2021; Collins, Lindström, & Sandbank, 2021; Cutting & Scarborough, 2006; Keenan & Betjemann, 2006; Keenan & Meenan, 2014; Nation & Snowling, 1997). Measures of reading comprehension employ some of the same tasks as oral language comprehension measures, except that in reading comprehension, the student has to do the reading rather than listen to content read aloud by the examiner. In addition to cloze or QA measures, maze assessments are often used, especially on CBMs for reading comprehension. A maze format is similar to cloze except that maze measures provide multiple-choice options for the blanks in items. Reading comprehension assessments vary in many other important ways besides task format, such as in the length and type of passages used (e.g., narrative or informational); whether a test is timed; whether students are allowed to look back in the text to find answers to questions; and whether questions are multiple-choice or open-ended.

A frequent finding from studies on reading comprehension assessment is that an individual student's performance may vary across different measures of reading comprehension depending on the features of specific tests and, sometimes, on the profile of the poor reader (Collins, Lindstrom, & Sandbank, 2021; Cutting & Scarborough, 2006; Keenan & Betjemann, 2006; Keenan, Betjemann, & Olson, 2008; Keenan & Meenan, 2014; Spear-Swerling, 2004). In measures with a QA format, it matters whether questions are passage-dependent or passage-independent (Keenan & Betjemann, 2006). Passage-independent questions can be answered without actually reading the passage, such as vocabulary questions (e.g., "What does the word *revived* mean in the sentence *The doctor revived the man who had fainted in the store?*"), or questions tapping common sense or background knowledge (e.g., "How do you think Mary felt when she found out that Karen lied to her?"). In contrast, passage-dependent questions require reading of the passage in order to respond correctly.

Here are a few examples of ways that a poor reader's profile may influence performance on reading comprehension tests with different features. Consider a student with specific word recognition difficulties (SWRD) who has poor decoding but strong vocabulary and background knowledge. This student may perform relatively better on a QA measure of reading comprehension with many passage-independent questions tapping vocabulary and background knowledge, than on a cloze measure with short, sentence-length passages. On these latter measures, decoding errors can have a greater impact on comprehension because there are fewer opportunities to gauge meaning from context than when test items involve longer passages (Keenan et al., 2008; Keenan & Meenan, 2014). Conversely, a student with SRCD who has weak vocabulary and background knowledge but good decoding may show the opposite pattern of performance, with stronger performance on the cloze measure and poorer performance on the QA measure. As another example, a poor reader with any profile who has serious fluency difficulties is likely to perform more poorly on timed than untimed reading comprehension assessments.

Because of this potential variability in performance, multiple measures of reading comprehension are warranted, particularly for students whose reading difficulties appear to include a comprehension component. These measures must be interpreted with a consideration of the specific features of individual tests, and in conjunction with more focused assessments of specific components of reading (Barquero & Cutting, 2021; Keenan & Meenan, 2014).

The Profiles Assessment Map

Form 3.1 (page 75) displays an assessment map that includes the key areas of reading discussed earlier and can help determine poor reader profiles. A variety of standardized assessments can be used to measure the emboldened areas on the map, as long as they are technically adequate and yield norm-referenced or benchmarked scores that compare a student to age or grade peers. However, because students' performance can change over time, the scores used should be from roughly similar time points, for instance, within a few months of each other. Also, not every emboldened area on the map is relevant for every student. For instance, a PA measure might not be given for a student whose word-reading skills are advanced and known to be grade-appropriate; a silent reading fluency measure might not be administered to a student with SWRD or if ORF data are available.

Table 3.1 provides examples of possible tests and subtests for assessing each of the emboldened areas on the map. Many other measures also could be used, as long as they are technically adequate and provide appropriate types of scores for the student's age or grade. In Table 3.1, unless otherwise noted, all tests are suitable for the K–12 grade range (and sometimes into adulthood).

To use the map in Form 3.1, begin by filling in a student's current test scores and highlighting the ones that are below benchmark or below average range (i.e., below 90 for standard scores, below 8 for scaled scores). The most relevant parts of the map for deciding on the profile are the two rectangular boxes with rounded corners on the left side of the form, labeled "Oral Language Comprehension" and "Word Reading." If a student's weaknesses cluster in the "Word Reading" box, with all of the "Oral Language Comprehension" measures in average range or higher, this pattern suggests a profile of SWRD. The opposite pattern, with at least one weakness in the "Oral Language Comprehension" box and all of the word-reading measures in average range or higher, a profile of SRCD is implied. Weaknesses in both boxes suggest a profile of mixed reading difficulties (MRD). Individual scores within both boxes should be examined to evaluate the severity of weaknesses in different areas.

The map illustrates how underlying weaknesses in word reading or language comprehension might relate to a student's difficulties in fluency and reading comprehension. For instance, suppose that a student has poor reading comprehension, but his or her word-reading skills are all grade-appropriate, including in both text-reading accuracy and out-of-context word reading. This is a profile of SRCD, suggesting that the student's poor reading comprehension is based in language comprehension or an area that directly impacts language comprehension, such as background knowledge. Other ways that the map can be useful include suggesting additional measures that should be administered to a student and deciding whether problems in text-reading fluency contribute to a student's poor reading comprehension.

The map is intended to summarize standardized assessment data for important areas of language and reading, but it does not include all of the data that would be important for educators to consider. For instance, if a student has been identified with

TABLE 3.1. Some Examples of Standardized Assessments for Components of Reading

Component	Examples of tests/subtests
Phonological/phonemic awareness	WIAT-4 Phonemic Proficiency; CTOPP-2 Phonological Awareness; WJ-IV Segmentation; DIBELS 8 Phoneme Segmentation Fluency (K–1 only)
Word-reading accuracy—real words (out of context)	WIAT-4 Word Reading; WJ-IV Letter–Word Identification
Word-reading accuracy—nonsense words	WIAT-4 Pseudoword Decoding; WJ-IV Word Attack
Automaticity of word reading (real or nonsense words)	WIAT-4 Orthographic Fluency; WIAT-4 Decoding Fluency (grades 3–12); DIBELS 8 Word Reading Fluency (K–3 only); TOWRE-2 Sight Word Efficiency and Phonetic Decoding Efficiency
Oral reading fluency—accuracy (in sentences or passages)	WJ-IV Oral Reading; DIBELS 8 Oral Reading Fluency, accuracy score (grades 1–8); Acadience Oral Reading Fluency, accuracy score (grades 1–6); GORT-5 accuracy score (grades 1–12)
Oral reading fluency—rate (in sentences or passages)	WIAT-4 Oral Reading Fluency (grades 1–12); DIBELS 8 Oral Reading Fluency, words correct per minute score (grades 1–8); Acadience Oral Reading Fluency, words correct per minute score (grades 1–6); GORT-5 rate score (grades 1–12)
Silent reading fluency	WJ-IV Sentence Reading Fluency; TOSCRF-2 (approximately grades 2–12)
Oral vocabulary	WIAT-4 Receptive Vocabulary and Expressive Vocabulary; WJ-IV Picture Vocabulary; PPVT-5
Oral language (broad listening) comprehension	WIAT-4 Oral Discourse Comprehension (QA/OE); WJ-IV Oral Comprehension (cloze); CELF-5 Receptive Language Index (varied tasks) and Understanding Spoken Paragraphs (QA/OE)
Reading comprehension (reading text under timed conditions)	GORT-5 Comprehension score (QA/OE, grades 1–12); DIBELS 8 Maze (grades 2–8, maze format); Acadience Maze (grades 3–6, maze format)
Reading comprehension (reading text under untimed conditions)	WIAT-4 Reading Comprehension (QA/OE); WJ-IV Passage Comprehension (mostly cloze)

Note. Acadience, Acadience Reading (Good et al., 2018); CELF-5, Clinical Evaluation of Language Fundamentals—Fifth Edition (Wiig, Semel, & Secord, 2013); CTOPP-2, Comprehensive Test of Phonological Processing—Second Edition (Wagner, Torgesen, Rashotte, & Pearson, 2013); DIBELS 8, Dynamic Indicators of Basic Early Literacy Skills—Eighth Edition (University of Oregon, 2018–2019); GORT-5, Gray Oral Reading Test—Fifth Edition (Wiederholt & Bryant, 2012); PPVT-5, Peabody Picture Vocabulary Test—Fifth Edition (Dunn, 2019); TOSCRF-2, Test of Silent Contextual Reading Fluency—Second Edition (Hammill, Wiederholt, & Allen, 2014); TOWRE-2, Test of Word Reading Efficiency—Second Edition (Torgesen, Wagner, & Rashotte, 2012); WIAT-4, Wechsler Individual Achievement Test—Fourth Edition (NCS Pearson, 2020); WJ-IV, Woodcock–Johnson IV Tests of Achievement/Tests of Oral Language—Fourth Edition (Schrank, McGrew, & Mather, 2014); QA, question-and-answer format; OE, open-ended questions.

problems in EF, these difficulties may affect performance on assessments, especially on listening or reading comprehension assessments (Wagner et al., 2021), and should be considered in interpretation of the student's performance. Further assessment of the student's application of EF skills in relation to reading comprehension, as well as written expression, may be especially informative for this kind of student; see Cartwright (2015) for a useful rubric. For all students, an analysis of their performance on diagnostic assessments, as well as their educational history, is also very important. These two areas are discussed later in the chapter.

A Sample Map: Ruben

Figure 3.1 displays an example of a completed assessment map for a third grader named Ruben. Unless otherwise indicated, map scores are all standard scores, with an average range of 90 to 109. As shown on the left side of the map, Ruben's weaknesses cluster in the area of word reading, and his language-comprehension scores are all in average range, so Ruben appears to have a profile of SWRD. Furthermore, his word-reading difficulties include automaticity as well as accuracy of real word reading, and the map suggests a phonological basis to those difficulties because Ruben's PA is below average. Ruben has difficulties reading both real words and nonsense words, but his real word reading is lower than his nonsense word reading, and for both types of words, his automaticity is poorer than his accuracy. This is a common pattern even in children who have received substantial phonics intervention (Compton et al., 2014; Kilpatrick, 2015), as is the case for Ruben.

The remaining parts of the map are consistent with the conclusion that Ruben has a profile of SWRD. Ruben has difficulties with both accuracy and rate of text reading, as expected given his word-reading difficulties. These difficulties impact his reading comprehension, even though his language comprehension is average. A comparison of Ruben's performance on different comprehension measures shows that he did relatively better on an untimed standardized test of reading comprehension from the Wechsler Individual Achievement Test—Fourth Edition (WIAT-4), only slightly below average range, than he did on a timed maze. Again, this makes sense given his underlying difficulties in automaticity of word reading and text-reading fluency, which would be expected to have a greater impact on comprehension under timed than untimed conditions. Also, the WIAT-4 Reading Comprehension (RC) subtest allows the student to look back in the text for answers, and the observations in the lower right corner of Figure 3.1, note that Ruben was diligent about looking in the text to try to find answers, although he worked slowly.

The impact of Ruben's word-reading difficulties is clear when one compares his oral comprehension with his reading comprehension. On the WIAT-4 Oral Discourse Comprehension subtest, in which students listen to verbally presented material and answer open-ended questions about it orally, Ruben's performance was solidly average. However, on WIAT-4 RC, a subtest that uses the same format as Oral Discourse Comprehension but requires reading, Ruben's performance was 17 points lower, likely because of the influence of his poor word reading.

Student *Ruben*   Grade *3*   Dates of Testing *Jan 14–Feb 9*

ORAL LANGUAGE COMPREHENSION

Oral Vocabulary (note receptive/expressive)

WIAT–IV Receptive Vocab 99

WIAT–IV Expressive Vocab 95

Oral Language (Listening) Comprehension (note format, e.g., cloze, maze, QA)

WIAT–IV Oral Discourse Comp (QA) 105

Other Oral Language

CELF–5 Receptive Lang Index = 101

WORD READING

Real Words—Accuracy
WIAT–IV Word Reading 82

Nonsense Words—Accuracy
WIAT–IV Pseudoword Decoding 88

Word Reading—Automaticity
WIAT–IV Orthographic Fluency 74

WIAT–IV Decoding Fluency 83

Phonological/phonemic awareness
CTOPP–2 PA composite 81

Oral Reading Fluency—Accuracy
DIBELS 8 88% intensive/at risk (2/1/23)
DIBELS 8 86% intensive/at risk (1/14/23)

Oral Reading Fluency—Rate
DIBELS 8 66 wcpm intensive/at risk (2/1/23)
DIBELS 8 72 wcpm intensive/at risk (1/14/23)
Silent Reading Fluency

Reading Comprehension (note test format, e.g., cloze, maze, QA, as well as other relevant features such as timing)

DIBELS 8 Maze intensive/at risk (timed CBM; 2/1/23)

WIAT–IV Reading Comp 88 (untimed; QA)

Observations

Comprehension errors appeared due to inaccurate decoding

On WIAT–IV RC, he repeatedly searched text for answers, took a long time to respond

FIGURE 3.1. Assessment map for Ruben.

Another Assessment Map: Lucas

Figure 3.2 displays another completed assessment map, this one for an eighth grader named Lucas. The left-hand side of Figure 3.2 shows that Lucas has weaknesses in both boxed areas, oral language comprehension and word reading, suggesting that he has an MRD. His specific oral language difficulties include vocabulary, as well as significant weaknesses on three subtests that assess students' academic knowledge in science, social studies, and humanities (e.g., literature, art, music). These subtests are administered orally and do not require any reading or writing.

Lucas's word-reading weaknesses include accuracy of real word reading, as well as automaticity of reading both real words and nonsense words. Unlike that of Ruben, Lucas's untimed nonsense word reading and PA are in the average range. Lucas's specific test scores suggest that his word-reading difficulties are a bit milder than his language-comprehension weaknesses. This does not mean that word reading and fluency should receive no attention in Lucas's intervention, but it underscores the importance of addressing Lucas's language-comprehension weaknesses. The conclusion that Lucas has a profile of MRD is also supported by the observations section of the map, which notes that his errors on the Gray Oral Reading Test—Fifth Edition (GORT-5) comprehension questions sometimes appeared to relate to decoding, but more often related to difficulties in vocabulary and other areas of language comprehension.

Additional assessment to determine Lucas's specific comprehension weaknesses would help inform his intervention. Some areas to assess, either formally or informally, include syntax, and understanding of text structure and cohesive ties. In addition, a speech–language evaluation may be warranted. This evaluation also could provide valuable information for planning Lucas's reading intervention.

Implications for Intervention

The assessment map is a useful starting point for planning interventions. For Ruben, it is clear that intervention needs to focus on word reading and fluency, not comprehension. Ruben should be able to receive his comprehension development within Tier 1 instruction, although some adjustments may be needed for him to fully benefit from that instruction, such as oral presentation of content from texts that Ruben cannot read. Within the area of word reading, intervention should focus on promoting accuracy and automaticity of word reading, especially real word reading, with transfer of those skills to text reading. Because Ruben has weaknesses in PA, his interventionist should also ensure that he has the PA skills he needs for successful decoding and spelling, especially phoneme blending and segmentation (Brady, 2020).

Lucas's intervention should address both language comprehension and word reading, and the pattern of his scores, as discussed earlier, suggests that language comprehension should receive relatively greater emphasis than word reading. Vocabulary and background knowledge (e.g., as shown by the Academic Knowledge subtests of the Woodcock–Johnson IV (WJ-IV) are particularly important areas to address in Lucas's intervention because of their key role in comprehension and because of Lucas's

Student *Lucas*   Grade *8*   Dates of Testing *Oct 14–29*

ORAL LANGUAGE COMPREHENSION

**Oral Vocabulary
(note receptive/expressive)**

PPVT-5 (receptive) <u>**80**</u>

WJ-IV Picture Vocab
(exp) <u>**77**</u>

**Oral Language
(Listening) Comprehension
(note format, e.g., cloze,
maze, QA)**

WJ-IV Oral
Comprehension 90 (cloze)

Other Oral Language

WJ-IV Science <u>**80**</u>
WJ-IV Social Studies <u>**76**</u>
WJ-IV Humanities <u>**74**</u>

WORD READING

Real Words—Accuracy
WJ-IV Word Identification
<u>**87**</u>

**Nonsense Words—
Accuracy**
WJ-IV Word Attack 92

**Word Reading—
Automaticity**
TOWRE-2 Sight Word
Efficiency <u>**85**</u>
TOWRE-2 Phonetic
Decoding Efficiency <u>**87**</u>

**Phonological/phonemic
awareness**
CTOPP-2 Phonological
Awareness Composite 92

**Oral Reading Fluency—
Accuracy**
GORT-5 Accuracy Scaled
Score 8

**Oral Reading Fluency—
Rate**
GORT-5 Rate Scaled Score
<u>**6**</u>

Silent Reading Fluency
WJ-IV Sentence Reading
Fluency <u>**84**</u>

**Reading Comprehension
(note test format, e.g.,
cloze, maze, QA, as well as
other relevant features
such as timing)**

GORT-5 Comprehension
Scaled Score <u>**5**</u> (timed; QA)

WJ-IV Passage
Comprehension <u>**78**</u>
(untimed; cloze)

DIBELS 8 Maze <u>**intensive
level /at risk**</u> (timed CBM;
maze)

Observations

GORT Comprehension
errors occasionally seemed
due to inaccurate
decoding, but more often
due to difficulties with
comprehension

FIGURE 3.2. Assessment map for Lucas.

weaknesses in these areas. Other areas of weakness relevant to literacy learning, if found in additional assessments, should also be addressed.

The Value of Diagnostic Assessment Data

Diagnostic assessments, assessments whose purpose is to identify specific skills that students need to be taught (Hougen & Smartt, 2020), are vital for planning SL interventions. Many diagnostic assessments are potentially helpful, depending on the individual poor reader's profile and specific skills. This section focuses on three useful types of assessment: criterion-referenced phonics assessments, oral reading inventories, and error analysis.

Criterion-Referenced Phonics Assessments

For students with SWRD or MRD, criterion-referenced assessments of phonics skills are extremely valuable. These assessments typically involve sets of words organized into categories from simple to more complex—for example, one-syllable consonant–vowel–consonant (CVC) words such as *lap*, then short-vowel words with consonant digraphs such as *fish*, and so on, through two-syllable or multisyllabic words. Often items involve both real and nonsense words. To be useful with poor readers who are beyond the early stages of reading, the inclusion of at least one or two categories of long words, those of more than one syllable, is essential.

The task for the student is simply to read the words in successive categories aloud, with testing discontinued when the words become too difficult. Scores involve percentages of words correct in each category, with a specific percentage (e.g., 80, 85, or 90% correct) set as a mastery level, and with intervention focused on word categories that are not mastered. This kind of assessment can help determine a starting point for phonics instruction, as well as help monitor a student's progress in learning specific decoding skills.

Performance of Ruben and Lucas on a Criterion-Referenced Phonics Test

Table 3.2 shows the performance of both Ruben and Lucas on a hypothetical criterion-referenced phonics assessment, the ABC Test of Phonics Skills (ABC Test), which defines 85% accuracy as the mastery level. As one might anticipate based on the fact that Lucas is older than Ruben and has milder word-reading weaknesses, Lucas demonstrates more skills on this assessment than does Ruben. Ruben has mastered decoding only the first three categories on the ABC Test, those involving short-vowel words, with his scores well below mastery level on all other word categories. In contrast, Lucas has mastered all the one-syllable word categories, and he also has many skills for reading easy two-syllable words and words with common suffixes (e.g., *rabbit*, *jumping*), a category on which his score was 75% correct. However, on more difficult two-syllable and multisyllabic words (e.g., *omit*, *citizen*) Lucas's score was only 55%,

TABLE 3.2. Two Students' Performance on a Criterion-Referenced Phonics Assessment

Phonics category (examples of words)	Ruben (sample errors)	Lucas (sample errors)
Consonant–vowel–consonant words (*lap, ten, mig*)	100%	100%
Short vowel words with consonant digraphs (*math, chip, shem*)	95%	100%
Short vowel words with blends (*limp, slat, frub*)	85%	95%
Silent e and open words (*shape, flu, blode, gly*)	50% (*hop* for *hope*, *slid* for *slide*, *shap* for *shape*, *rud* for *rude*, *chip* for *chipe*; only 1/10 nonsense words correct)	85%
Vowel r words (*stir, burn, glor*)	35% (*star* for *stir*, *born* for *burn*, *from* for *form*, *spack* for *spark*; only 1/10 nonsense words correct)	90%
Vowel team words (*cheap, aim, bloot*)	40% (*am* for *aim*, *chee* for *chew*, *blot* for *bloot*, *tron* for *troin*; only 2/10 nonsense words correct)	100%
Easy two-syllable words/ words with common suffixes (*magnet, needy, ladle, glamping*)	20% (read a few real words correctly that he seemed to know by sight; no other words, and no nonsense words, correct)	75% (*laddle* for *ladle*, *stiffle* for *stifle*; *shuggle* for *shugle*; all other real words and 8/10 nonsense words read correctly)
Harder two-syllable and multisyllabic words (*excitement, unpredictable, infortuning*)	Not administered	55% (cit-EYE-zen for *citizen*; UN-i-kwa for *unique*; OM-it for *omit*; p-SOOD-nime for *pseudonym*; CAT-uh-strop-he for *catastrophe*; 4/10 nonsense words read correctly)

well below mastery level, and problematic for an eighth grader expected to read texts containing many multisyllabic words.

Analysis of Decoding Errors

In addition to determining students' mastery level, it is important to analyze specific error patterns in students' performance (Farrall, 2012). On a phonics assessment that includes both real and nonsense words, one pattern to consider involves students' ability to read real words as opposed to nonsense words. If a student can read all or most nonsense words within a category, this pattern suggests that the student has the ability to decode unfamiliar words in that category; the student is not merely reading specific words from memory. On the ABC Test, both Ruben and Lucas had good ability to read nonsense words within categories they had mastered. However, as Table 3.2 shows, Ruben's ability to decode nonsense words dropped off dramatically for all categories beyond one-syllable short-vowel words with blends. Lucas could read nonsense words for all of the one-syllable categories on the test but had more difficulty decoding longer nonsense words. This supports the idea that Ruben's phonics instruction needs to focus first on one-syllable words with patterns such as silent *e*, VR, and VT, whereas Lucas's phonics instruction should emphasize words of more than one syllable.

Closer analysis of specific errors can provide additional instructionally useful information. Table 3.2 shows some sample errors that each student made on the test, on categories that were not mastered. Ruben's errors suggest that he has difficulty decoding the long vowel in silent-*e* words—for example, he read *hop* for *hope* and *slid* for *slide*. His errors on other categories suggest that he may not know sounds for VR and VT patterns, such as the *ir* in *stir* or the *ai* in *aim*. These are all skills that can be explicitly and systematically taught to improve Ruben's decoding.

Lucas's specific error patterns differ from Ruben's. In the category for easy two-syllable words, he had trouble reading consonant-*le* words in which the first syllable is open and has a long vowel; he read these words with a short vowel (e.g., *laddle* for *ladle*). In the final multisyllabic category, he made some errors involving sounds for letter patterns that are more common in long words than in one-syllable words, such as the *-ique* in *unique*, the initial *ps* in *pseudonym*, and the *ph* in *catastrophe*. Another pattern is that Lucas decoded all sounds in many words, such as *omit* and *citizen*, correctly but placed the accent on the wrong syllable when combining syllables into a whole word. Again, these are all skills that can be addressed in instruction, through teaching of specific grapheme–phoneme relationships for long words, teaching about etymology, and flexibility training (Kearns et al., 2022).

Oral Reading Inventories

Oral reading inventories (ORIs) involve graded word lists and graded passages that a student reads aloud, with comprehension questions asked orally by the examiner after the student reads each passage. Students start at a grade level that is easy for them and proceed until the reading is too difficult for them to go further; that is, in a K–8 or K–12 ORI, a given student reads only a subset of all word lists and passages. The word lists can be evaluated for both accuracy and automaticity of real word reading. The passages are scored for both word accuracy (the percentage of words read correctly out of total words in the passage) and comprehension (the percentage of comprehension questions about each passage answered correctly). The student's performance on each word list and passage is then categorized into one of three levels: *independent*, meaning the level at which students can read words or text independently, without the help of a teacher; *instructional*, the level at which they should be placed for instruction;

and *frustration*, the level at which the reading material is too difficult for either of the preceding purposes.

Commercial ORIs provide their own specific guidelines and cutoffs for these three levels, as well as guidelines for scoring of oral reading and comprehension errors. Because of issues with standardization and technical adequacy (Farrall, 2012), scores from ORIs are not suitable for the assessment map. However, ORIs can be useful for more fine-grained observations of a student's reading skills across multiple word lists and passages, as well as for suggesting a possible type or grade level of text to try in initial instruction or intervention.

Performance of Ruben and Lucas on an ORI

Table 3.3 shows the performance of Ruben and Lucas on a hypothetical ORI, the XYZ Oral Reading Inventory, with Ruben's performance on the left and Lucas's on the right. Both students took the inventory under untimed conditions.

Ruben's ORI results show that the examiner was not able to establish an independent level for him in either the word lists or passages, even when testing in the very first passage, preprimer level (about end of kindergarten). Ruben's highest instructional level, for both the word lists and passages, was grade 1, roughly the end of first grade on an ORI. In grade 2, again for both word lists and passages, Ruben's reading was at a frustration level. Across the first three passages, even as his word accuracy declined, Ruben's comprehension remained good, perhaps in part because of the use of passage-independent questions about vocabulary, a strength for Ruben. However,

TABLE 3.3. Two Students' Performance on an Oral Reading Inventory

Ruben (grade 3)	Lucas (grade 8)
Graded word lists	
Preprimer—Instructional	Grade 5—Independent
Primer—Instructional	Grade 6—Instructional
Grade 1—Instructional	Grade 7—Instructional
Grade 2—Frustration	Grade 8—Frustration
Graded passages	
Preprimer—Instructional (word acc = 94%, comp = 100%)	Grade 4—Independent (word acc = 100%, comp = 100%)
Primer—Instructional (word acc = 92%, comp = 100%)	Grade 5—Instructional (word acc = 97%, comp = 80%)
Grade 1—Instructional (word acc = 91%, comp = 90%)	Grade 6—Instructional (word acc = 96%, comp = 75%)
Grade 2—Frustration (word acc = 80%, comp = 70%)	Grade 7—Frustration (word acc = 94%, comp = 50%)

Note. The typical lower limit for instructional-level word accuracy is about 90–93%, and for comprehension is about 75%, but specific cutoffs vary depending on the ORI. Word acc, word accuracy (percentage of words read correctly in the passage); comp, comprehension (percentage of comprehension questions answered correctly).

in the grade-2 passage, his word-reading difficulties began to have a bigger impact on his comprehension.

Lucas's ORI shows that his highest independent level in the word lists was grade 5, with his highest instructional level grade 7. However, his performance in passages was lower, due to difficulties in comprehension. In passages, his highest independent level was in the grade-4 passage and his highest instructional level in the grade-6 passage. These results support the view that Lucas has difficulties in both word reading and comprehension, in line with the standardized testing shown on his assessment map.

Error Analysis of ORI Performance

Ruben's performance on the grade-2 frustration-level passage, about a boy's trip to a zoo, is shown in Figure 3.3. Although Ruben used some sight-word knowledge in reading this passage, he had substantial difficulty decoding it because of the many words that were beyond his current level of phonics skills—words such as *raccoons*, *paced*, *peacock*, and *feathers*. He did try to self-correct two word-reading errors and was successful doing so once. More often, however, he substituted words that fit the context but were not the actual words on the page, reading *Saturday* for *Sunday*, *in a different cage* for *in another cage*, *were* for *looked*, and *liked seeing* for *loved to see*. As these

---

"The Zoo"—Grade 2 Passage

Word accuracy errors

Saturday   *EP*   *1) br- 2) friend*
On ~~Sunday~~ Matt went to the ~~park~~. His Mom and Dad took him there. His little ~~brother~~ Ben went,

with them   *nice*   *rabbits*
~~too~~. At the park was a ~~small~~ zoo with all kinds of ^animals. There were two ~~raccoons~~

   EP   *1) cag 2) SC   a different*   *EP*   *that was*
who ~~paced~~ back and forth in a big <u>cage</u>. In ~~another~~ cage was a big ~~snake called~~ a rat snake.

                      EP   *EP*   *had*   *EP*
There was also a pen with a ~~peacock~~. Sometimes the ~~peacock showed~~ its ~~feathers~~, in a big fan.

                                                        were   *liked seeing*
The feathers were blue, purple, and yellow. They ~~looked~~ very pretty. Matt and Ben ~~loved to see~~

                              going to
the peacock. That was the best thing about ^the zoo.

Comprehension errors

When did Matt go to the park? *On Saturday*

Who was Ben? *Matt's friend*

Which animals were pacing back and forth in a cage? *Some rabbits*

FIGURE 3.3. Ruben's performance on an ORI passage. A strikeout indicates a word that was read incorrectly or skipped. A carat shows words the student inserted. Words in italics above a strikeout or carat show the student's substitution or insertion errors. Underlined words were self-corrected. Numbers show the student's first and second attempts at a word. SC, self-correction (not counted as an error); EP, examiner-provided word (i.e., student could not respond within allowed time frame; counts as error).

examples show, Ruben sometimes substituted words that bore little resemblance to the printed word. To put it another way, Ruben did not consistently pay close attention to the details of printed words—not an effective strategy for success in reading.

Another notable aspect of Ruben's performance is that all of his comprehension errors related to decoding. For instance, because he misread *Sunday* as *Saturday*, he gave the wrong answer to a question about when Matt went to the park. His other comprehension errors were similar, as Figure 3.3 shows. This pattern supports the idea that Ruben's reading difficulties revolve around word reading rather than language comprehension.

Lucas's performance on the grade-7 passage from the XYZ Oral Reading Inventory, called "Richard's Summer Job," is shown in Figure 3.4. Lucas made three successful self-corrections when reading this passage orally, and his word accuracy in the passage was not nearly as poor as Ruben's was in the grade-2 passage. Lucas did not make wild guesses at words, as Ruben often did; Lucas consistently looked carefully at words and tried to decode. When he made errors, those errors sometimes reflected the same difficulty he evidenced on the ABC Test, sounding out the parts of a word correctly, but failing to put the syllables back together into the correct word (e.g., reading *calamity* as *CAL-a-mitty*).

"Richard's Summer Job"—Grade 7 Passage

Word accuracy errors

> *1) de- 2) SC*

Richard <u>despised</u> his job working in a furniture store for the summer. His boss Mr. Wilson, who happened to be a friend of Richard's Uncle Joe, was a demanding employer. He had Richard

> *1) cat- 2) SC   mer-CHAND-iss*

spend long hours in a back room <u>cataloging</u> ~~merchandise~~. This task was so boring that it

> *comma   ma-ha-GO-ny*

practically sent Richard into a coma. When Richard accidentally scratched a ~~mahogany~~ desk, his

> *1) infur- 2) EP   1) ambi- 2) EP*

carelessness ~~infuriated~~ his boss. He yelled at Richard for not being ~~ambitious~~ enough. Then he informed Richard that he was fired. Richard had no idea how he was going to tell Uncle Joe

> *1) emba- 2) SC   CAL-a-mitty*

about this <u>embarrassing</u> ~~calamity~~.

Comprehension errors

Where did Richard work for the summer? *A place where there are catalogs; maybe a bookstore?*

Who was Richard's boss? *His Uncle Joe*

What task did Richard have to work on for long hours? *Reading catalogs*

What does the word "merchandise" mean? *I'm not sure—types of catalogs?*

Why was Richard worried about talking to his Uncle Joe at the end of the passage? *I don't know*

FIGURE 3.4. Lucas's performance on an ORI passage. A strikeout indicates a word that was read incorrectly or skipped. Words in italics above a strikeout show the student's substitution errors. Underlined words were self-corrected. Numbers show the student's first and second attempts at a word. SC, self-correction (not counted as an error); EP, examiner-provided word (i.e., student could not respond within allowed time frame; counts as error).

Lucas's decoding was not automatic in this passage, and poor fluency likely impacted his performance on the comprehension questions. However, Lucas's comprehension errors also appear to be influenced by language-comprehension factors. For example, he was confused about who was Richard's boss, incorrectly specifying the boss as Uncle Joe instead of Mr. Wilson. This error might relate to syntax, the center-embedded clause in the second sentence of the passage (*His boss Mr. Wilson, who happened to be a friend of Richard's Uncle Joe, was a demanding employer*). This initial confusion likely also contributed to Lucas's inability to answer the last question in Figure 3.4, about why Richard was worried about talking to his Uncle Joe. Vocabulary weaknesses also appear to have influenced Lucas's comprehension performance. For instance, Lucas did not know the meaning of the word *merchandise*, which may have added to his confusion about where Richard worked, leading him to focus on the word *catalog* instead of recalling from the beginning of the passage that Richard worked in a furniture store.

Notice that, for both Ruben and Lucas, the results of these diagnostic assessments align with each other, as well as with the testing shown on the assessment map. For example, the ORI results are consistent with each student's profile—SWRD for Ruben, with reading difficulties centered on decoding, and MRD for Lucas, with reading difficulties involving both word reading and language comprehension. Considering the consistency of assessment results across different measures of similar constructs (e.g., word reading or comprehension) is important. If there are significant inconsistencies across assessments, educators should try to figure out why, such as by considering how differences in test characteristics, as well as student factors such as attention, might account for these disparities.

More Implications for Intervention

The diagnostic assessments discussed earlier provide some additional implications for designing reading interventions. One key decision involves the type and level of text a student should read, as text reading is very important to effective interventions (Kilpatrick, 2015). Both the ABC Test and ORI results suggest that Ruben needs decodable text because he does not yet have sufficiently developed phonics skills to read uncontrolled text successfully. Decodables are usually organized by skill rather than grade level. Ruben should do well in a decodable text with CVC words and other one-syllable short-vowel words with digraphs and blends, all categories he has mastered on the ABC Test. As Ruben learns to decode additional word patterns, he can advance to other decodables including those patterns, and then to uncontrolled text.

Lucas's assessments indicate that he does not require a decodable series because he has the phonics skills to decode a wide range of one-syllable words and even many longer words. However, he will probably have considerable difficulty reading grade-level texts, especially if he is expected to read those texts independently. For independent reading, such as homework, he will likely need some support (e.g., via assistive technology). For reading in school, texts at approximately a grade-6 level would be his instructional level, although with teacher scaffolding (e.g., preteaching of vocabulary needed to understand a particular text), Lucas might be able to function in some grade-appropriate texts.

In choosing texts for students to read, the roles of motivation and background knowledge should also be considered. For example, Lucas might be better able to read a grade-appropriate text that he is highly motivated to read or for which he has relatively strong background knowledge. For both boys, these initial decisions about text reading should be reconsidered after specific texts have been tried in intervention, with adjustments as needed.

In addition, the diagnostic assessments provide some ideas for specific skills to target first in intervention. Ruben's phonics intervention could focus initially on teaching skills for reading silent-*e* words (e.g., long vowels and the silent-*e* syllable type), although other word patterns could be appropriate as well, depending on the specific phonics sequence being used in the decodable series Ruben is reading. In the text reading part of Ruben's intervention, the interventionist should emphasize looking carefully at words and applying decoding skills, not guessing based on context.

Lucas's intervention should focus initially on two-syllable words, such as teaching him the rule for dividing consonant-*le* words—that is, to keep the consonant-*le* pattern together. Thus, a word like *ladle* divides as *la-dle*, with a first syllable that is open and has a long vowel. Intervention should then advance quickly to teaching about specific grapheme–phoneme correspondences that Lucas does not know (e.g., *ph*), etymology, and especially, the need for flexibility in decoding long words. Any phonics intervention used with Lucas should not require him to start far below his current level of decoding skill because he already has good skills for one-syllable decoding. Developing automaticity of word reading and text fluency are also important needs. In the area of comprehension, Lucas's intervention must address vocabulary, including morphology, and should consider other possible contributors to his comprehension difficulties, such as syntax and background knowledge, in relation to the specific texts he is reading.

Information from Spelling Assessments

Although spelling is technically a component of written expression, students' spelling abilities are closely related to their word-reading skills (Ehri, 2005; Moats, 2022). Underlying weaknesses in areas such as phonology or morphology manifest in students' spelling, as well as their word reading. For this reason, spelling assessments can be useful both in initial screening for reading difficulties and in informing students' interventions. Some important error patterns to look for in students' spelling include difficulties with the following:

- Phonological skills, such as frequently omitting sounds when spelling words or representing sounds incorrectly (e.g., *jup* for *jump* or *lit* for *let*)
- Spelling common phonetically irregular words (e.g., *the, to, do, of, was, come*), which are important to writing sentences and longer text

- Spelling rules and conventions, such as misspelling words that require spelling changes when adding a suffix to a base word (e.g., *shaking* as *shakeing* or *fanned* as *faned*)
- Morphological knowledge, such as misspelling common suffixes (e.g., *lookt* for *looked*, *smallist* for *smallest*) or roots of Latin or Greek derivation in long words (e.g., *teligram* for *telegram*)

Although students with any profile may have spelling difficulties, these difficulties occur often in those with SWRD and MRD, for whom spelling generally must be included in SL interventions. Spelling and word reading can be used to reinforce each other; for instance, as students are learning certain grapheme–phoneme correspondences or morphemes in reading, they can also practice those relationships in their spelling. Therefore, spelling and word-reading instruction should not be taught as completely separate areas.

Both Ruben and Lucas had spelling difficulties that involved many of the same weaknesses reflected in their word reading. Ruben was able to spell most one-syllable words with short vowels, including most words with common digraphs and many blends. However, he still needed some work on segmenting and spelling words with more difficult blends (e.g., *shr, thr, str*), and he made many spelling errors on other one-syllable word patterns, such as those involving silent *e*, VR, and VT words. Ruben also could not spell many common irregular words correctly, which affected his ability to write sentences, since it is almost impossible to write a sentence without any irregular words.

Lucas could spell many one-syllable words correctly, including common irregular words, but he had trouble spelling long words. For example, he often had difficulty spelling words with schwa, for which multiple vowel spellings are possible and the student needs to use morphemic knowledge or study specific words to learn their spellings (e.g., misspelling *treatment* as *treatmint*). For both students, these are skills that can be taught explicitly and systematically, and that should be incorporated into their interventions.

Educational History.

Information about students' educational histories can be very valuable in understanding the nature of their reading difficulties. This information can help confirm individual poor readers' profiles and provide additional insights about students' intervention needs. Educational histories include students' past assessment results, as well as the kinds of instruction they have received. Poor reader profiles are not necessarily stable over time; in the best outcomes, struggling readers may be brought to grade expectations in some or all areas through effective interventions and may never have further problems in reading. Nevertheless, many students do continue to experience some challenges, and the underlying strengths and weaknesses associated with each profile often manifest in predictable ways as students encounter escalating literacy demands across grades.

Table 3.4 displays the three poor reader profiles in relation to relatively early stages of reading, involving students like Ruben, or more advanced stages of reading, like Lucas. In general, students at early stages tend to be those in the early to middle elementary grades, whereas those at later stages tend to be in the upper elementary grades or beyond. However, the term "stage" refers to students' level of literacy functioning, not their grade placement. For example, a seventh grader (Shakira, discussed in Chapter 4) with a very severe reading difficulty could be functioning at a level that is similar to Ruben's, and therefore would be at an early stage of reading.

In the early stages of reading, students with SWRD typically have difficulties with PA, learning letters, and/or basic decoding and spelling skills. These areas should be the focus of students' interventions. Oral language comprehension is often recognized as a strength in students with SWRD. Because the texts used at this stage are relatively simple and students with SWRD have good language comprehension, the students may rely heavily on using context to compensate for poor word reading. This description fits Ruben very well. He struggled greatly with learning letters in kindergarten, as well as with PA, even with appropriate intervention provided by his school. He still struggles with basic decoding skills and overrelies on context in reading passages.

At more advanced stages of reading, students with SWRD often still have problems with word reading, but frequently their difficulties revolve around reading long words and reading fluency rather than basic phonics. Demands for volume—sheer amount—of reading are much greater as students advance to the upper elementary grades and middle school, and meeting these demands is challenging for adolescents with SWRD. Also, meeting expectations for written expression at later grade levels is often difficult, especially in relation to basic writing skills such as spelling. However, these students generally are still viewed as having good ability to learn verbally and to grasp content.

In the early stages of reading, students with SRCD, shown in the second row of Table 3.4, often have weaknesses in specific areas of oral language comprehension, such as vocabulary or narrative language, which may be noted in listening activities such as teacher read-alouds. These weaknesses may have some impact on reading comprehension, but unless the student's language weaknesses are severe, this impact may be mild and go unnoticed in the early grades. Furthermore, these students show appropriate progress in learning PA and phonics skills, so they may not be seen as at risk in reading (Clarke et al., 2014).

At more advanced stages of reading, the language weaknesses of students with SRCD impact their reading comprehension more seriously, especially in content areas such as social studies, history, and science, in which students usually are expected to read independently to learn content. These students' underlying language difficulties also make writing increasingly difficult for them. However, their writing difficulties tend to involve different components of written expression than those of students with SWRD. The writing difficulties of students with SRCD typically involve text-generation aspects of writing—translating one's thoughts into language. For students with SRCD, foundational writing skills may be a strength.

As shown in the third row of Table 3.4, at early stages of reading, students with MRD evidence a combination of weaknesses in beginning word-reading skills (e.g., in

TABLE 3.4. Difficulties Common to Each Profile at Early and Advanced Stages of Reading

Profile	Early stages of reading	More advanced stages of reading
Specific word recognition difficulties (SWRD)	• Difficulties with phonemic awareness (PA), learning letter sounds, and/or learning basic (one syllable) decoding skills • Spelling also a weakness • Overreliance on sentence or picture context to compensate for poor word reading is common • Oral language comprehension (e.g., understanding teacher read-alouds) is a strength, grade appropriate or higher • If student has received intervention, the focus usually is on PA and decoding	• Difficulties with reading unfamiliar long words (two or more syllables) • Continued difficulties with spelling • Poor reading fluency, due to poor word reading, may influence the student's ability to meet grade-level demands for reading volume and may drain reading comprehension • Increasing difficulties with grade-level written expression demands; student is often said to have good ideas but difficulties writing them down due to poor spelling/basic writing skills • Ability to learn content verbally remains grade appropriate or higher
Specific reading comprehension difficulties (SRCD)	• Weaknesses in areas of language comprehension, such as vocabulary, syntax, or background knowledge, may be noted in listening activities, such as teacher read-alouds • Language weaknesses may not affect reading comprehension at first but begin to impact reading as the student advances in school • Word reading and phonological skills at least grade appropriate • Any interventions usually have focused on comprehension rather than word reading	• Difficulties meeting text comprehension demands, especially in content areas • Written expression often a weakness, especially text-generation aspects of writing (translating one's thoughts into language, e.g., word choice, elaboration) • Rate of reading may sometimes be slow, not due to poor word reading, but because the student reads slowly to try to comprehend • Word reading and phonological skills continue to be at least grade appropriate
Mixed reading difficulties (MRD)	• Difficulties with PA, learning letter–sound correspondences, and/or basic decoding skills • Weaknesses in language comprehension (e.g., vocabulary) may be noted in listening activities in some students • Word-reading weaknesses often more noticeable than comprehension problems early on because of relatively low text demands for comprehension • Interventions may have focused on PA and phonics, only to have concerns about reading comprehension emerge later	• Comprehension weaknesses may be most noticeable in these stages, especially if word reading problems are mild • Poor reading fluency is common, and based both in word reading and language comprehension • Written expression is a weakness, with difficulties typically involving both basic writing skills (e.g., spelling) and higher-level aspects of writing such as text generation

PA and basic phonics) and in specific areas of language comprehension (e.g., vocabulary, syntax, background knowledge). At first, the word-reading problems of students with MRD may be more noticeable than their language-comprehension weaknesses because of the limited impact of the latter on reading comprehension in simpler texts. A student with MRD may receive phonics intervention in the primary grades, only to have concerns about reading comprehension emerge later, related to language-comprehension weaknesses that went undetected early on.

As students with MRD advance in reading, and assuming there has not been effective intervention, lingering problems in word reading coupled with language-comprehension weaknesses can have a substantial impact on the students' reading comprehension, as is true for Lucas. In the later grades, students' comprehension weaknesses may be more noticeable than their decoding difficulties, especially if the latter are mild or have been partially addressed through intervention. Reading fluency and written expression are also weak areas for these students, whose patterns of difficulty in written expression tend to be broad, involving both basic writing skills such as spelling, and text-generation aspects of writing such as word choice.

Students with the same profile and similar specific skills usually have similar intervention needs in relation to reading, regardless of age or grade. For instance, a seventh grader with a profile of SWRD and specific word-reading skills similar to Ruben's would be a more severely impaired reader than Ruben but would still need to be taught the same basic decoding skills, with the same emphasis on applying those skills in text reading. Of course, educators would want to try to find intervention activities appropriate to the older student's age, and the older student would have additional needs relating to his or her grade level, beyond the intervention itself, such as requiring more extensive accommodations to access general-education content. Still, the fundamental skills to be addressed in each student's intervention would be largely the same.

Therefore, the remaining chapters of this book are organized around the three profiles, with two chapters for each profile, one involving early and the other more advanced stages of reading. We turn to those chapters next, beginning with students who have SWRD.

SUMMING UP: Assessment for Planning SL Interventions

Here are key points from this chapter:

- An understanding of the student's poor reader profile is an important first step in planning effective SL interventions.

- To identify the student's profile, use technically adequate, standardized measures of key component areas, ones providing norm-referenced or benchmarked scores, in the domains of word reading and language comprehension.

- Essential components to assess in the domain of word reading are real-word reading, nonsense-word reading, automaticity of word reading, and (for many poor readers) PA; in the area of language comprehension, assess oral vocabulary and broad oral language comprehension, with more in-depth language assessment as warranted for individual students.

- Assessments of reading fluency and reading comprehension are also essential.
- Diagnostic assessments, such as criterion-referenced phonics measures, informal reading inventories, and error analysis, can provide more detailed assessment data to help determine specific skills to address in students' interventions.
- Information about a student's educational history can yield important additional insights about the nature of a student's reading problems.

APPLIED EXERCISES

Exercise 1

Polly is a fifth grader whose parents and teachers have raised concerns about her reading comprehension since the middle of grade 4. There were no concerns about Polly's reading in the primary grades, and she met both accuracy and rate benchmarks for ORF in these grades. Educators conducted an in-depth evaluation of Polly's reading, with the results detailed below.

Polly's standard scores on specific WJ-IV subtests were as follows: Word Identification, 108; Word Attack, 101; Sentence Reading Fluency, 87; Passage Comprehension, 70; Picture Vocabulary, 80; Oral Comprehension, 78; Segmentation, 111.

Here are Polly's standard scores on several additional reading-related measures. On the Peabody Picture Vocabulary Test—Fifth Edition (PPVT-5), she had a standard score of 78. On the Test of Word Reading Efficiency—Second Edition (TOWRE-2), she had a Sight Word Efficiency score of 99 and a Phonetic Decoding Efficiency score of 97. On the GORT-5, on which scaled scores have an average range of 8 to 12, Polly's scaled scores were as follows: Accuracy, 9; Rate, 9; and Comprehension, 5.

Fill out the assessment map shown in Form 3.1 with these scores. Does Polly have difficulties in reading comprehension, and if so, are these difficulties based in word reading, language comprehension, or both areas? What is Polly's poor reader profile?

Answer

Yes, Polly has difficulties in reading comprehension, and these difficulties appear to be based in broad language comprehension, including vocabulary. Her poor reader profile is SRCD. Her completed assessment map can be found in Figure 3.5. Because Polly's difficulties center on language comprehension, a more in-depth evaluation by a speech–language pathologist could be very helpful in informing her reading intervention. Administration of the three WJ-IV subtests involving academic knowledge (as was done for Lucas) might also provide useful information.

Student *Polly*   Grade *5*   Dates of Testing *Feb 10–27*

ORAL LANGUAGE COMPREHENSION

**Oral Vocabulary
(note receptive/expressive)**

PPVT–5 (receptive) **78**

WJ–IV Picture Vocab
(exp) **80**

**Oral Language
(Listening) Comprehension
(note format, e.g., cloze,
maze, QA)**

WJ–IV Oral
Comprehension **78** (cloze)

Other Oral Language

WORD READING

Real Words—Accuracy
WJ–IV Word Identification
108

**Nonsense Words—
Accuracy**
WJ–IV Word Attack 101

**Word Reading—
Automaticity**
TOWRE–2 Sight Word
Efficiency 99
TOWRE–2 Phonetic
Decoding Efficiency 97

**Phonological/phonemic
awareness**
WJ–IV Segmentation 111

**Oral Reading Fluency—
Accuracy**
GORT–5 Accuracy Scaled
Score 9

**Oral Reading Fluency—
Rate**
GORT–5 Rate Scaled Score
9

Silent Reading Fluency
WJ–IV Sentence Reading
Fluency **87**

**Reading Comprehension
(note test format, e.g.,
cloze, maze, QA, as well as
other relevant features
such as timing)**

GORT–5 Comprehension
Scaled Score **5** (timed; QA)

WJ–IV Passage
Comprehension **70**
(untimed; cloze)

Observations

GORT Comprehension
errors did not appear to
reflect problems in
decoding or reading
fluency

FIGURE 3.5. Assessment map for Polly.

Exercise 2

Is Polly's educational history consistent with her poor reader profile? Why or why not?

Answer

Yes, Polly's history is consistent with a profile of SRCD because in the primary grades she met benchmarks for accuracy and rate in ORF, and she did not have difficulties in word reading. Even in these early grades, she may have had weaknesses in vocabulary and other areas of oral language comprehension that did not impact her reading comprehension until she advanced to the middle elementary grades and the reading comprehension demands became more challenging.

Exercise 3

Notice that Polly's WJ-IV Sentence Reading Fluency (SRF) score was slightly below average range, with a standard score of 87 (although her rate on the GORT-5 was in average range). Do you think this SRF score reflects problems in word reading? Why or why not? What might explain Polly's performance on this subtest?

Answer

It is unlikely that Polly's SRF score reflects problems in word reading because, as her assessment map shows, all of her word-reading scores were average, as were her accuracy and rate on the GORT-5. WJ-IV SRF is a silent measure, and it includes a check on comprehension; the student has to respond "yes" or "no," depending on whether the sentence is true or false (e.g., for the sentence *A car always has three wheels*, the student circles *no*). Polly's performance on this subtest might reflect her comprehension weaknesses, and/or reading slowly in order to try to comprehend.

Exercise 4

What kinds of diagnostic assessments could be helpful to use in informing intervention with Polly?

Answer

The most important diagnostic assessments to use would be related to comprehension, for example, assessments of Polly's vocabulary and background knowledge for the specific texts that she is reading in school, as well as her performance on different types of comprehension questions (e.g., literal and inferential questions).

Profiles Assessment Map

Student   Grade   Dates of Testing

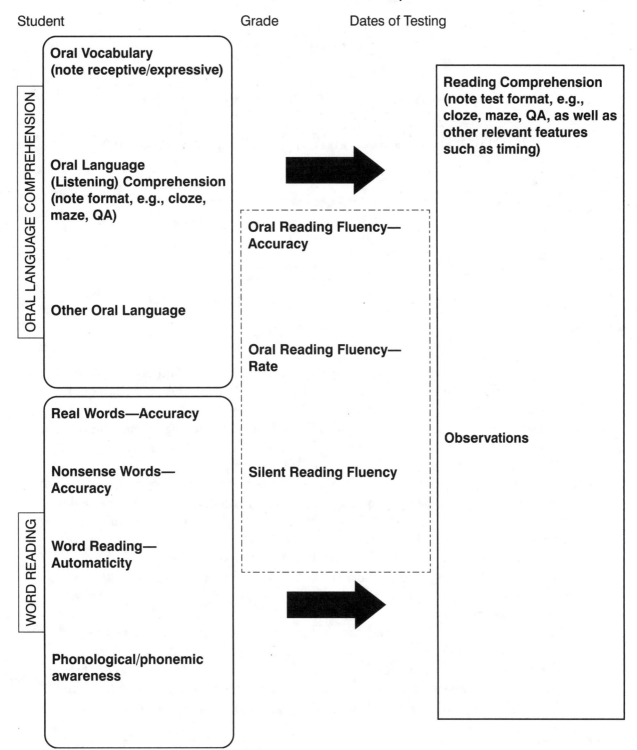

ORAL LANGUAGE COMPREHENSION

Oral Vocabulary (note receptive/expressive)

Oral Language (Listening) Comprehension (note format, e.g., cloze, maze, QA)

Other Oral Language

WORD READING

Real Words—Accuracy

Nonsense Words—Accuracy

Word Reading—Automaticity

Phonological/phonemic awareness

Oral Reading Fluency—Accuracy

Oral Reading Fluency—Rate

Silent Reading Fluency

Reading Comprehension (note test format, e.g., cloze, maze, QA, as well as other relevant features such as timing)

Observations

CHAPTER 4

Structured Literacy Interventions for Specific Word Recognition Difficulties

Early Stages

This chapter focuses on students with specific word recognition difficulties (SWRD) who are functioning at relatively early stages of reading—like Ruben, the third grader described at length in the previous chapter. Ruben's assessment map showed that his core reading weaknesses center upon word reading, not language comprehension. Additional assessments of Ruben's specific phonics skills revealed that Ruben had mastered decoding short-vowel, one-syllable word patterns, but that he had little ability to decode other one-syllable patterns (e.g., silent *e* [SE], vowel-*r* [VR], vowel team [VT]) or longer words; that is, he still required substantial instruction involving one-syllable words. Ruben struggled when reading text that was not phonetically controlled, even text at a grade-2 level, tending to guess wildly at words based on their first letters and sentence context. Ruben has recently been identified with dyslexia.

Chapter 3 also mentioned an older student, a seventh grader, Shakira, with a profile and skill level similar to Ruben's, as well as similar intervention needs. Shakira provides an example of a student who not only has a profile of SWRD, but who, like Ruben, is functioning at a relatively early stage of reading, with mastery only of short-vowel, one-syllable word patterns. Because of some compensatory skills, Shakira reads text at a slightly higher grade level than Ruben, a second- to early third-grade level. Still, given her age and grade, Shakira's reading difficulties are severe. Although many students in the early stages of SWRD are in the beginning to middle elementary grades, some are much older, like Shakira.

Readers of this chapter might wonder how a student could possibly get as far as seventh grade with reading difficulties as serious as Shakira's. A couple of factors may explain why Shakira's identification with reading problems came so late. First, Ruben's school had a core Tier 1 reading curriculum that explicitly taught important components of reading and used appropriate universal screening procedures, which led to Ruben receiving supplemental reading intervention in grade 1. In contrast, Shakira attended a school lacking these practices. The Tier 1 reading curriculum at Shakira's school did not emphasize explicit teaching of foundational reading skills and espoused a "three cueing systems" approach to reading. Furthermore, Shakira had some strengths that enabled her reading difficulties to go unnoticed by her teachers in the earliest grades: She had better-than-average language comprehension and was skilled at using context to guess at words, and she also had relatively strong sight-word knowledge. Shakira's strengths allowed her to function adequately in easy texts at first, and in the absence of effective screening of phonological skills, she was seen as progressing appropriately in reading. In fact, like Ruben, Shakira has dyslexia, which was identified when Shakira's reading difficulties became more apparent in later grades. Shakira finally began receiving SL intervention in special education in grade 6.

Not all students with SWRD have dyslexia or other disabilities, but students in the early stages of SWRD can benefit from the kinds of SL interventions discussed in this chapter, regardless of whether they have disabilities. In addition to sample intervention activities for both Ruben and Shakira, the chapter discusses effective activities for other early-stage readers with SWRD, and it introduces a format for intervention lessons for these students. The chapter also addresses intervention issues that are especially relevant to this group of poor readers, such as when a student can transition from decodable to less controlled texts and how to adapt basic SL reading activities to make them more suitable for older students.

About Early-Stage Readers with SWRD

As Ruben and Shakira illustrate, early-stage readers with SWRD can vary widely in age. What students in this group all have in common is (1) a poor reader profile with difficulties centered on word reading, not language comprehension and (2) a need for intervention in basic (one-syllable) decoding and spelling skills as opposed to more advanced, multisyllabic words. Whatever their age, these students have some similar intervention needs, although they can vary in other, potentially important ways. For instance, older students such as Shakira typically have different social–emotional needs as compared to younger poor readers, and they often require more extensive accommodations to function in general education classes. Also, by definition, older students functioning at early stages of reading have more severe reading problems than younger children at the same reading level; therefore, older students often require more intensity of intervention in order to progress. Intensity of intervention may be increased by providing longer intervention sessions, more frequent intervention sessions, longer-duration interventions (e.g., lasting months or years vs. weeks), and a smaller group size in intervention. Intensifying certain characteristics of the intervention (e.g., by increasing explicitness, breaking instruction into smaller steps, or providing more practice opportunities with feedback) can also be beneficial (Vaughn, Wanzek, Murray, & Roberts, 2012).

Key intervention needs of early-stage readers with SWRD involve PA, grapheme–phoneme and phoneme–grapheme knowledge, basic phonics (decoding) skills, reading of phonetically irregular words, and spelling. Even at an early stage of reading, transfer of word-reading skills to text reading is vital, so text reading accuracy and fluency are also key intervention needs. Considerable research exists to inform interventions for readers in the early stages of SWRD, as summarized in the next section.

Research on Interventions for Early-Stage Readers with SWRD

PA and Letter Knowledge

Many abilities are ultimately important in learning to read, but in the beginning stages of reading, the two most essential skills are PA and knowledge of grapheme–phoneme/phoneme–grapheme correspondences, that is, knowledge of letters (NRP, 2000; Roberts et al., 2020). PA, awareness of individual sounds (phonemes) in spoken words, is necessary for students to understand the logic of an alphabet and begin mapping sounds to letters. Without knowledge of letter names and especially letter sounds, progress in beginning reading is impossible. Moreover, in the early stages of reading, PA and letter knowledge are strongly related, with growth in one contributing to growth in the other (Lerner & Lonigan, 2016). Most students with SWRD have initial difficulties in one or both of these areas.

Phonological awareness includes more rudimentary levels of awareness than PA, such as rhyming. Especially with young children, it may be helpful to begin instruction with these easier tasks (Foorman et al., 2016). However, requiring children to master a lengthy sequence of rudimentary levels of awareness is not necessary. Teachers can begin with, or rapidly progress to, PA tasks involving phoneme identity—first, initial sounds in words, followed by final sounds, then medial vowels (Brady, 2020). Instruction can then focus on full phoneme blending and phoneme segmentation of simple words, such as CVC words. Letters should be integrated into PA instruction for children in kindergarten and beyond (Brady, 2020; Brown, Patrick, Fields, & Craig, 2021; NRP, 2000). Children with limited letter knowledge can initially perform PA tasks with pictures and colored counters, then transition to using letter tiles representing phonemes as their letter knowledge develops (see, e.g., Al Otaiba et al., 2022; Foorman et al., 2016). Initial activities focused on phoneme segmentation and spelling of words can be even more effective in promoting growth in word decoding than traditional phonics instruction alone (Herron & Gillis, 2020).

Students with difficulties in PA may benefit from using articulatory cues to increase their awareness of phonemes in words (Castiglione-Spalten & Ehri, 2003), such as looking in a mirror to see the shape of their lips when articulating various sounds. It can also be helpful to begin PA instruction with words containing continuous sounds, sounds that can be articulated continuously or stretched (e.g., /f/, /m/, /n/, /s/), rather than stop consonants such as /b/, /g/, or /t/. A CVC word such as *sun* is easier to blend and segment than *bug*, even though both words are CVC words with three phonemes and the same vowel, because *sun* involves continuous sounds, whereas *bug* contains two stop consonants.

For at-risk children and those who have difficulty learning letters, simple exposure to letters in contextualized situations—such as in books or in their own or classmates' names—will not suffice for efficient learning (Roberts et al., 2020). Highly explicit and systematic instruction in letter names and sounds, including decontextualized instruction focused specifically on letters, is often needed. Even for preschoolers, decontextualized instruction involving features of SL—such as highly explicit teaching, many opportunities for practice, and active responding with teacher feedback—has been found more effective in improving learning of letter sounds and PA than contextualized letter instruction focused on presenting letters in storybooks and children's names (Roberts et al., 2020). Contrary to many teachers' beliefs that decontextualized instruction is not engaging to children, Roberts and colleagues (2020) also found greater student engagement in a decontextualized than in a contextualized intervention.

Another effective approach for students who have difficulty learning letters involves the use of mnemonic cues, including systems of mnemonics. For example, Roberts and Sadler (2019) studied an intervention involving integrated mnemonics, with letter forms embedded within pictures of letter characters whose character name contained the relevant letter sound, and with short narratives about the different letter characters. The integrated mnemonics intervention was more effective in promoting letter-sound learning and PA than a control condition involving plain letters and alphabet books. Integration of handwriting instruction in teaching of letter knowledge and phonological skills also is valuable (Ray, Dally, Rowlandson, Tam, & Lane, 2022). As children learn to form letters properly—as much as possible, in a single stroke and in a manner that will facilitate developing speed of writing—they can reinforce their knowledge of the shape of the letter and its sound.

Basic Phonics Skills, Spelling, and Irregular Words

Many studies and literature reviews (e.g., Brady, 2020; Christensen & Bowey, 2005; Fletcher et al., 2019; Foorman et al., 2016; NRP, 2000; Stanovich, 2000) have documented the effectiveness of explicit, systematic phonics interventions both for reading and spelling words. As discussed in Chapter 1, varied methods for teaching phonics exist, but post-NRP research has favored the one common to SL approaches, synthetic-phonics with initial instruction at the grapheme–phoneme level, especially for reading transfer words and advanced words (Brady, 2020; Christensen & Bowey, 2005). In this latter approach, phonics instruction is integrated with PA instruction and emphasizes basic grapheme–phoneme (as well as phoneme–grapheme) correspondences, such as correspondences for single letters (e.g., the letter *m* corresponds to the phoneme /m/) and common consonant digraphs (e.g., the letter pattern *sh* corresponds to /sh/). A common problem for many students at this stage is blending phonemes. For these students, the use of connected phonation, in which students learn to pronounce phonemes without breaking the speech stream, may be useful (Gonzalez-Frey & Ehri, 2021).

Later, students learn correspondences for larger units such as VR patterns (e.g., *ar*, *er*, *or*) and common inflectional endings (e.g., *-ing*, *-est*). As students progress beyond short-vowel words, the variability of vowel sounds in English is challenging. Teaching them about syllable types may help address this problem (Foorman et al., 2016; Spear-Swerling, 2009).

Initial spelling instruction should be integrated with students' phonics instruction so that students are learning to spell the same types of words, with the same grapheme–phoneme correspondences, they are learning to decode. In general, the emphasis should be on using the same word *patterns* in spelling and decoding, not exactly the same *words*, because the goal is for students to develop skills for decoding and spelling unfamiliar words rather than to memorize specific words. For instance, if students are learning to decode and spell CVC words with the vowels *a* and *i*, their decoding practice within a particular lesson might include the words *mat*, *map*, *lag*, *lip*, and *sit*, whereas spelling practice could focus on other CVC words with *a* and *i* (e.g., *sat*, *sag*, *hip*, *rid*, *tin*). When students can spell simple short-vowel words, teachers can introduce basic spelling generalizations such as the "floss" rule (doubling the *f*, *l*, and *s* at the end of a one-syllable, short vowel word; e.g., *stuff*, *will*, *mess*). Phoneme–grapheme mapping, word building, and word sorts are effective for teaching spelling, as well as decoding (Foorman et al., 2016; Moats, 2022).

Early word-reading instruction must also encompass teaching of phonetically irregular (exception) words, words that do not entirely conform to common phonics relationships, for example, a word such as *some*, which should be pronounced to rhyme with *dome* but is not, or *Wednesday*, which should be pronounced with three syllables but only has two. Although it has been common in education to approach these kinds of words as requiring rote memorization, more recent research and thinking (e.g., Moats, 2020, 2022; Seidenberg, 2017) have emphasized that irregular words typically contain regularities, as well as irregularities; therefore, phonological skills do help students in reading these words. For instance, the *s* and *m* in *some* conform to their usual pronunciations, as do the letters at the beginning and end of *Wednesday*. Several instructional strategies have been found useful for irregular words, including pointing out the regularities, as well as irregularities, to students; mnemonic cues (e.g., *where* contains the word *here*); and grouping similar patterns together, such as *some* and *come* (Moats, 2022). Coupled with these strategies, multisensory activities involving repeated tracing and saying of words can improve both reading and spelling of irregular words (Spear-Swerling, 2009; Spear-Swerling & Brucker, 2004).

In the early stages of phonics instruction, SL approaches use decodable texts that focus on specific, learned word patterns that provide students with practice applying their decoding skills to text reading and help students avoid maladaptive strategies such as guessing based on context. To be maximally useful for these purposes, decodables should have a high lesson-to-text match; that is, the sequence of phonics skills taught in individual phonics lessons should correlate well with the texts children are reading (Murray, Munger, & Hiebert, 2014). Sometimes teachers do not have access to a comprehensive program that provides this kind of matching of lessons to texts. In this situation, an alternative is to examine the sequence of skills in the decodable series teachers are using and to adopt that sequence for teaching phonics in lessons.

Reading Fluency

Most students with SWRD struggle with developing reading fluency, the ability to read text accurately, effortlessly, and with appropriate speed. These students' fluency weaknesses are based in word-reading problems involving inaccurate or nonautomatic decoding, not language comprehension. Common general education practices for fluency building, such as instructional time devoted to sustained silent reading, are ineffective for these students, who require explicit fluency instruction (Rasinski, Homan, & Biggs, 2009).

For students with early-stage SWRD, developing automaticity on specific word-reading skills—identifying letter sounds, reading various regular word patterns, and reading common irregular words—can help provide a foundation for fluent text reading. Brief but frequent timed practice, such as flash card activities for 1 or 2 minutes in each lesson reviewing letter sounds or previously taught irregular words, may help students develop automaticity as well as accuracy. SL lessons typically include this kind of practice (see, e.g., Carnine, Silbert, Kame'enui, & Tarver, 2009; Wilson, 2018).

Instruction that fosters accuracy of text reading, such as guided oral reading of text with appropriate teacher feedback, benefits these students (NRP, 2000). Guided oral reading of text with appropriate teacher feedback helps ensure that students look carefully at the details of printed words and consistently apply their phonics skills to text reading. Nevertheless, many students with SWRD require additional interventions focused on building rate. Research reviews (e.g., Stevens, Walker, & Vaughn, 2017) suggest that repeated reading, in which students read the same text repeatedly, usually under timed conditions (see, e.g., Hudson et al., 2022), is the most effective intervention for increasing reading fluency. In elementary students with learning disabilities, such as Ruben, repeated reading often benefits comprehension, as well as fluency. In older students like Shakira with severe, long-standing reading problems, achieving strong growth in fluency may be particularly difficult, but repeated reading may still provide some improvements in rate (Wexler, Vaughn, Edmonds, & Reutebuch, 2008).

Certain features can increase the effectiveness of repeated reading interventions. These include the use of relatively easy texts, providing a model of fluent reading, providing performance feedback to students, and setting an accuracy or rate goal for students (Stevens et al., 2017). Timing can be valuable for monitoring fluency progress, but for the student who tends to rush reading to the detriment of accuracy or comprehension, or who is made anxious by timing, the timing can be done covertly, without the student's awareness. Improvements in accuracy of text reading are very important, even if they are not accompanied by equivalent rate gains. Students who read accurately at grade level can perform much better in general education classes than those who cannot, even if their rate does not meet grade expectations. Therefore, teachers should monitor students' progress in both accuracy and rate of text reading.

Sample SL Intervention Activities

An Intervention Routine for Teaching PA and Letter Knowledge

Emily Odesky, a reading interventionist who is working with a group of four first grad-ers, provides a good example of SL intervention for students at the earliest stages of SWRD. Ms. Odesky's students all struggle with PA and letter knowledge. The children have some ability to perform phoneme identity tasks; they can usually identify initial sounds of spoken words, but they still have some difficulty with final sounds. Also, they have some knowledge of letters, especially of capital letters, but their knowledge of lower-case letters and their sounds is much more limited. Below is a useful SL inter-vention routine that Ms. Odesky uses for these skills. The routine can be varied to suit students' needs and used for teaching grapheme–phoneme patterns such as consonant digraphs, as well as single letters. It is partially based on the decontextualized inter-vention of Roberts and colleagues (2020), as well as activities from Slingerland (1994).

1. Using flash cards, Ms. Odesky quickly reviews previously learned letters, both lower- and uppercase. (Lower- and uppercase letters are presented on separate cards.) Students chorally give the name and sound for each letter. The aim of this step is to build automaticity on letters children generally know, and Ms. Odesky deliber-ately moves at a fast pace, but if mistakes are made, she puts the letter card aside for increased review.

2. Every 2 or 3 days, Ms. Odesky introduces a new letter name and sound that children need to learn, prioritizing lowercase letters and explicitly teaching both the name and the most common sound together. For example, for the letter *n*, Ms. Odesky holds up the letter card *n* and says, "Today we are going to learn a new letter. The name of this letter is *n*, and its sound is /n/, as in *nut*. What is the letter name? What is the letter sound?" Children respond chorally, several times.

3. A tracing activity helps students practice the new letter–sound correspondence and also incorporates handwriting. Ms. Odesky gives students a large piece of paper with lines for handwriting—solid top and bottom lines, as well as a lighter middle line (see Figure 4.1). The paper is folded in thirds, with the new letter written on the far left section of the paper. Ms. Odesky models on a whiteboard how to form the letter correctly (e.g., lowercase *n* starts on the middle line, goes straight down to the bottom line, has a hump that goes back up to the middle line, then ends on the bottom line). The children repeatedly trace over the letter with their pencils, while at the same time saying the letter name and its sound; Ms. Odesky monitors their letter formation as they do so, before telling them to proceed to the center section of the paper. The center section has a dotted-line version of the letter for children to trace and say, repeating the process already used for the left-hand section. Finally, children fold the left-hand section of the paper over the center section, so that only the blank section on the right is visible; they write the letter from memory and repeatedly trace it, saying the corre-sponding name and sound.

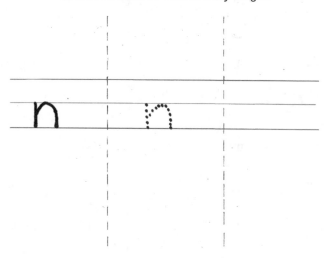

FIGURE 4.1. Tracing activity for letter–sound correspondence.

4. Ms. Odesky gives each student a set of five or six letter cards involving any newly introduced letter, along with several review letters. Then, using a separate set of picture cards without letters (e.g., a picture of a nail), Ms. Odesky shows the picture, names it, and asks individual students to hold up the letter that corresponds to the first sound in the word (e.g., *n* for nail) and then the last sound (*l* for nail). If the student being called upon shows the correct card, other students have learned also to hold up the correct card; otherwise, they are supposed to remain silent while Ms. Odesky helps the individual student correct his or her error. Then all students respond chorally with the correct card, letter name, and sound. This procedure helps maintain students' attention and gives all students practice even when an individual child is responding (see, e.g., Slingerland, 1994).

5. To further build automaticity of students' letter-sound knowledge, Ms. Odesky uses a brief timed practice activity. The activity uses arrays of printed lowercase letters that children have learned, randomly ordered and repeated (see Figure 4.2). In 20-second increments, children are asked to mark several specified letters when the teacher gives the sound, while simultaneously whispering to themselves the letter sound they are marking. For instance, Ms. Odesky might say, "Now we are going to find letter sounds. Work as fast as you can without making mistakes. First, circle the letter with the sound /s/ as in *sun*. Find all of them. Ready, set, go. Stop [after 20 seconds]. Next, we'll do the letter with the sound /b/ as in *boy*. Put a line through every letter with the sound /b/, and find all of them," and so on. Ms. Odesky uses individual children's papers to help monitor their progress in learning letters; the child whose performance is shown in Figure 4.2 was accurate in identifying all three letters in the activity—*s, b,* and *f* —but appears to need more practice to become automatic on *b* and *f*.

6. Individual letter books encourage children to practice the letters they have been taught, including at home with their parents. Each letter is displayed on a separate

f	(s)	t	a	f
m	l	r	i̶	(s)
a	i̶	l	f	m
t	m	f	(s)	r
l	a	m	t	b
r	l	a	f	t
b	(s)	l	a	r
r	t	(s)	b	m

FIGURE 4.2. A first grader's timed letter–sound practice.

page in enlarged font. Pictures are provided for the initial sound of each letter to help children practice the correct letter–sound relationship (e.g., a picture of the sun for the letter *s*). Children are also taught to trace over the letter with their index fingers, using correct letter formation, while practicing the letter name and sound.

With the above routine, Ms. Odesky is developing children's knowledge of two short vowels, for *a* and *i*, as well as their knowledge of single consonants, because she wants students to move into decoding and spelling simple words as quickly as possible. Students do not have to have perfect knowledge of letter sounds to begin decoding and spelling simple words; words can use the letter sounds that students know. One especially helpful intervention activity for students at early stages of decoding and spelling is word building. Ms. Odesky's students will soon be ready for this activity, described next.

Word Building for Decoding and Spelling

Word building has long been employed in SL teaching of phonics skills, using varied materials and procedures. For her group of first graders, Ms. Odesky plans to use a pocket chart on an easel, with large letter cards that are easy for all the children to see. The teacher arrays the cards to spell different words that children take turns reading, with a focus only on letter sounds and word patterns that children know, and with cards substituted, added, or deleted to form new words. For instance, after using the *s*, *a*, and *t* cards to spell *sat*, the teacher substitutes the *s* card in *sat* with the card for *m*, to spell *mat*, or changes the *a* to *i* to form *sit*. Initially, Ms. Odesky emphasizes words with continuous sounds that are easiest to blend. Instead of the pocket chart, teachers can also use letter tiles, especially with small groups or in one-to-one instruction.

A key requirement of the materials is that the cards or tiles should be at the phoneme–grapheme level. For instance, consonant digraphs such as *sh* and *th* should be represented on one card, not with two separate cards. Unfamiliar word patterns and irregular words must be screened out of the activity. Using chains of highly patterned words can be especially effective, with single-phoneme changes made in unpredictable places in the word—that is, not always the first letter, not *sat* to *bat* to *hat* to *rat*, but instead, say, *sat* to *sap* to *sip* to *tip*. This activity encourages students to look carefully at the internal details of words (McCandliss et al., 2003), an important habit to develop for successful decoding. Furthermore, if structured appropriately and done at a brisk pace, like a game, the activity can be very engaging to students. Figure 4.3 displays an example of a sequence of words in a word-building activity that Ms. Odesky might use with her first graders, when they know the short vowels *a* and *i*, as well as many single-consonant sounds. In a typical 10- to 15-minute activity, more words

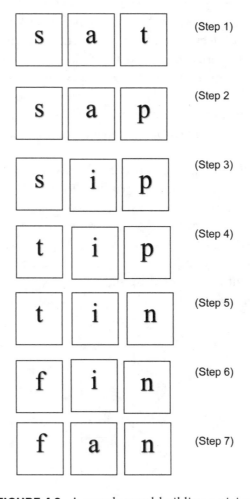

s a t	(Step 1)
s a p	(Step 2
s i p	(Step 3)
t i p	(Step 4)
t i n	(Step 5)
f i n	(Step 6)
f a n	(Step 7)

FIGURE 4.3. A sample word-building activity.

might be practiced beyond those shown in the figure, for example, *fan* to *ran* to *rag* to *rig* to *dig* and so on.

If reversed, with the teacher dictating words and the students using letter cards or tiles to spell them, word building is also valuable for teaching spelling, as is a paper-and-pencil activity, phoneme–grapheme mapping. In phoneme–grapheme mapping, the teacher dictates a series of patterned words, and students write the words into boxes, with one grapheme per box. Figure 4.4 displays an example of a phoneme–grapheme mapping activity for children who are learning to spell short-vowel words with blends and digraphs. Phoneme–grapheme mapping can be used to help students learn to spell a range of word patterns, not just short-vowel words; for detailed discussion and examples, see Moats (2020, 2022).

Word Sorts for Syllable Types

Syllable types were discussed in Chapter 2, which includes a list of syllable types, with concise definitions and examples of words, in Table 2.1. Teaching students about syllable types can help them determine the vowel sounds of unfamiliar words, which are highly variable in English. Although the teacher must know clear, concise definitions of syllable types for effective teaching, instructional activities for students should emphasize looking for patterns in printed words and applying knowledge of syllable types to read unknown words, not verbalization of rules. Sorting tasks can be very valuable in teaching syllable types. The main prerequisite for students to begin learning syllable types is being able to classify single letters as either vowels or consonants. To apply syllable types in reading words, students must also know the relevant letter–sound relationships.

A student such as Ruben, who can decode short-vowel words and has learned the closed-syllable type, but who needs to learn how to decode other one-syllable words such as SE syllables, could benefit from a sorting task involving closed, SE, and "other" words. An "other" category ensures that the student has to look carefully at words; without this category, Ruben could sort closed and SE merely by looking at the final letter of each word to see if it ends in an *e*. Teachers should also include many examples of words that the student cannot read by sight because the point of learning syllable types is to have a useful strategy for decoding unfamiliar words.

s	i	p		
s	a	p		
s	n	a	p	
s	l	a	p	
f	l	a	p	
f	l	a	sh	
f	l	u	sh	

FIGURE 4.4. Sample grapheme–phoneme mapping activity.

Figure 4.5 shows examples of words that would be appropriate in a sorting task for Ruben. Because SE is the new concept, that category has the most words. Below is a sample intervention routine for teaching syllable types that Ruben's teacher could use.

1. Ruben's teacher explains the SE syllable type to Ruben, using a clear, concise definition and a specific example of a word. (See Table 2.1: A silent-*e* word ends in a vowel–consonant–*e* [-VC*e*] pattern; the first vowel will be long and the *e* silent.) She models looking at a few additional words and deciding whether the word has a -VC*e* pattern, including potentially confusing words such as *dance*, which end in a silent *e* but are not considered SE syllables because they have two consonants before the *e*, not one. In this initial step, the focus is on looking for the letter pattern in the word rather than reading the word.

2. For SE words, after highlighting the -VC*e* pattern, the teacher emphasizes that the first vowel in the -VC*e* pattern will be long and the final *e* will be silent (e.g., "So, this word [pointing to *flame*] has a vowel–consonant–*e* pattern [underlining the *ame* part of the word]. It is a silent-*e* syllable; the *a* will say its name, and the *e* will be silent. The word is *flame*"). She then guides Ruben through classifying several additional words as SE or not-SE.

3. Using the words shown in Figure 4.5, written on index cards and mixed together, she asks Ruben to sort the words into three piles: closed, SE, and other. She provides coaching as needed by asking questions about the letter pattern in the word (e.g., "Does this word have a vowel–consonant–*e* pattern at end? So is it a silent-*e* syllable?").

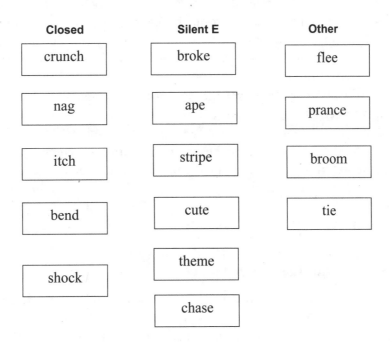

Closed	Silent E	Other
crunch	broke	flee
nag	ape	prance
itch	stripe	broom
bend	cute	tie
shock	theme	
	chase	

FIGURE 4.5. A sample word sort for Ruben.

4. When the sorting task is complete, the "other" category is set aside. Ruben is asked to give the vowel sound for each SE syllable, then read the word (e.g., for the word *broke*, Ruben says "Long /o/," then reads the entire word). As he becomes more skilled at reading these words, the step of giving the vowel sound first can be dropped. Ruben also reads the closed-syllable pile as a review.

Activities for Phonetically Irregular Words

Some phonetically irregular words must be explicitly taught to early-stage readers with SWRD because without knowledge of common irregular words, students cannot read or write even the simplest sentences. For groups of children, the three-part activity shown in Figure 4.1 can be adapted for irregular words. Instead of writing a letter or letter pattern in the first two sections of the paper, the teacher writes the irregular word, first as normally written and then in a dotted-line version in the center part of the paper. The right-hand section is again blank, and children write the word from memory, using the basic procedure described previously in the chapter. As they repeatedly trace over the word with their pencils or write it from memory, they say the letter names (rather than the sounds), then the whole word (e.g., *p -u -t, put*).

A variant of this activity involves writing the word on an index card or piece of paper, having the student use the tracing-and-saying routine, then turning over the card and writing the word from memory. If the student makes a mistake, the tracing-and-saying routine is repeated until the student remembers the word and spells it correctly. The tracing procedure is only used to introduce new words or practice words the student continues to read or spell incorrectly. Learned words—those on which the student is usually accurate but needs to develop automaticity—can be practiced on flash cards without tracing. When introducing new words, teachers should mention any helpful mnemonic cues for specific words and should point out the regularities in the word. For example, for the word *put*, both the *p* and the *t* have their usual sounds; only the vowel *u* is irregular.

Although students' learning to spell these words often lags behind learning to read them, the kinds of activities described can facilitate growth in both reading and spelling of irregular words (Spear-Swerling, 2009; Spear-Swerling & Brucker, 2004) Also, it is important to attend to lesson-to-text match in relation to irregular words, as well as phonics elements. In choosing which irregular words to teach, teachers should first take these words from the texts that students are reading in intervention, so that students will not repeatedly encounter unknown irregular words during the text-reading part of the lesson.

Oral Text Reading with Teacher Feedback

Oral reading of text is an essential part of interventions for students with early-stage SWRD. Teachers cannot assume that these students will naturally transfer skills learned in phonics lessons to text reading because children may overrely on context when reading text, as Ruben does. Also, text reading requires coordinating multiple skills, not just reading individual words. Moreover, text reading is motivating for many students, especially if texts are well chosen. Adequate time for text reading in lessons is therefore very important. For students with SWRD, text reading in lessons must include oral reading because of the need to monitor these students' accuracy and provide feedback to word-reading errors.

As noted previously, decodable texts are generally most appropriate for these students, especially in initial instruction. Once students have mastered a variety of one-syllable word patterns, they should have the phonics skills to decode many words they will encounter in less controlled texts at their instructional levels, and they can transition out of controlled decodables. The appropriate transition point varies depending on factors such as the student's sight-word knowledge, automaticity of word reading, and motivation to read a particular text. Teachers can check whether a specific text is suitable for a student by monitoring the student's word accuracy in text reading, with a minimum of at least 90–93% word accuracy typically suggested for instructional level. Conversely, if the student's word accuracy and automaticity are flawless, a harder book should be tried. Comprehension during text reading is not usually an issue for an early-stage reader with SWRD, assuming the student's word accuracy in a text meets criteria for instructional level. However, if the student does evidence poor comprehension in this situation, teachers should consider whether, despite good word accuracy, a student's word reading may be effortful, thus creating a drain on comprehension.

Whether students are reading decodables or other types of text, an important aspect of SL instruction involves teacher feedback to students' word-reading errors. Apparently minor, contextually appropriate errors (e.g., *this* for *that* or *a* for *the*) should not be ignored because text-reading accuracy is a foundation for building fluency, and even contextually appropriate errors can impair comprehension (Daane, Campbell, Grigg, Goodman, & Oranje, 2005). Feedback should be provided immediately, and it should include having the child read the word correctly and reread the sentence (Archer & Hughes, 2011). Lengthy verbal feedback to errors during text reading, which may be inadvertently confusing and drain comprehension, is best avoided. However, non-verbal cues such as pointing can be very useful in focusing the student's attention on the details of printed words without draining comprehension. If verbal cues are used, they should be brief and concise (Heubusch & Lloyd, 1998). Below is a sequence of steps that teachers can try in providing feedback to students' word-reading errors during oral text reading:

- Wait for a few seconds to see if the student tries to self-correct; attempts at self-corrections are a positive sign and should be encouraged, even if the student cannot independently arrive at the correct word.
- If it is clear that the student will not or cannot self-correct, use a pointing cue, such as pointing to a word the student has skipped or read incorrectly. Pointing cues can also focus on parts of words; for example, if a student has read the word *spoon* as *soon*, the teacher can point to the *p*.
- If pointing cues do not work, try a brief verbal cue (e.g., in the *spoon* example, feedback such as, "Notice the *p*").

- If this fails, then tell the student the word and have him or her repeat it.
- The final step should involve having the student reread the sentence.
- Students should be taught to cross-check *after* decoding that the word they have read makes sense in context.

If teachers use this kind of feedback procedure regularly, students become accustomed to it, and the teacher does not have to repeatedly remind the student to reread the sentence at the end. Also, one exception to this procedure may occur when a student is having difficulty reading a phonetically irregular word. In this situation, it is generally best simply to tell the student the word right away, since attempts at decoding will not usually succeed. If teaching of irregular words in lessons is coordinated with the sequence of these words in the texts students are reading, such errors should be uncommon. Table 4.1 displays some examples of student errors during text reading, with sample teacher feedback depending on the type of error.

Finally, it is important to note several variations in students' text reading that do not count as decoding errors. These are variations in pronunciation of words due to dialect or regional differences, foreign accent, or articulation, all of which are generally not counted as errors on standardized testing of oral reading. For example, students who speak African American English (AAE), a common variety of English, may read *bath* as *baf*, or words containing final -*ing* with a dropped *g* (e.g., *runnin* for *running*), because those pronunciations are consistent with AAE (Washington & Seidenberg, 2021). Similarly, a child who articulates *rabbit* as *wabbit* might read the word that way. If the teacher constantly stops a child during oral text reading to provide feedback to such variations, fluency and comprehension may be severely disrupted. The child may become discouraged and embarrassed. A better way to address these kinds of language differences is to provide phonics and spelling instruction that reviews the standard pronunciation of these words in relation to common phoneme–grapheme correspondences (Washington & Seidenberg, 2021). Of course, teacher feedback should still be provided to text-reading errors that reflect poor decoding, as well as to spelling errors.

SL Intervention Plans for Early-Stage Readers with SWRD

Table 4.2 displays a basic lesson format that can be useful in intervention with students such as Ruben and Shakira, who have SWRD and are functioning at early stages of reading. The plan is adapted from Spear-Swerling (2022a) and contains broad segments for four areas: word recognition and spelling; fluency; text reading; and writing. For each lesson segment, Table 4.2 includes a description, sample activities, and suggested time allocations. Total lesson time is 40–60 minutes. However, the plan can be adapted, depending on student needs. For example, for students with milder difficulties, different lesson segments might be alternated across days rather than being implemented every day. For all students, the time allocations for lesson segments can be adjusted to suit individual students' needs. Data from progress monitoring assessments

TABLE 4.1. Specific Examples of Word-Reading Errors with Sample Teacher Feedback

Type of error	Text	Specific student (S) error	Sample teacher (T) feedback
Student tries but struggles to read a word he or she has the skills to decode.	*At last, Jan got her wish. Her mom and dad gave her a pet cat as a gift.*	"At last, Jan got her wish. Her mom and dad gave her a pet cat as a g-, git." [S pauses, knows word is wrong but has trouble correcting it.]	T points to the letter *f*. S says, "gif," then pauses, still struggling to sound out the word. T points to the letter *t*. S says, "gif–t," without blending. T says, "Say it fast." S says, "gift." T says, "Well done!" Asks S to reread the sentence.
Student makes an error on a small function word he or she knows.	*Gus is a little fish in a big pond.*	"Gus is a little fish in the big pond."	T points to the word *a*. S self-corrects word to *the*. T asks S to reread the sentence.
Student skips a word.	*Jupiter is the largest of the nine planets.*	"Jupiter is the largest of the planets." [S skips over the word *nine*.]	T points to the word *nine*. S reads "nine" correctly. T asks S to reread the sentence.
Student struggles to read an irregular word.	*Maria felt that Mr. Crandall was not an honest man.*	"Maria felt that Mr. Crandall was not an hoan. . . . "[S tries to sound out the irregular word *honest*.]	T points to word and says, "honest." T says, "What word?" [S repeats, "honest."] T asks student to reread the sentence.
Student fails to try to correct a contextually inappropriate error.	*At last, Jan got her wish. Her mom and dad gave her a pet cat as a gift.*	"At last, Jan got her wash. Her mom and dad gave her a pet cat. . . ." [S keeps reading.]	T points to the letter *i* in the word *wish*. S sounds out "w-e-sh." T says, "I says /i/." S sounds out "w-i-sh, wish." T says, "Yes. Now read the sentence again, and make sure the word makes sense." [S rereads.] T says, "Does that make more sense?" [S nods.] T says, "Good job!"

should be used to inform decisions about time allocations and make any necessary changes on an ongoing basis.

Some details of the plan in Table 4.2 should be underscored. The first segment, word recognition and spelling, involves multiple bulleted areas, including PA, phoneme–grapheme correspondences, generalizations for decoding and spelling, decoding phonetically regular words in isolation, spelling, and irregular words. Not every bulleted area will necessarily be covered in every session. For instance, a student with SWRD

TABLE 4.2. Format for an Intervention Plan for Students with SWRD

Component(s)	Description	Sample activities
Word recognition and spelling (~20–25 minutes)	Skills for reading and spelling printed words	
• Phonemic awareness (PA)	• Key PA skills such as phoneme blending and segmentation	• Oral practice with teacher modeling, counters, letter tiles
• Phoneme–grapheme, grapheme–phoneme, and morphological relationships	• Correspondences for single letters, letter patterns (e.g., *sh, ch, oy*), and morphemes (e.g., *-ing, -ed*)	• Explicit teaching with letter cards; tracing and saying activities
• Generalizations (rules or strategies for decoding and spelling unfamiliar words)	• Generalizations for decoding (e.g., syllable types) and spelling (e.g., "floss" rule)	• Explicit teaching of generalizations with guided practice; word sorts
• Decoding words	• Apply above skills to read unfamiliar, phonetically regular printed words	• Word-building activities; decoding sorted words
• Spelling	• Apply above skills to spell phonetically regular words	• Word-building activities with letter tiles; writing dictated words; phoneme–grapheme mapping
• Irregular (exception) words	• Read and spell words that contain exceptions to typical phonics relationships	• Tracing and saying activities; teach similar patterns together (e.g., *could, should, would*)
Fluency (~5–10 minutes)	Practice reading words automatically and reading text fluently	Timed flash-card practice on common irregular words; repeated readings of text
Text reading (~10–15 minutes)	Application of word reading skills to reading an unfamiliar text aloud, with accuracy, and while maintaining good comprehension	Guided oral reading of decodable or instructional-level text with immediate teacher feedback to decoding errors; alternating reading
Writing (~5–10 minutes)	Using writing to teach or reinforce foundational skills (e.g., phonemic awareness, decoding, spelling)	Apply learned spelling and basic writing skills in writing tasks (e.g., dictated sentences)

Note. From Spear-Swerling (2022a). Copyright © 2022 The Guilford Press. Reprinted by permission.

might already have mastered the PA skills required for basic decoding and spelling; therefore, that area might be routinely omitted. As another example, students often take some time to master a new phonics or spelling generalization, so a session might focus on practicing previously taught generalizations rather than introducing a new one.

Because this plan is for students with SWRD, the text-reading part of the lesson focuses mainly on developing accuracy and fluency of text reading, not on teaching comprehension. Comprehension instruction is certainly important for all students, but these students do not need *intervention* in the area of comprehension; they can usually receive their comprehension development as part of Tier 1 instruction, with any necessary accommodations. Of course, students should always attend to meaning as they read text, so interventionists will still want to ask some questions and ensure that students are maintaining good comprehension as they read. Nevertheless, comprehension development is not the focus of the lesson segment. Likewise, the writing segment of the intervention lesson is intended to reinforce these students' needs in the area of foundational skills, so it emphasizes basic skills such as spelling. It is not intended to comprise a complete writing intervention; please see Smith and Haynes (2022) for a much fuller discussion of SL interventions for written expression.

A Sample Intervention Lesson for Ruben

Table 4.3 shows a sample, 60-minute intervention lesson for Ruben, based on the intervention plan just discussed. Ruben's teacher, Ms. Rice, has grouped him with one other third grader, Evan, who is well matched to Ruben in terms of instructional needs. The lesson incorporates several activities discussed earlier in the chapter, including a sorting task for teaching the SE syllable type and a tracing-and-saying activity, using an adaptation of the folded-paper task shown in Figure 4.1, for spelling irregular words. For fluency, Ms. Rice does a quick flash card review of common irregular words with both boys, then has one student orally reread a familiar decodable text (i.e., a text the student has read before), with timing and charting of results for both accuracy and rate. The student rereading the text orally with timing is alternated each session; this session, it is Ruben's turn. While Ruben is timed by the teacher, the other student rereads the text silently.

For the text reading segment of the lesson, the boys take turns orally reading a new decodable text, one they have not previously read. The texts the boys read primarily contain a variety of short-vowel, one-syllable words, as well as irregular words that the boys have learned. Ms. Rice reviews several words that she anticipates might be difficult to decode, or might be unfamiliar vocabulary, before the students begin the reading; she also asks a few initial questions to activate background knowledge. As the boys read, she monitors their accuracy of reading and provides the kind of scaffolded feedback to word-reading errors discussed previously in this chapter. She also asks occasional comprehension questions to ensure they are comprehending what they read and to engage them in the story.

TABLE 4.3. Sample Intervention Lesson for Ruben (with Evan)

Component(s)	Activity
Word recognition and spelling (25 minutes)	
• Review short- and long-vowel sounds.	• Teacher uses flash cards to quickly review previously learned long- and short-vowel sounds.
• Review closed syllable type.	• Teacher elicits from students how syllable types are helpful (i.e., in determining the vowel sound of a syllable); reviews closed (CL) by having each student look at a word, tell if it is CL, and if so, what the vowel sound will be.
• Teach silent-*e* (SE) generalization.	• Teacher explains SE syllable type with multiple examples (i.e., it has a -VC*e* pattern, first vowel will be long); models classifying several words as SE or not SE; students complete a sorting task involving CL, SE, and other words, with teacher guidance as needed; take turns giving vowel sound for CL and SE words.
• Decode unfamiliar words, closed and SE.	• Teacher has students take turns reading sorted CL and SE words.
• Spell common phonetically irregular words.	• Teacher introduces two new phonetically irregular words for spelling, *does* and *done*, using each in a sentence and pointing out their grammatical relationship and shared letters. • Students practice both words using the folded-paper task that involves tracing, saying, and writing each word from memory.
Fluency (10 minutes)	Teacher quickly reviews previously learned irregular words using flash cards; Ruben does repeated reading of a familiar decodable text, with monitoring of both accuracy and rate, and with charting of results. (Student is alternated each session.)
Text reading (15 minutes)	Students alternate in guided oral reading of an unfamiliar (new) decodable text; teacher begins by briefly reviewing three to four difficult words; asks questions during and after reading to monitor students' comprehension and engage them in the story.
Writing (10 minutes)	Students write three sentences dictated by the teacher, with a focus on applying learned spelling skills (both regular, short-vowel words and irregular words, including *does* and *done*), as well as basic writing skills (capitalizing first word and *I*, correct ending punctuation).

The final writing segment of the lesson involves having the boys apply previously learned spelling, punctuation, and capitalization skills in dictated sentences. While the writing skills the boys are learning are quite basic, the repeated practice they receive will help them retain these skills and have a foundation for learning more advanced writing skills.

Adaptations of the Intervention Lesson for Shakira

Shakira's intervention needs are similar to Ruben's and Evan's in terms of the skills that need to be addressed in her intervention. Thus, most of the skills addressed and approximate time allocations on a lesson plan for Shakira would look much like Ruben's plan. However, because of her age, Shakira's special education teacher, Mr. Chen, has made some significant adaptations to his approach with Shakira. First, he is seeing Shakira one-to-one, partly because of Shakira's needs for intensity of instruction, but also because of the difficulty of finding appropriate students at Shakira's grade placement to group with her. Also, he has made several changes to the instructional activities that he uses with Shakira. Most of these changes relate to Shakira's resistance to activities that she perceives as too juvenile. She is sensitive about this issue even though she is receiving one-to-one intervention.

• Shakira's teacher uses some computer-based activities for learning and practicing phoneme–grapheme relationships and spelling, in lieu of letter tiles or tracing-and-saying activities. Shakira especially enjoys building words in spelling using computer-based activities. Mr. Chen leads, guides, and monitors the activity, as well as provides feedback. Dictated sentences and other writing activities also give Shakira continued practice with spelling and basic writing skills.

• Mr. Chen uses a phonics sequence that allows Shakira to begin working on longer, two-syllable words more quickly than does the sequence that Ruben's teacher is using. Specifically, in the "generalizations" step of the lesson, he uses short-vowel and SE nonsense words that can be parts of real, two-syllable words for Shakira to sort by syllable type (e.g., *dis*, *seg*, *bap*, *ig*, *gust*, *nite*, *tize*, *ment*); then he assembles real words for her to read from those word parts (e.g., *disgust*, *segment*, *baptize*, *ignite*). Shakira is very motivated to read these longer words.

• Because Shakira was extremely resistant to reading decodable texts, Mr. Chen has her read high-interest texts written for adolescents with reading difficulties. He has found texts sufficiently close to Shakira's instructional level (end of grade 2/early grade 3) that she can read these texts adequately with some advance teaching of harder words and scaffolding from him during her oral reading. He also alternates oral reading with Shakira, in which he reads a section of text (especially a more difficult section), and she reads the next one. While he reads, he models appropriate accuracy, prosody, and rate.

During text reading, Mr. Chen provides appropriate feedback to Shakira's oral reading errors, which initially did involve some overreliance on context—in particular, substitutions of small words such as *a* for *the*. He has also explained the importance of reading the words on the page correctly, as well as how minor errors of this type may affect comprehension, especially in more advanced texts (e.g., *a* car could be any car, whereas *the* car often refers back to a car previously mentioned in the text). With practice, Shakira has become more accurate in her oral text reading, and she now generally avoids these types of errors.

Additional Considerations for Written Expression

In written expression, students with SWRD, including many of those with dyslexia, often have strengths in text generation, the ability to translate their thoughts into language (e.g., vocabulary, word choice, elaboration of content), but weaknesses in foundational writing skills, particularly spelling. Students' weaknesses in foundational skills may create a drain on their ability and motivation to perform extended writing tasks. For example, students might be able to dictate a sophisticated story orally to a teacher but be unable to write any of it down due to poor spelling.

Addressing spelling, as well as word reading, in intervention is therefore very important for early-stage readers with SWRD. Incorporating explicit teaching of other basic writing skills—such as handwriting, capitalization, punctuation, and sentence structure—into students' interventions, such as in sentence dictation tasks, can help ensure that students have the skills they need to eventually learn more advanced types of writing. For older students such as Shakira, assistive technology for writing (e.g., speech-to-text technology) often is required for them to meet advanced grade-level demands. However, explicit instruction in spelling and other foundational writing skills should still be incorporated into these students' interventions.

SUMMING UP: SL Interventions for Early-Stage Readers with SWRD

Here are key points from this chapter:

- Students in the early stages of SWRD typically require interventions focused on PA, basic phonics skills, reading irregular words, spelling, and accuracy and fluency of text reading.

- Most early-stage readers with SWRD are in the beginning to middle elementary grades, but some are older; older students often need increased intensity of intervention to progress.

- Examples of effective SL activities for early-stage readers with SWRD include word-building, phoneme–grapheme mapping, word sorts, guided oral reading of text with appropriate teacher feedback, and repeated reading of text.

- Decodable texts are usually most appropriate for these students in initial intervention, but after students can decode a variety of one-syllable word patterns, they can generally transition to less controlled texts at their instructional levels.

- In written expression, early-stage readers with SWRD often have relatively strong text-generation abilities in writing but weaknesses in foundational writing skills, particularly spelling, that may affect their ability and motivation to complete extended writing tasks.

APPLIED EXERCISE: TERESA

Teresa, a fourth grader with SWRD, is receiving SL intervention. Her current reading level is about grade 2. She has made considerable progress in intervention but still needs phonics instruction at the one-syllable level. Teresa's intervention-ist does not have access to a comprehensive intervention program that coordinates lessons and texts, but she has a strong background in SL and has assembled good materials for teaching word-reading skills, including an engaging decodable series for Teresa's text reading. Teresa is doing well in this series and likes it. The order in which various phonics patterns are introduced in the series is as follows: (1) CVC words; (2) short-vowel words with consonant digraphs; (3) short-vowel words with blends; (4) SE; (5) open syllables; (6) VR; (7) VT; (8) consonant-*le*, and (9) other two-syllable word patterns such as VCCV and VCV.

Figure 4.6 displays Teresa's recent performance on the ABC Test from Chapter 3, the criterion-referenced test with a mastery level set at 85%. Examine Teresa's performance on this assessment, including her sample errors, and answer the

Phonics category (examples of words)	Teresa (sample errors)
Consonant–vowel–consonant words (*lap*, *ten*, *mig*)	100%
Short-vowel words with consonant digraphs (*math*, *chip*, *shem*)	100%
Short-vowel words with blends (*limp*, *slat*, *frub*)	95% (one error, *shemp* for *shremp*; all other nonsense words correct and all real words correct)
Silent-*e* and open words (*shape*, *flu*, *blode*, *sny*)	90% (two errors, *dree* for *dry* and *snee* for *sny*; 9/10 real words and 9/10 nonsense words correct)
Vowel-*r* words (*stir*, *burn*, *glor*)	55% (*steer* for *stir*, *bun* for *burn*, *spairk* for *spark*; *thrip* for *thirp*; nearly all errors on words with *ar*, *ir*, *ur*; 4/10 nonsense words correct)
Vowel-team words (*cheap*, *aim*, *bloot*)	65% (*chep* for *cheap*, *throw* [to rhyme with *cow*] for *throw*, *digt* for *dight*, *tro-in* for *troin*; errors on a range of vowel-team words; 3/10 nonsense words correct)
Easy two-syllable words/words with common suffixes (*magnet*, *needy*, *ladle*, *glamping*)	40% (most closed and silent-*e* words with -*ed*, -*ing*, -*s*, -*es*, -*y* read correctly; many errors on words with consonant-*le*, VCCV, or VCV patterns; 2/10 nonsense words correct)
Harder two-syllable and multisyllabic words (*excitement*, *unpredictable*, *infortuning*)	15% (a few words read correctly by sight; did not have strategies to decode longer words; read first few letters, then guessed; 0/10 nonsense words correct)

FIGURE 4.6. Applied exercise: Teresa's performance on a criterion-referenced phonics test.

questions below. Assume that Teresa's assessment results are consistent with her day-to-day performance in intervention, and that she knows the syllable types for the phonics categories she has mastered.

Exercise 1

Given the skills that Teresa has mastered/not mastered on the ABC test and the decodable series that the interventionist is using, which phonics skills should be introduced next?

Answer

Teresa has met mastery criteria for the first four categories, involving short-vowel (closed) words, SE, and open syllables. Her errors on the fourth category suggest that she would benefit from some review of open syllables, especially those with the vowel *y*, but she also is ready to learn some new phonics skills. The skills the interventionist should introduce are VR sounds (especially *ar*, *ir*, and *ur*) and the VR syllable type because Teresa will need these skills to continue reading in her decodable series.

Exercise 2

The interventionist has been using sorting tasks effectively to teach Teresa syllable types. Suppose that the interventionist has also had time to teach Teresa three new VR sounds, for *ar*, *ir*, and *ur*, and that Teresa now knows these sounds consistently. Describe an appropriate instructional activity for Teresa that introduces the new syllable type and includes a sorting task.

Answer

Teresa's interventionist should begin by giving a clear, concise definition of the VR syllable type (see Table 2.1), with several examples of VR words (e.g., *turn*, *ark*, *short*). She should model classifying several additional examples of words that are VR (e.g., *tar*, *chirp*, *urn*) and are not VR (*strap*, *hush*), as well as guide Teresa through several practice examples. She should then have Teresa complete a sorting task, with the teacher providing guidance as needed. Teresa knows syllable types for closed, SE, and open, so these can be included in a sorting task, along with the new syllable type, VR. Because of the variety of syllable types that Teresa can now sort, an "other" category is optional. Once Teresa has sorted the words, she should give the vowel sound for each VR word, then read it. The closed, SE, and open words can also be read, as a review. For the open syllables, some words with the vowel *y* should be included, and Teresa should give the vowel sound first, since she seems to need some additional review on these words.

Exercise 3

Give some specific examples of VR words that would be appropriate to use with Teresa in the sorting task.

Answer

It is important to use VR words with just one vowel, and not to include words with a VR-SE (e.g., *spire, cure, flare*) or VR-VT (e.g., *cheer, stair, oar*) pattern, because the vowel sound for these words is not the same as for those with just one vowel followed by an *r*. The VR unit should appear in varied positions in the word, not just at the end. All VR units (*ar, er, ir, ur, or*) should be used, but Teresa seems to need the most practice reading words with *ar, ir,* and *ur*, so the interventionist should include ample words with those patterns. Examples of VR words that could be used are *skirt, blur, short, arm, shark, herd, thirst, churn,* and *irk.* Distractor (non-VR) words should include some with an *r* that is not part of a VR unit, such as *trash*.

Exercise 4

Given her current level of phonics skills, do you think Teresa should be reading decodable text in intervention lessons, or less controlled text, such as grade-2 children's literature? Why or why not?

Answer

Teresa still needs considerable work on one-syllable word patterns such as VR and VT; she also is doing well in her decodable series, and she enjoys it. Therefore, it is appropriate for her to continue in it for the time being. Decodables do provide Teresa with more practice applying specific decoding skills in text than would a less controlled text, and this factor is important. However, Teresa is approaching the point at which a less controlled text could be tried. This should be a text at her instructional level, which will probably not be the same as her grade placement. Some advantages of these latter texts are that they are more similar to what Teresa will be expected to read in general education classes, and that the comprehension demands may be more appropriate for Teresa's language comprehension level.

CHAPTER 5

Structured Literacy Interventions for Specific Word Recognition Difficulties

Advanced Stages

Destiny, a beginning fourth grader, attends an urban school serving primarily minority students, most from low-income backgrounds. Historically, poor reading achievement has been a chronic problem at the school. However, a couple of years ago, Destiny's school began participating in a reading reform effort that greatly improved their core reading instruction and use of tiered interventions. Destiny had struggled with basic word-reading skills since kindergarten, but she finally began receiving effective, SL intervention, and she made strong progress. Although Destiny has come a long way, she still requires some intervention involving long words and reading fluency.

Conor is a ninth grader at a suburban high school. Recently, his school district agreed to an independent educational evaluation of his reading, requested by his parents. They had long-standing concerns about his slow reading and poor spelling, which led to Conor spending many hours every night completing homework that his classmates completed in less than half that time. Conor acknowledged that textbook reading was difficult for him; he said he relied heavily on class discussions to fully understand his textbooks.

Conor had a history of reading difficulties in the elementary grades. He had received phonics interventions in grades K–2, and then again in grades 4 to 5. At that point, he was said to have caught up in reading and intervention was discontinued. Conor has generally performed at or near goal on state accountability testing in reading; he is also a strong math and science student who is earning solid grades in accelerated classes in these subjects. Educators at his school pointed to both factors as evidence that Conor no longer required intervention in reading. Nonetheless, Conor's independent evaluation showed that, like Destiny, he needed intervention involving reading and spelling long words, as well as reading fluency.

This chapter addresses the needs of students with specific word recognition difficulties (SWRD) who are functioning at relatively advanced stages of word reading, beyond the one-syllable level, such as Destiny and Conor. Like early-stage readers with SWRD, advanced-stage readers with SWRD can vary in age, as well as other characteristics. Let's consider some additional background and assessment data for both of these students.

Destiny

Destiny did not attend preschool and knew few letters upon entering kindergarten. From the beginning of formal schooling, despite good oral language comprehension, she was behind with regard to grade expectations in foundational reading skills. One factor in Destiny's literacy difficulties may have been that, like many other students in her school, her home language involved a variety, sometimes termed a *dialect*, of English. Research suggests that dialect use is associated with lower reading achievement, independent of other variables that also correlate with reading achievement, such as vocabulary size and socioeconomic status (Brown et al., 2015; Gatlin & Wanzek, 2015; Washington & Seidenberg, 2021).

All languages have varieties. African American English (AAE), used by Destiny and some of her classmates, is one common variety of American English, different from General American English (GAE), sometimes termed Standard English. AAE and GAE are both systematic and rule-governed, considered linguistically—though not socially—equal (Washington & Seidenberg, 2021). AAE and GAE have numerous linguistic differences, but with regard to learning basic word-reading skills, phonological differences between the two are especially relevant. For example, as noted in Chapter 4, in AAE, final unvoiced /th/ as in *bath* or *with* may be pronounced /f/ (e.g., *baf*, *wif*), and in words that end with -*ing*, the g may be dropped (e.g., *runnin*, *playin*). Final consonant clusters may be reduced, with a word such as *fold* pronounced like *fole* and *past* as *pas*. Thus, while children who use AAE typically perform similarly to users of GAE in phoneme identity tasks involving initial sounds, they may find identification of final sounds more difficult (Washington & Seidenberg, 2021).

Most students who use AAE also have some familiarity with GAE. Nevertheless, when students use a variety of English that differs from the one taught in school, learning basic reading skills may be a more complex task for them (Brown et al., 2015), requiring additional steps to translate from one variety of English to the other. These students may need more time, more targeted instruction, and more opportunities for practice in order to learn certain word recognition skills (Washington & Seidenberg, 2021). Furthermore, if teachers lack knowledge about dialect or view it negatively, as "bad English," of if they are unaware of the systematic differences between AAE and GAE, their teaching may be ineffective in important ways. For instance, teachers may misconstrue the nature of children's difficulties, fail to provide appropriate feedback, and even, in some cases, unintentionally confuse or embarrass children. Unfortunately, in her early schooling, Destiny experienced this kind of problematic instruction.

However, as part of reading reform in Destiny's school, teachers received professional development not only in reading science and SL interventions, but also in AAE. Destiny's interventionist was knowledgeable about these areas, and Destiny made excellent progress in her small-group SL intervention. She is now on a trajectory to catch up to grade expectations. She also switches easily between AAE and GAE.

Figure 5.1 displays Destiny's recent performance on the criterion-referenced phonics test from Chapter 3, the ABC Test. Destiny's scores are in the center column, which shows that she has mastered all one-syllable categories of this assessment. She still needs work on two-syllable and multisyllabic words, the last two categories of the test. Her specific errors on easy two-syllable words suggested that she had the ability to decode many words with a vowel–consonant–consonant–vowel (VCCV) pattern (e.g., *magnet, rabbit*). She also could decode most short-vowel, SE, open, VR, and VT words with common suffixes such as *-s, -es, -ing, -er,* and *-est*, sometimes termed *inflectional endings*. However, she struggled to decode words with a VCV pattern (e.g., *lemon, robot*) or *-cle* syllables (e.g., *ladle*). Also, her ability to read words of three or more syllables was quite limited.

On informal measures of oral vocabulary and listening comprehension, Destiny performed solidly at grade level. Nevertheless, on an oral reading inventory (ORI), Destiny's highest independent level in reading graded passages was grade 2, and her highest instructional level was in a grade-3 passage, roughly 6 months to a year below her grade placement. She could read many common words, and her word reading errors were primarily on long words, consistent with the ABC Test. Spelling assessments suggested that Destiny had grade-appropriate phonological spelling skills. Because she generally represented all sounds in a word, in the correct order, the intended word was generally recognizable even when it was misspelled (e.g., *steem* for *steam, rideing* for

Phonics Category—ABC Test	Destiny (sample errors)	Conor (sample errors)
One-syllable word categories, CVC words through VT words	All ≥ 90%	All ≥ 90%
Easy two-syllable words/words with common suffixes (*magnet, needy, ladle, glamping*)	50% (Read some VCCV words such as *magnet* correctly; errors included *laddle* for *ladle, stiffle* for *stifle, ROB-ot* for *robot, play-NET* for *planet*; 2/10 nonsense words read correctly.)	90%
Harder two-syllable and multisyllabic words (*excitement, unpredictable, infortuning*)	20% (Sounded out a few two-syllable, real words correctly but lacked strategies for breaking up and decoding most of these words; 0/10 nonsense words read correctly.)	50% (kuh-TIZ-in for citizen; puh-SODE-nim for pseudonym; disrageous read as dis-ruh-GEE-us, with a hard g; regirnium read as re-GERN-ee-um with a hard g; 3/10 nonsense words read correctly.)

FIGURE 5.1. Criterion-referenced phonics data for Destiny and Conor.

riding, pland for *planned, ternup* for *turnip*). However, she lacked knowledge of certain spelling generalizations, such as those that involve adding endings to a base word, and she needed to learn to spell many grade-appropriate words that required learning word-specific spellings, such as the need to use *ea*, not *ee*, in the word *steam*.

Children who use AAE can have dyslexia, but this does not appear to be true for Destiny. In addition to her strong progress in intervention, Destiny does not have risk indicators for dyslexia, such as a family history of dyslexia or a history of early language delay. Although her school's implementation of appropriate reforms has provided her with effective intervention to this point, she still needs continued intervention involving advanced word-reading skills.

Conor

Figure 5.1 shows Conor's performance on the ABC Test in the right-hand column. Like Destiny, he has mastered all one-syllable word categories on the test, and he also has mastered the category for easy two-syllable words. His only weaknesses were on the final category, involving more difficult two-syllable and multisyllabic words. Conor's skills on the test were stronger than Destiny's, and his weak performance on this one category may not seem important. However, given the prevalence of multisyllabic words in the ninth-grade texts that Conor is expected to read in school, his weaknesses have a significant impact on his text reading, fluency, and comprehension. On an ORI, Conor's highest independent level was in a grade-5 passage, well below his grade placement, especially problematic given expectations for high school students to read textbooks and other curriculum materials independently. His highest instructional level was in a grade-7 passage. His comprehension difficulties in passage reading related heavily to effortful and sometimes inaccurate decoding, not language comprehension.

Spelling assessments showed that Conor had good ability to spell most one-syllable words, consistent with his performance on the ABC Test, and even good ability to spell many longer, common words. However, on more complex words of two or more syllables, he often made phonologically based spelling errors, such as the following:

- *Satisfaction* misspelled as *satifaction*
- *Obedient* misspelled as *obedent*
- *Identify* misspelled as *idenfy*
- *Infiltrate* misspelled as *infitate*
- *Electrical* misspelled as *eletical*

Figure 5.2 displays Conor's scores from his independent evaluation, using the assessment map from Chapter 3. As the map shows, Conor had clear strengths in vocabulary and broad oral language comprehension, with above-average scores in these areas, but weaknesses in word-reading and text-reading fluency. Although his score for real-word reading was in average range, his scores on WIAT-4 Pseudoword Decoding, Orthographic Fluency, and Decoding Fluency were all below average, as

Student *Conor*   Grade *9*   Dates of Testing *Sept 15–Oct 5*

ORAL LANGUAGE COMPREHENSION

Oral Vocabulary (note receptive/expressive)

WIAT-4 Receptive Vocab 118

WIAT-4 Expressive Vocab 115

Oral Language (Listening) Comprehension (note format, e.g., cloze, maze, QA)

WIAT-4 Oral Discourse Comp (QA) 128

Other Oral Language

WORD READING

Real Words—Accuracy
WIAT-4 Word Reading 103

Nonsense Words—Accuracy
WIAT-4 Pseudoword Decoding 86

Word Reading—Automaticity
WIAT-4 Orthographic Fluency 88

WIAT-4 Decoding Fluency 80

Phonological/phonemic awareness
WIAT-4 Phonemic Proficiency 84

Oral Reading Fluency—Accuracy
GORT-5 Accuracy Scaled Score 6

Oral Reading Fluency—Rate
GORT-5 Rate Scaled Score 6

WIAT-4 ORF 78

Silent Reading Fluency

Reading Comprehension (note test format, e.g., cloze, maze, QA, as well as other relevant features such as timing)

GORT-5 Comprehension (timed; QA) 7

WIAT-IV Reading Comprehension (untimed; QA) 109

Observations

Worked hard on WIAT-4 RC, searched for answers in text, sometimes took a long time to answer questions

Decoding errors influenced comprehension performance

FIGURE 5.2. Assessment map for Conor.

was his text-reading fluency. This pattern of results demonstrates that Conor's fluency difficulties are attributable to problems in word reading, and that he has a profile of SWRD. Furthermore, Conor's poor word reading has a basis in phonology, as shown by his below-average WIAT-4 Phonemic Proficiency score, a measure of PA, as well as by other assessments.

Interestingly, despite his problems in word reading and fluency, Conor's reading comprehension on the WIAT-4 was at the upper end of the average range, and his performance on GORT-5 Comprehension, though below average, was not extremely low. Observations of his performance indicated that he worked slowly on the untimed WIAT-4 Reading Comprehension subtest, consistent with his homework difficulties. Conor's school district viewed his performance on these standardized, individually administered reading comprehension tests as further evidence that he did not require intervention. However, few reading comprehension tests approximate the demands of everyday schooling at Conor's grade level, involving a high volume of independent reading and increasingly complex literacy expectations (e.g., reading two novels and writing an essay comparing their themes). Conor struggled with these expectations, mainly due to his slow reading and weak spelling.

Moreover, Conor's family history revealed that he had an aunt and an uncle who had been diagnosed with dyslexia. When Conor's school considered the results of his independent evaluation, as well as their own comprehensive evaluation and other data such as family history, he was finally found eligible for special education services in the category of specific learning disability/dyslexia.

SL interventions for long words can help Conor, Destiny, and other students like them, whether or not they have dyslexia. This chapter provides sample intervention activities for students at relatively advanced stages of SWRD, discusses some key intervention issues for these students, and includes sample intervention lessons for both Destiny and Conor.

About Advanced-Stage Readers with SWRD

Advanced-stage readers with SWRD all have the following in common: (1) a poor reader profile with difficulties centered on word reading, not language comprehension and (2) a need for intervention involving more advanced word-reading skills, as opposed to basic skills at the one-syllable level. Although these students can be in the elementary grades, most are in middle school or high school. As discussed in Chapter 4, older students often require more intensity of intervention to progress, and they typically have other needs as well, such as different social–emotional needs as compared to younger children. The primary intervention needs of advanced-stage readers with SWRD involve learning to read long words, those of two syllables or longer; morphology, especially advanced morphology (e.g., Latin- and Greek-derived roots and affixes); spelling; and text-reading accuracy and fluency. Learning to be flexible in reading long words is also essential for them.

Research on Interventions
for Advanced-Stage Readers with SWRD

A Word about Late-Emerging SWRD

Many advanced-stage readers with SWRD are like Destiny and Conor in having a history of word-reading difficulties from the earliest grades. However, some students with SWRD are late-emerging poor readers, usually defined as reading problems that emerge after grade 3 (Leach et al., 2003). In late-emerging SWRD, the reading problem usually emerges by grade 4 or 5 (Catts et al., 2012), and primarily involves decoding of long or complex words. These are not students whose early reading problems were overlooked by schools. Rather, they may have relatively mild phonological or working memory difficulties that did not greatly affect their ability to learn to read simple words, but that had a greater impact later on, when they had to learn more complex, multisyllabic words (Lipka et al., 2006). All three poor reader profiles can be early- or late-emerging (Catts et al., 2012). One important implication of research on late-emerging reading difficulties is that screening and identification efforts must continue past kindergarten and grade 1, even for SWRD.

Whether a student's SWRD is early- or late-emerging, if the student is functioning at an advanced stage of word reading, with instructional needs focused on long words, it is important to avoid interventions with rigid requirements for all students to start at a low, beginning level (e.g., CVC words). Such requirements may impede students' reading progress, as well as cause them to lose motivation. Like other struggling readers, advanced-stage readers with SWRD generally do require cumulative review of lower-level skills. However, this kind of review can be incorporated into lessons, including during reading of long words and text, without requiring students to start over from the beginning.

Reading and Spelling Long Words

In order to read unfamiliar long words, students typically need to accomplish several steps. First, they must be able to break the word into manageable parts. To do this, knowledge about generalizations for syllabicating words, such as VCCV and VCV, can be helpful, as is knowledge about morphology, such as recognizing common roots and affixes. Second, students must be able to pronounce the parts of the word. Being able to read the six syllable types can help students pronounce word parts in a longer word, but knowledge of syllable types is not essential as long as students can successfully decode the individual syllables of the word. Other skills are also valuable, such as knowing sounds for common prefixes and suffixes, as well as sounds for letter patterns that are more common in long words than in one-syllable words (e.g., the /k/ sound for *ch* in words of Latin derivation, as in *chemist* and *chorus*). Some letter sounds usually taught at the one-syllable stage, such as soft *c* and *g*, become more common in long words and may require teaching or reteaching for some students.

Finally, students must synthesize the parts they have read into an approximation of a recognizable word, a tricky step that requires dealing with accent patterns and

schwa sounds. Accent patterns in English are somewhat unpredictable, with unaccented vowels often taking a schwa sound. A word can sound quite different depending on where the accent is placed. Recall the *canopy* example from Chapter 2, which
can be plausibly read as cuh-NOP-ee rather than CAN-up-ee. The student has to try
different possible pronunciations to arrive at the correct word, and to know they have
pronounced the word correctly, they must have heard it before. Flexibility is important
even in reading one-syllable words, such as VT words associated with more than one
possible pronunciation (e.g., *ow* in *cow* vs. *slow*). However, the need for flexibility
and the ability to try alternative pronunciations become especially important when
students are learning to read long words (Kearns et al., 2022) because most of these
words have more than one possible pronunciation.

In interventions with poor readers learning to decode long words, including adolescents, researchers have found teaching these kinds of steps effective in improving
word reading. These interventions typically incorporate teaching of both phonological decoding strategies and larger-unit, morphological approaches (Archer, Gleason,
& Vachon, 2003; Lovett, Lacerenza, & Borden, 2000; Lovett, Lacerenza, DePalma,
& Frijters, 2012). One example is the BEST strategy of O'Connor and her colleagues
(2013), which involves having students approach a multisyllabic word by breaking off
the word parts they know (e.g., affixes); examining what's left and underlining vowels;
saying each part; then trying the whole word in context.

These interventions can help improve students' spelling, as well as their reading,
because spelling and word reading tap similar types of linguistic knowledge (Ehri,
2005; Moats, 2020, 2022). However, spelling is more difficult than word reading
because it requires recall of all letters in a word in the correct sequence, whereas word
reading only requires recognition of the word (Treiman, 2017). In early-stage readers
with SWRD, individual students often have similar needs for word reading and spelling, usually involving phonological skills. For instance, a student who needs to work
on reading CVC words generally also needs to work on spelling CVC words. But, as
students advance, their reading skills tend to outstrip their spelling skills. In advanced-
stage readers with SWRD, the skills that are appropriate to teach individual students
may differ somewhat for spelling as compared to reading. For example, although Destiny can read one-syllable words with common inflectional endings, she is still having difficulty spelling those words. Intervention plans for advanced-stage SWRD may
therefore need to differentiate spelling instruction from word-reading instruction relatively more than for early-stage SWRD.

Reading Fluency

Most advanced-stage readers with SWRD do not require decodable text because they
have mastered a sufficient variety of word patterns to read text that is not controlled
with regard to phonics skills. However, in intervention, they should generally read
texts at their instructional levels, which may not be grade-level texts. Estimates of independent and instructional levels are only approximations, and many factors can influence an individual student's ability to read a particular text. Struggling readers might

successfully read more challenging texts than expected if the text is on a familiar topic, one about which a student has considerable background knowledge; if the text is "considerate" (Armbruster & Anderson, 1985), that is, well-structured and clearly written; and/or if the student is highly motivated to read the text. With appropriate teacher support, students can also benefit from some practice in lessons reading "stretch text," challenging texts that they cannot read independently, often texts at or near their grade level (Vaughn et al., 2022). But if all texts are difficult for students, both comprehension and motivation to read may be affected. Also, the use of easier texts in fluency interventions may improve fluency outcomes for some students (Stevens et al., 2017).

Repeated reading interventions, discussed in Chapter 4, can improve reading rate in advanced-stage readers with SWRD, even in high school students like Conor (Wexler, Vaughn, Edmonds, & Reutebuch, 2008). These improvements do not necessarily transfer to comprehension, perhaps because of the more complex comprehension demands of upper-grade-level texts. Nevertheless, improvements in rate alone can be helpful in increasing students' ability to meet demands for reading volume in the later grades. For example, if Conor could read faster while maintaining good accuracy and comprehension, he might be able to complete homework within a more reasonable time frame. The research synthesis of Wexler and colleagues (2008) suggests that rate results could be improved through the inclusion of listening passage previewing, which involves having a student listen to an audio version of the passage or to a teacher's read-aloud of it, providing a good model of fluent reading prior to the student's own reading. In addition, providing a different purpose for each rereading—such as first reading to identify difficult multisyllabic words, then chorally with the teacher, then individually with good prosody—may be more effective and engaging than simply rereading three or four times, particularly with older students (Vaughn et al., 2022).

Researchers also have compared repeated reading interventions with continuous, nonrepetitive reading of text. In continuous reading, rather than rereading the same text several times, students read a comparable amount, but in different texts or different consecutive passages within the same book. These comparisons in studies involving older students suggest that continuous reading can be as effective as repeated reading in improving reading rate, and it may have other advantages as well (O'Connor, White, & Swanson, 2007; Wexler et al., 2008). For example, older students may find it more motivating to read varied texts than the same text repeatedly; varied texts provide greater exposure to vocabulary and background knowledge; and varied texts may benefit students' word accuracy (Wexler et al., 2008). Considered as a whole, these studies support the importance of including oral text reading as part of interventions for reading fluency in SWRD, even for older, advanced-stage readers, including in varied texts such as continuous reading in books.

Independent Pleasure Reading

Struggling readers often dislike reading and are not usually inclined to read for enjoyment. However, there are many reasons to encourage pleasure reading in all students, including those with reading difficulties. Voluntary pleasure reading is associated with many potential literacy benefits, including better reading fluency, vocabulary, spelling, and reading comprehension (Mol & Bus, 2011; Spear-Swerling, Brucker, & Alfano, 2010; Stanovich, 2000). Pleasure reading also can provide students with increased exposure to models of good writing (Graham & Hebert, 2010). Although good readers are more likely to read for enjoyment than poor readers, a meta-analysis of print exposure concluded that poor readers do benefit from independent reading for enjoyment and, in fact, that leisure time reading was especially important for them (Mol & Bus, 2011). Encouraging an interest in reading is desirable for all readers, at any stage, but early-stage readers with SWRD may have skills too limited for them to find texts they can enjoy, or reading may simply be too effortful to be enjoyable. However, advanced-stage readers with SWRD have increased options for text reading. Students do not have to read at grade level for interesting texts to become accessible to them; for instance, once they can read at a second- or third-grade level, more texts written specifically for older poor readers, including texts on topics of interest to adolescents, are available.

Independent pleasure reading is not a substitute for effective intervention in school, but it could be a valuable adjunct to it for many students. Some steps that teachers can take to encourage independent reading for enjoyment include helping students find books at their reading levels on topics that interest them; assigning independent reading (with student choice) as homework, with teacher monitoring; forming book clubs of students with a shared interest in reading a particular book; and using a topic interest inventory or specific intervention plan that targets reading for enjoyment (Wei, Spear-Swerling, & Mercurio, 2021).

Sample SL Intervention Activities

Word Sorts for Advanced-Stage Readers with SWRD

If designed appropriately, word sorts, discussed in Chapter 4 for teaching syllable types, can be as useful in teaching advanced-stage readers as early-stage readers with SWRD. For example, word sorts can be used to practice syllable division in two-syllable words with students like Destiny. Destiny's performance on the ABC Test suggested that she could decode many VCCV words, but she had difficulty reading -*cle* and VCV words.

Destiny, who is being seen for intervention with another student, Mia, has now learned and can apply the syllable division rules for VCCV and -*cle*, as well as decode words with these patterns. The interventionist, Mr. Hewitt, is currently introducing VCV, often the most difficult rule for students because they have to try more than one way to read the word. Also, as with other long words, the unaccented syllable may take a schwa sound. Here is Mr. Hewitt's intervention routine for teaching these words.

1. Mr. Hewitt begins by eliciting from both students how the syllable division rules are helpful (i.e., they give you a way to break up a long word to help read it). He also briefly reviews the generalizations for VCCV (i.e., divide between the two consonants) and -*cle* (i.e., divide right before the -*cle* syllable), by having each student show the appropriate place to divide a sample word with each pattern.

2. Next, he tells the students that they are going to learn to read a new word pattern. These words are a bit different than the others they have learned so far because there can be more than one way to divide them. He presents several words with a VCV pattern, highlighting the pattern within each word. He explains that the students should first try dividing before the consonant; pronouncing the parts based on the syllable types they have learned; then put the parts together into a whole word. If that does not result in a recognizable word, they should try dividing after the consonant and repeat the same process.

3. He then coaches the students through several examples of these words, including words that must be divided before the consonant (V/CV; e.g., *fro/zen*, *si/lent*), as well as after it (VC/V; e.g., *shad/ow*, *rob/in*). He tries to use words that the students will recognize orally if they sound them out correctly rather than words they are unlikely to have heard before. He also avoids using common sight words that the students know and will not have to decode.

4. He has the students practice all three rules using the word sort shown in Figure 5.3. Similar to the activity for Ruben in Chapter 4 involving syllable types, the words on the cards are mixed together, and the students must sort them into three piles: VCCV, *-cle*, and VCV. Then, they take turns showing where each word should be divided and reading the word.

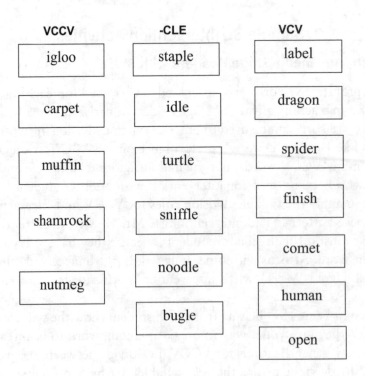

FIGURE 5.3. Sample word sort for syllable division rules.

Destiny has correctly sorted the word *dragon* as VCV and is now showing where to divide it. As taught, she first points to the space between the *a* and the *g*, dra/gon.

TEACHER: That's right, first try dividing before the consonant. How would you read the first syllable?

DESTINY: Druh.

TEACHER: Try again. What's the syllable type?

DESTINY: Open.

TEACHER: Good. So what sound will the *a* have?

DESTINY: Its name.

TEACHER: Exactly. So try it now.

DESTINY: Dray (*pronouncing with long a*).

TEACHER: Yes. Now add the second syllable.

DESTINY: Dray–gon.

TEACHER: Is that a real word?

DESTINY: (*Shakes her head no.*)

TEACHER: Right. What do you do next?

DESTINY: Divide here (*pointing to the space between the g and the o*).

TEACHER: Now how would you read the first syllable?

DESTINY: Drag.

TEACHER: Yes. Now add the second syllable.

DESTINY: Drag–on. Drag–on (*struggling to come up with the correct word*).

TEACHER: Can you blend it into a real word?

DESTINY: Drag–on (*still not coming up with the correct word*).

TEACHER: Remember, in long words some syllables can have a schwa sound, like uh.

DESTINY: Drag–un. Oh, *dragon*! (*reading word correctly*).

TEACHER: Is that a real word?

DESTINY: Yes.

TEACHER: You've got it. Great job!

FIGURE 5.4. Teacher feedback to Destiny on a VCV word.

5. If either student has trouble trying alternative ways to read the VCV words, Mr. Hewitt provides appropriate feedback. Figure 5.4 shows an example of teacher feedback to difficulties that Destiny had decoding the word *dragon*.

Using Morphology

Attention to morphology is very important in reading long words. Knowledge about morphology can benefit struggling readers' spelling and vocabulary, as well as their reading (Goodwin & Ahn, 2013). Conor's performance on the ABC Test suggested that he needed not only to learn morphology but also to review the rule for soft *c* and *g*. Furthermore, he sometimes made errors in blending the syllables in long words, specifically, by putting the accent on the wrong syllable (see Figure 5.1; e.g., kuh-TIZ-in for *citizen*); that is, like Destiny, he would benefit from flexibility practice.

Conor and one other student with similar skills and instructional needs, named Ryan, are being seen together for their special education instruction. Their teacher, Ms. Williams, has been teaching them new affixes and root words, including their sounds and spellings, as well as how to use these word parts to break up and read a longer word. She has previously emphasized to the students that to be an affix or root, a letter pattern must be part of a long word and carry meaning within the context of that word (e.g., the *aud* in *Claude* is not a root). She has also reviewed the rule for soft *c* and *g*, which involves attending to whether these letters are followed by *e*, *i*, or *y* within a word. (See Chapter 2.) Figure 5.5 shows how Conor has learned to analyze long words by circling affixes and underlining recognizable roots. If a word has no affixes or obvious roots (e.g., *Lebanon*), he has learned to underline the vowels in the word, determine the number of syllables based on the number of vowels, and try syllable division rules. Sometimes he applies one of the syllable division rules to the remainder of a word after circling affixes, putting a vertical line between syllables. He also marks the sounds for the letters *c* and *g* when they are soft, as shown in Figure 5.5.

After Conor and Ryan have analyzed a word, they try to decode it; if they have difficulty, Ms. Williams provides feedback to help them. This feedback includes reminders to be flexible in trying different possible pronunciations, including shifting accent patterns and vowel sounds. Ms. Williams' feedback is similar to what Destiny's teacher did in Figure 5.4, but with a focus on words of three or more syllables.

Here are a couple of additional points about the activity in Figure 5.5. First, there can be multiple ways to break up a multisyllabic word, and Ms. Williams accepts these as long as they make sense and can lead to successful reading of the word. For example, for the word *uninterrupted*, Conor could break up and decode the word in

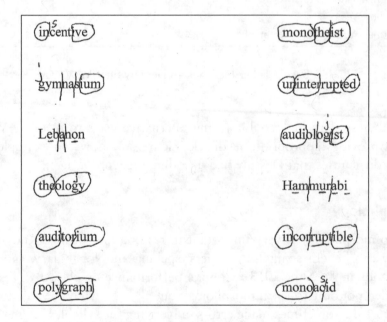

FIGURE 5.5. Conor's analysis of multisyllabic words.

other ways besides the one shown in Figure 5.5. He could identify *un* as a prefix, *-ed* as a suffix, and *rupt* as a root, then apply VCCV to read *inter* (i.e., *in/ter*). Alternatively, he could identify *un* as a prefix, *-ed* as a suffix, and *interrupt* as the base word. These can all lead to successful reading and spelling of the word; so, although she might sometimes point out a previously taught morpheme that Conor has overlooked, Ms. Williams does not belabor one particular way to break up a word. Also, Conor usually recognizes the correct pronunciations of words after producing them, but if the word is unfamiliar to him orally, then she just tells him the word once he has produced it, as does Destiny's interventionist.

Column Activities for Spelling

Column activities can be useful in practicing spelling rules. Students are given contrasting columns on a worksheet or whiteboard, and the teacher dictates relevant spelling words orally. Students must first decide which column the word belongs in, then write the word. For example, if students have been taught the rule for when to use *-tch* (i.e., immediately after a short vowel, at the end of a one-syllable word), the headings for the two contrasting columns would be *ch* and *-tch*. The teacher dictates a series of words such as *chin*, *hatch*, *ditch*, *chop*, *chat*, *Dutch*, and so on, and students write them in the correct column. The activity draws their attention to the difficult element of the word and has them decide the spelling of that element first, before attempting the entire word.

Figure 5.6 shows a slightly more complex column activity appropriate for Destiny and Mia. (For a template version of this activity optimized for student use, see Form 5.1 on page 125.) This column activity is aimed at spelling closed-syllable base words

1 Consonant	2+ Consonants
rub	wish
rubbed	wishing
shop	end
shopping	ended
plan	stuff
planned	stuffing
sit	blast
sitting	blasted
chop	bump
chopped	bumped

FIGURE 5.6. Column activity for spelling closed syllables with *-ed* and *-ing* (completed example).

with the suffixes *-ing* and *-ed*. Later the teacher will address other suffixes, including those beginning with a consonant (*-ful*, *-ly*, *-ness*). However, like many students, Destiny finds spelling words with inflectional endings confusing, so Mr. Hewitt wants to begin with only closed syllables and two of the most common suffixes. Another consideration is that these kinds of words may be especially confusing for students who use AAE (Gatlin-Nash, Johnson, & Lee-James, 2020), such as both Destiny and Mia, because of certain features of AAE such as possible reduction in consonant clusters at the ends of words, omissions of *-ed* for past tense, and dropping of *g* in *-ing*. Destiny and Mia both now switch easily between AAE and GAE, and they can readily spell closed-syllable base words (e.g., *fast*, *spot*, *slump*). Still, Mr. Hewitt wants to ensure their mastery of these potentially challenging words before moving on to other base words and suffixes.

In the column activity, the main contrast involves the number of consonants at the end of the closed-syllable base word. If the base word ends in a single consonant (e.g., *sit*, *flop*), that consonant must be doubled when adding *-ed* or *-ing* (e.g., *sitting*, *flopped*). If the base word ends in two or more consonants (e.g., *jump*, *crunch*), the suffix is added without any doubling (e.g., *jumped*, *crunching*). Mr. Hewitt has introduced the rule to the students in a previous lesson, as well as the spellings of the *-ed* and *-ing* suffixes, including the fact that *-ed* has three possible sounds—for example, *How do you spell the suffix at the end of the word <u>landed</u>? How about in the word <u>jumped</u>? How about in <u>fanned</u>? Right, they are all spelled with -ed.*) Now the girls are trying to spell these words themselves, with the teacher's guidance as needed.

1. The teacher says a closed-syllable word *with a suffix* and in standard dictation format (e.g., "Shopping, Mrs. Smith went shopping at the store, shopping"). The students take turns deciding what the base word is (i.e., *shop*), as well as which column the word belongs in (i.e., the left, one-consonant column, because *shop* ends in a single consonant). They write the word in the correct column.

2. If either girl makes a mistake—such as choosing the wrong column—Mr. Hewitt lets her write it to see if she realizes the word actually has only one consonant at the end and belongs in the other column. If necessary, he provides corrective feedback.

3. Finally, he repeats the word *shopping*, and the students write the entire word below the base word, with the final consonant doubled, as shown in Figure 5.6. Words are dictated in an unpredictable sequence, not alternated predictably from one column to the other.

Mr. Hewitt avoids telling the students the base word if possible, and instead consistently dictates the whole word, including the suffix. He wants the students to generate the base word themselves because he wants them to learn a process that they can eventually apply independently when they are trying to spell an unfamiliar word with one of these suffixes.

Syllable Segmentation Activity for Spelling Multisyllabic Words

Conor's spelling errors show that he has a pattern of omitting phonemes in multisyllabic words. Figure 5.7 displays an example of a syllable segmentation activity to help improve Conor's spelling of these words. (For a template version of this activity optimized for student use, see Form 5.2 on page 126.) The point of this activity is not to teach Conor syllable segmentation, which is easy for him; rather, it is to encourage him to listen more carefully for the interior phonemes in long words. Here is how Conor's teacher implements this activity, which is adapted from Moats (2022).

1. After giving Conor the worksheet shown in Figure 5.7, with the series of blanks in it, Ms. Williams dictates a multisyllabic word, such as *electrical*, in standard dictation format and enunciating clearly (e.g., "Electrical; There was an electrical fire at the factory last night; electrical"). Conor repeats the word, and if he does not articulate the word clearly, the teacher has him try again until the word is clearly articulated.

2. She asks Conor to count the number of syllables in the word, and to mark off with a vertical line on the worksheet where the word will end (see Figure 5.7).

3. Conor then writes the word syllable by syllable, articulating the word slowly and writing one syllable per blank as shown in Figure 5.7, with his teacher providing tailored feedback to any errors. For example, when Conor initially omitted the first *c* in *electrical* (i.e., *eletrical*), Ms. Williams pointed to the second blank. She told him to say the word again and listen carefully for a sound he had left out in this part of the word. As another example, Conor originally misspelled the word *identify* as *identafy*. For this word, since the misspelled sound involves a schwa, Ms. Williams encouraged

1.	e	lec	tric	al |			electrical
2.	in	fil	trate |				infiltrate
3.	i	dent	✗ i	fy |			identify
4.	sat	is	fac	tion |			satisfaction
5.	an	ti	grav	i	ty |		antigravity
6.	mis	un	der	stand	ing |		misunderstanding
7.	pre	dict	ive |				predictive
8.	in	vest	i	ga	tion |		investigation
9.							
10.							
11.							
12.							

FIGURE 5.7. Multisyllabic segmentation activity for spelling (completed example).

a morphemic rather than phonemic strategy. She told Conor to look for any affixes on the word and to check that he had spelled them correctly. Conor had learned the suffix *-ify* and he was able to self-correct with this feedback.

4. Once the individual syllables of the word have been spelled correctly, Conor writes the entire word in the blank on the right side of the paper. He reads it back slowly to make sure he has not left out any letters or made other errors.

As with the morphology activity shown in Figure 5.5, there may be more than one way that individual words can be syllabicated, and the teacher accepts these alternatives as long as they make sense, include the correct number of syllables, and facilitate spelling of the word. For instance, syllabicating *electrical* as *e-lect-ric-al* or *e-lec-tri-cal* instead of *e-lec-tric-al* would be acceptable, but *elect-r-ic-al* would not. Also, although whole words may be repeated for Conor as needed, the teacher avoids segmenting the words for him if possible because, as in Mr. Hewitt's activity with Destiny, Ms. Williams is trying to teach Conor a process that he can eventually apply independently in spelling long words.

Reading Fluency Activities

Destiny's interventionist uses the timed repeated-reading activities described for Ruben in Chapter 4, but with grade-3 text instead of the controlled decodable text that Ruben needed. Also, unlike Ruben, Destiny and Mia are reading short chapter books, texts that cannot be completed in one session. For fluency practice, Mr. Hewitt often has the girls reread the final passage from the book that they read in the previous intervention session. This not only serves to practice fluency, but also to remind the girls of what was happening in the book the last time they were reading it. As did Ruben's teacher, Mr. Hewitt alternates timing across the two students, so each student is timed every other session, with monitoring and charting of both accuracy and rate. The student not being timed rereads the passage silently.

For fluency practice with her high school students, Ms. Williams often uses curriculum-related materials, easier texts at or near the students' instructional level but on topics they are studying in content classes. She also uses a somewhat different approach to repeated reading involving purposeful fluency activities (see Vaughn et al., 2022). In this approach, Conor and Ryan first skim the passage for words that they find difficult to read. The teacher helps them decode these words using the kind of approach illustrated in Figure 5.5. Then, the students listen to Ms. Williams read the passage aloud, with appropriate prosody and phrasing. The listening step is followed by choral reading of the passage, with teacher and students reading the passage aloud together. Finally, the students take turns reading the passage aloud with appropriate accuracy and prosody. Ms. Williams does use timing periodically to monitor the students' progress in relation to both accuracy and rate of text reading. In general, however, with her secondary students, Ms. Williams has found purposeful fluency activities focused on accuracy and prosody more useful than traditional repeated readings with timing. Purposeful fluency activities have been more appealing to the students, as well as more suited to the dense informational texts that secondary-level students are expected to read.

Mr. Hewitt and Ms. Williams also use activities to promote independent reading for enjoyment. Destiny's interventionist assigns independent reading for homework, with student choice of texts and teacher monitoring to ensure that the books Destiny and Mia pick are appropriate for their independent reading. To show that they have done the reading, the girls must answer a few basic questions about the texts they have read.

Conor's teacher has found the use of book groups especially helpful with her adolescent students. Conor and Ryan had a strong, shared interest in a fantasy novel that was written for adolescents at their independent reading level, about grade 5. Their homework includes reading one chapter per week in the novel. To monitor that they are doing the reading, Ms. Williams allocates about 15 minutes, once a week, for them to discuss the reading they have done that week and respond to a writing prompt related to the chapter they have read. This has become the students' favorite activity of the week.

SL Intervention Plans for Advanced-Stage Readers with SWRD

The same lesson format can be used for advanced-stage readers with SWRD as for early-stage readers with SWRD. This format is shown in Chapter 4, in Table 4.2. The same four broad lesson segments—for word recognition and spelling, fluency, text reading, and writing—also apply to advanced-stage readers with SWRD. However, a few specific areas within these segments may be less relevant for advanced-stage readers as compared to early-stage readers and may be routinely omitted. For instance, most advanced-stage readers do not require instruction in PA, at least not instruction separate from their learning of word recognition and spelling skills. Furthermore, some of them may not require work on common phonetically irregular words, particularly in relation to reading. This was true for Conor, who had good reading and spelling of common irregular words. In contrast, Destiny could read common irregular words but did need some continued work on spelling them. The lesson format can be further adapted to meet individual students' specific needs, and with adjustments to time allocations as warranted, as previously discussed in Chapter 4.

A Sample Intervention Lesson for Destiny

Table 5.1 shows a sample 45-minute intervention lesson for Destiny and her classmate, Mia, that uses the lesson format in Table 4.2 and incorporates several of the activities discussed in this chapter. The lesson begins with a brief flash card review of sounds for letters and common letter patterns, with a focus on those especially relevant for this lesson: long and short vowels, *-cle* syllables (e.g., *-fle*, *-ble*, *-tle*), and common inflectional endings (e.g., *-ing*, *-ed*). Mr. Hewitt then implements the word sort activity

TABLE 5.1. Sample Intervention Lesson for Destiny (with Mia)

Component(s)	Activity
Word recognition and spelling (20 minutes) • Review short- and long-vowel sounds; sounds for *-cle* patterns; sounds for common suffixes (inflectional endings).	• Teacher uses flash cards to quickly review these previously learned sounds.
• Review VCCV and *-cle* syllable division rules.	• Teacher elicits from students how syllable division rules are helpful (i.e., can help break up a long word into parts you can read); reviews VCCV and *-cle* syllable division by having each student show where to divide a sample word.
• Teach VCV syllable division rule.	• Teacher explains VCV rule with several examples; models classifying several words as VCV or not VCV; emphasizes importance of flexibility in reading these words. • Then students complete a sorting task involving VCCV, *-cle*, and VCV words, with teacher guidance as needed.
• Decode unfamiliar two-syllable words with VCCV, *-cle*, and VCV patterns.	• Teacher has students take turns reading sorted words.
• Practice spelling closed-syllable words with endings *-ing, -ed*.	• Teacher reviews previously taught rule for adding these endings to a closed-syllable base word by eliciting from students the key thing to look for (i.e., how many consonants are at the end of the closed syllable). • Students practice writing teacher-dictated words using a column activity, first writing the base word in the appropriate column, then the word with the ending underneath it.
Fluency (10 minutes)	Teacher quickly reviews previously learned irregular words using flash cards; Destiny does repeated reading of a familiar grade-3 passage, with monitoring of both accuracy and rate, and with charting of results. (Students are alternated each session.)
Text reading (10 minutes)	Students alternate guided oral reading of next chapter in grade-3 book; teacher begins by briefly reviewing three to four difficult words; asks questions during and after reading to monitor students' comprehension and engage them in the story.
Writing (5 minutes)	Students write three sentences dictated by the teacher, with a focus on applying previously taught spelling and basic writing skills (e.g., spelling closed syllables, including with *-ed* and *-ing*; spelling common irregular words; ending punctuation; use of apostrophe to show possession or in a contraction; capitalization of first word, *I*, and proper nouns).

shown in Figure 5.3, along with the accompanying intervention routine described in that section of the chapter. Destiny and Mia have already learned to recognize and decode two-syllable words with VCCV and -*cle* syllables, so the primary new reading skill being introduced in this section of the lesson is learning to decode two-syllable words with VCV.

For spelling, the lesson focuses on spelling closed-syllable words with the inflectional endings -*ed* and -*ing*. Mr. Hewitt uses the column activity for spelling shown in Figure 5.6 and described in the related section of the chapter. The main purpose of this lesson's spelling activity is to review and provide further practice applying the rule, which often takes time for students to learn. Mr. Hewitt will not teach any new irregular words in spelling during this lesson. However, he will review some previously taught irregular words by incorporating them into dictated sentences in the final writing step of the lesson.

The fluency step of the lesson addresses automaticity of irregular word reading through a quick flash card review of these words. Most of the fluency time, however, is spent on the repeated reading activity described previously, involving a familiar passage from a grade-3 chapter book that Destiny and Mia are reading in lessons.

In the text reading segment of the lesson, the girls alternate oral reading of the next chapter of the grade-3 book, new text that they have not read before. Mr. Hewitt initiates this segment of the lesson by briefly reviewing any difficult words contained in the upcoming text, as well as asking a few questions about what has happened in the book thus far and what the students think might happen next. As the students read, he provides the kind of feedback to errors described in Chapter 4, beginning with pointing cues. He also asks occasional questions to ensure that the girls are engaged and maintaining good comprehension of what they are reading. If a chapter is too long to finish in the allotted time, he chooses a point to leave off, with further reading in the chapter to be completed next time. The lesson concludes with dictated sentences that incorporate previously taught spelling and basic capitalization and punctuation skills.

A Sample Intervention Lesson for Conor

Conor's sample lesson, implemented with his classmate Ryan, is shown in Table 5.2. Conor and Ryan have mastered many basic phoneme–grapheme relationships, but they both need work on learning morphemes to help them read and spell long words. Ms. Williams begins this lesson with a quick review of previously taught morphemes (e.g., *un-*, *dis-*, *-tion*, *-ive*, *-ify*, *-ology*), including those most relevant to the current lesson, using flash cards. She also reviews the rule for soft *c* and *g* by asking the students how they will know which sound to use for these letters. Students should reply that they will look at the letter following the *c* or *g*; if it is an *e*, *i*, or *y*, *c* will usually have the sound /s/, and *g* will usually have the sound /j/. Otherwise, *c* has the sound /k/ and *g* the sound /g/.

Ms. Williams then introduces several new morphemes: *mono*, *poly*, and *the/theo*. She selects these particular morphemes because they will help the students read and

TABLE 5.2. Sample Intervention Lesson for Conor (with Ryan)

Component(s)	Activity
Word recognition and spelling (20 minutes)	
• Review previously taught morphemes (e.g., -*ology*, -*ive*, *pre-*, *aud/audi*, *rupt*).	• Teacher uses flash cards to quickly review sounds for these morphemes and their meanings.
• Teach new morphemes: *mono*, *poly*, *theo* (content-related, from Ancient History).	• Teacher writes morphemes and sample words on board (e.g., *theology*, *monotheism*, *polytheism*); provides rationale for selecting these (i.e., to help read/spell/understand words in content area); briefly discusses meaning.
• Review *c/g* rule.	• Teacher reviews rule by asking students, "How can you tell the sound of this letter?" (i.e., look to see if the following letter is *e*, *i*, *y*).
	• Students are given a list of words with new and review morphemes; they find and circle any affixes in each word, underline roots, mark *c/g* sounds, divide the rest of the word as needed.
• Read unfamiliar multisyllabic words.	• Students take turns reading the list of words, including practicing flexibility, with teacher feedback and coaching.
• Spell two-syllable or multisyllabic words with previously taught morphemes.	• Teacher dictates several words for students to spell to reinforce spelling of new/review morphemes (e.g., *monorail*, *polygon*, *monotone*, *theology*, *theocrat*).
Fluency (10 minutes)	Conor and his classmate complete a purposeful fluency activity in a grade-7-level passage on Hammurabi's code. Students (1) scan to find three to four difficult words, which the teacher helps them decode; (2) listen to the teacher read the passage; (3) read chorally with the teacher; and (4) take turns reading orally with appropriate prosody and teacher monitoring.
Text reading (15 minutes)	Students alternate in oral reading of a novel from the grade-9 curriculum, from their English class; teacher begins by briefly reviewing three to four difficult words and what has been happening in the novel; asks questions during and after reading to monitor students' comprehension and engage them in the reading; provides immediate feedback to oral reading errors.
Writing (15 minutes)	Students discuss the chapter they have read independently this week from a grade-5 fantasy novel and begin a response to a writing prompt related to the chapter; incorporate learned spelling and basic writing conventions and complete for homework.

understand words from a content class that they are finding particularly difficult—Ancient History. She introduces the new morphemes in the context of Ancient History content words (e.g., *monotheism, polytheism, theology*), discussing their pronunciation and meaning in relation to each word (i.e., *mono* means one, *poly* means many, and *the* or *theo* means God). As she explains, she circles the morphemes in each word.

Next, Ms. Williams implements the paper-and-pencil activity for analyzing multisyllabic words shown in Figure 5.5 and described earlier in this chapter. She elicits from students how they will begin (i.e., look for and circle affixes) and reminds them that while most of the words do have affixes, not all of them do (e.g., *Lebanon, Hammurabi*). Then, the students take turns reading the words, with Ms. Williams providing feedback as needed and encouraging flexibility in decoding. For example, Conor initially read *Lebanon* as leh-BAN-on, with the accent on the second syllable. The teacher asked him if he recognized that as a real word, and when he shook his head, she encouraged him to try again, reminding him that the accent might fall on a different syllable, and that unaccented syllables often have a schwa or brief /uh/ sound. Conor then was able to read the word successfully. Ms. Williams also thought that *Hammurabi* might be tricky, but after decoding the first two syllables correctly, Conor recognized the word as one he had heard in his Ancient History class and was able to read it.

Next, Ms. Williams uses a spelling activity to reinforce the new morphemes that students have learned in this lesson, dictating several words with these morphemes (e.g., *monotone, polygon*) for the students to write. For this initial introduction, she deliberately chooses transparent words without spelling changes or shifts in accent (not, e.g., *monotony* or *polygamy*). She also uses standard dictation format, including the word in a sentence and briefly discussing the meaning of each word. However, the main purpose of this activity is simply to anchor the spellings of the new morphemes in students' memories. If a morpheme or word is misspelled, Ms. Williams provides appropriate feedback.

For fluency, the students complete the purposeful fluency activity described previously in this chapter, using an approximately grade-7-level passage and the four steps shown in Table 5.2. The students' Ancient History textbook is too difficult for them to read for now, but for fluency practice, Ms. Williams has chosen an internet passage with content relating to their history class, on the subject of Hammurabi's code. She monitors the students' accuracy of reading to ensure the passage is not too difficult for them, but in this activity, Ms. Williams does not use timing; she takes a more prosodic approach to fluency instruction. However, in other lessons, she uses occasional CBM probes to monitor progress in students' rate, as well as accuracy of reading. She has seen substantial growth in their accuracy, as well as some improvements in rate and prosody.

For the text-reading lesson segment, the students are reading a novel from their English class, one that is easier reading than their Ancient History textbook and within their reach in an instructional setting. The students alternate text reading, with Ms. Williams providing guidance and feedback. In the final writing step of the lesson, Ms. Williams devotes time for the students to discuss the fantasy novel that they are reading independently for homework. To show that they have done the reading, as well as to practice writing, the students answer a writing prompt (e.g., *Discuss the most important event in this chapter and explain why you think it matters*). The students complete the prompt for homework. In their writing, they are expected to spell previously taught words correctly and implement basic writing conventions they have learned, with subsequent editing as needed. For other lessons with Conor and Ryan, the writing segment of the lesson involves different activities, such as responding to a writing prompt relating to the text reading from that session or dictated sentences.

Additional Considerations for Written Expression

Like early-stage readers, advanced-stage readers with SWRD typically have strengths in their broad language abilities and in text-generation aspects of writing. However, poor spelling often is a lingering problem for them because learning to spell words is even more difficult than learning to read them (Moats, 2022; Treiman, 2017). Like early-stage readers with SWRD, many advanced-stage readers have good ideas for writing and can grasp key points in content areas just as well as typical students but have trouble writing down their ideas due to weaknesses in spelling and other basic writing skills.

At this stage students' spelling often lags behind their word reading. A student might be able to decode two- and three-syllable words but still need work on spelling one-syllable words. Including spelling as part of their interventions therefore remains important for most of these students, as does teaching of other writing skills. Although assistive technology for writing can be a valuable tool for these students in keeping up with content-area demands at advanced grade levels, technology does not eliminate the need to teach spelling explicitly (Joshi et al., 2008). Furthermore, teaching spelling helps to promote word reading and can even lead to increases in speed of word reading (Ouellette et al., 2017), a common weakness in advanced-stage readers with SWRD.

SUMMING UP: SL Interventions for Advanced-Stage Readers with SWRD

Here are key points from this chapter:

- Advanced-stage readers with SWRD typically need interventions focused on morphology, reading long words, spelling, and reading fluency.

- Most of these students are in middle school or high school, but some can be younger.

- Examples of effective intervention activities for these students include teaching strategies for breaking up long words, such as syllable division rules; instruction in morphology such as teaching about common prefixes, suffixes, and roots; flexibility practice; purposeful fluency activities; and continuous reading.

- Usually, these students do not require decodable texts, and some may be able to read grade-level texts, especially with teacher support; however, students should not always read difficult texts because they may lose comprehension and motivation to read.

- Like early-stage readers with SWRD, in written expression, advanced-stage readers tend to have weaknesses in spelling but strengths in the text generation aspects of writing.

- The spelling skills of advanced-stage readers with SWRD usually lag behind their word-reading skills, and continuation of spelling intervention remains important for them.

APPLIED EXERCISES

Exercise 1

Ms. Torres, an interventionist, is working with a group of fifth-grade poor readers. The students have learned to decode all common one-syllable word patterns (i.e., closed, SE, open, VR, VT), as well as those patterns with common inflectional endings (e.g., *trapping, liked, farmer*) and words with *-cle* (e.g., *marble, rifle, bundle*). Next, Ms. Torres plans to teach students words with VCCV patterns, beginning with the rule for dividing those words to help read them. Which of the following sets of words would be best to use as examples in introducing VCCV?

A. *rabbit, trigger, hammer, button, muffin*
B. *conductor, apricot, understand, envelope*
C. *snorkel, rather, invite, napkin, Rachel*
D. *window, attic, cartoon, publish, rescue*

Answer

The best list to use is D because this list uses a range of two-syllable VCCV words, without any exception words or potentially confusing words. List A uses only words in which the two consonants in the VCCV pattern are the same, which may lead students to infer this is a requirement for the pattern, which is not the case. List B uses words of three syllables, whereas introduction of the rule should start with two-syllable words. List C has two problematic examples, *rather* and *Rachel*. Both words have a consonant digraph as part of the VCCV pattern and are exceptions that are best introduced after the students have learned the VCV rule.

Exercise 2

What is flexibility practice and why is it especially important as students begin learning to read long words?

Answer

Flexibility practice involves practicing different possible ways to pronounce long words, consistent with the letters and letter patterns in the word. This usually involves shifting vowel sounds and accent patterns, with the goal of matching the printed word to one the student has heard before. Flexibility practice is especially important for long words because these words are likely to have more than one possible pronunciation.

Exercise 3

Rob, an eighth grader, is struggling to spell the word *resident*. He keeps misspelling the word as *resadent*. His teacher has repeatedly encouraged him to say the word to himself and listen for the second vowel sound, but Rob still misspells the word with an *a*. What is better feedback that his teacher could give him?

Answer

Encouraging Rob to listen for the second vowel sound is not the best feedback for this word because the second vowel sound is a schwa and can be represented by a range of vowel letters, including *a*. Morphemic feedback would probably be more successful in this situation. Rob's teacher could point out that the base word for *resident* is *reside*, helping him spell the base word if necessary, then ask him to determine the correct spelling of *resident* given that base word.

Column Activity for Spelling Closed Syllables with *-ed* and *-ing* (Template Version)

1 Consonant	2+ Consonants

Multisyllabic Segmentation Activity for Spelling (Template Version)

1. _____ _____ _____ _____ _____ _____

2. _____ _____ _____ _____ _____ _____

3. _____ _____ _____ _____ _____ _____

4. _____ _____ _____ _____ _____ _____

5. _____ _____ _____ _____ _____ _____

6. _____ _____ _____ _____ _____ _____

7. _____ _____ _____ _____ _____ _____

8. _____ _____ _____ _____ _____ _____

9. _____ _____ _____ _____ _____ _____

10. _____ _____ _____ _____ _____ _____

11. _____ _____ _____ _____ _____ _____

12. _____ _____ _____ _____ _____ _____

CHAPTER 6

Structured Literacy Interventions for Specific Reading Comprehension Difficulties

Early Stages

Jane Woody, a third-grade teacher, felt her heart sink when she saw the most recent progress monitoring results for one of her students. Mary, nicknamed Mamie, had consistently done well on the oral reading fluency (ORF) curriculum-based measure (CBM) that her school used for universal screening and progress monitoring, beginning in the middle of grade 1. As is common in CBM screening, the school began using an additional CBM for maze comprehension in grade 3. On the maze assessment, Mamie's fall results were a little below the benchmark. Ms. Woody had hoped that this borderline performance reflected Mamie's adjustment to reading third-grade text and the fact that it was the beginning of the school year. Unfortunately, in the most recent winter screening, Mamie's performance was well below the benchmark, in a range that was clearly at risk. Moreover, this result aligned with some increasing concerns Ms. Woody had with Mamie's comprehension during classroom reading instruction. Still, she was somewhat puzzled by Mamie's difficulties because Mamie had no history of poor comprehension in previous grades, and because most of Ms. Woody's poor readers had problems in decoding or reading fluency, something that was not true of Mamie.

The focus of this chapter and Chapter 7 is specific reading comprehension difficulties (SRCD), a different profile of poor reading than in the previous two chapters. SRCD involves different underlying patterns of strengths and weaknesses in reading than do specific word recognition difficulties (SWRD). This chapter addresses students with SRCD who are functioning at early stages of reading, like Mamie. SRCD is a relatively uncommon profile of poor reading in the primary grades (Leach et al., 2003) but becomes more common among poor readers in the later grades (Catts et al., 2012;

127

Leach et al., 2003; Lesaux & Kieffer, 2010). An SRCD profile is also relatively more common among specific populations of students, such as those with autism spectrum disorders (ASD; Huemer & Mann, 2010; Norbury & Nation, 2011). While some early-stage poor readers with SRCD are in the elementary grades, others are older, in middle school or beyond. Nathan, a sixth grader, provides an example of this latter kind of student.

Nathan was identified with ASD at age 3. In preschool and the primary grades, his teachers struggled to maintain his attention and to deal with certain behaviors, such as tantrums related to frustration and changes in routine, which often affected his academic learning. Nevertheless, learning to read and spell words came easily to Nathan, and his skills in these areas were always on grade level. In contrast, he struggled with comprehension. Nathan's comprehension difficulties worsened as he advanced in school and was expected to read more challenging texts. Below is some additional information about both Mamie and Nathan.

Mamie

After Mamie's difficulties on the winter screening with the maze CBM, Ms. Woody administered an ORI to her. On this assessment, Mamie's highest instructional level in graded word lists was grade 4, above grade placement, but in passages, her highest instructional level was grade 2, about a year below grade expectations. Mamie could read the grade-3 passage with 97% accuracy; her problems in passage reading were entirely due to comprehension. On comprehension questions, she had a pattern of difficulties with vocabulary and background knowledge, a pattern that Ms. Woody has also noticed in classroom read-alouds, as well as informal comprehension assessments. Mamie has some difficulties in writing as well. Her spelling is on grade level, but Ms. Woody has noted problems with Mamie's word choice and lack of elaboration in writing. For instance, Mamie often responds to a writing prompt with a single sentence, when a paragraph or more is expected.

Mamie's parents say that her early language development was on target, and Mamie passed a language screening by the school's speech–language pathologist. Mamie has no indications of any other disabilities. Nevertheless, she is now evidencing significant difficulties in reading comprehension. She has been selected for supplemental intervention with the school reading specialist.

Nathan

Students with ASD, such as Nathan, can vary greatly in their underlying profiles of language abilities, including in their phonological, vocabulary, and syntactic abilities (Geurts & Embrechts, 2008; Norbury & Nation, 2011). One aspect of language that is often impaired in students with ASD is pragmatic language, the use of language in a social context (Nelson, 2010). Examples of pragmatic language include the ability to have an age-appropriate conversation, to express emotions, and to recognize when a listener has not understood something and provide clarification. Students with ASD may also have difficulties with various aspects of narrative language, such as retelling a narrative, taking the perspective of others, and understanding the emotions or motivations of characters in a story (Dodd, Ocampo, & Kennedy, 2011; Whalon, 2018). Difficulties with pragmatics and narrative language are not unique to ASD or to students with disabilities; however, pragmatic weaknesses may be especially enduring in ASD (Geurts & Embrechts, 2008).

The variability in underlying language abilities associated with ASD aligns with the variability in reading profiles seen in these students (Nation, Clarke, Wright, & Williams, 2006; Norbury & Nation, 2011). Not all students with ASD have reading difficulties, but for those who do, the most common profiles involve SRCD or MRD, not SWRD (Whalon, 2018). As with all poor readers, however, going beyond the profile to identify the specific language and reading weaknesses of individual students is crucial.

Figure 6.1 displays an assessment map with selected scores involving Nathan's reading and language performance in his most recent triennial evaluation in special education, an evaluation done every 3 years to determine whether students' educational needs have changed and whether they still are eligible for special education. Nathan had strengths in word reading and phonological skills, with scores in these areas all in average range or higher. In the area of oral language, his vocabulary scores were also solidly average. However, Nathan's broad language comprehension was well below average. His lowest score was on the Test of Pragmatic Language—Second Edition (TOPL-2; Phelps-Terasaki & Phelps-Gunn, 2007). Nathan's reading comprehension was also poor on two different measures, as shown on the right-hand side of Figure 6.1.

Interestingly, despite his good word reading and phonological skills, Nathan's scores suggested some problems in reading fluency. These problems were not due to word reading, however, but to language comprehension. On the GORT-5, which involves oral reading of passages, his examiner observed that Nathan did not appear to monitor comprehension—that is, actively think about meaning while reading—especially as passages became more difficult. At the end of a line of text, he would sometimes simply stop, even though he was in the middle of a sentence, and was reading words easily. These pauses affected his score for rate but did not reflect difficulties in reading words. On the sentence-reading fluency subtest of the WJ-IV, which has a comprehension component requiring students to tell whether various statements are true or false, Nathan completed many items but made numerous errors. Again, his difficulties on this subtest, considered in conjunction with his good performance on measures of out-of-context word-reading and text-reading accuracy, did not appear to reflect poor decoding, but rather problems with comprehension.

Nathan just transitioned to middle school, and he has a new special education teacher this year, Mr. Thorpe. Nathan's reading progress has been very slow in the past few years and his planning and placement team (PPT)—the educators who work with Nathan, school administrators, and his parents—wants to improve his progress. Like Mamie, Nathan currently reads at about a grade-2 level, although the underpinnings

Student *Nathan*   Grade *6*   Dates of Testing *Jan 20–Feb 12*

ORAL LANGUAGE COMPREHENSION

Oral Vocabulary (note receptive/expressive)

WJ-IV Picture Vocabulary 95 (exp)

Peabody Picture Vocabulary Test–5, 98 (rec)

Oral Language (Listening) Comprehension (note format, e.g., cloze, maze, QA)

WJ-IV Oral Comprehension (cloze), 82
CELF-5 Understanding Spoken Paragraphs (QA), 78
CELF-5 Receptive Index, 80

Other Oral Language

Test of Pragmatic Language (TOPL-2), 68

WORD READING

Real Words—Accuracy

WJ-IV Word Identification 98

Nonsense Words—Accuracy

WJ-IV Word Attack 112

Word Reading—Automaticity

TOWRE-2 Sight Word Efficiency, 95

TOWRE-2 Phonemic Decoding Efficiency, 106

Phonological/phonemic awareness

CTOPP Composites all > 95

Oral Reading Fluency—Accuracy

GORT-5 Accuracy Scaled Score 10

Oral Reading Fluency—Rate

GORT-5 Rate Scaled Score 7

Silent Reading Fluency

WJ-IV Sentence Reading Fluency 82

Reading Comprehension (note test format, e.g., cloze, maze, QA, as well as other relevant features such as timing)

GORT-5 Comprehension (timed; QA) 4

WJ-IV Passage Comprehension (untimed; cloze) 75

Observations

On the GORT-V, especially as passages became more difficult, he did not appear to monitor comprehension

FIGURE 6.1. Assessment map for Nathan.

of his comprehension difficulties are quite different from Mamie's. In addition to problems with pragmatic language, comprehension monitoring, and understanding characters' emotions in narratives, Mr. Thorpe has noticed that Nathan has some difficulties with cause and effect, such as understanding why something has happened, even when this information is explicitly stated in a text. Mr. Thorpe recently had some professional development in SL. He and the other members of Nathan's PPT hope that SL interventions will help increase Nathan's reading progress.

SL interventions are not only for teaching phonics or for students with SWRD. They can also help students like Mamie, Nathan, and many other students with comprehension-based reading difficulties. This chapter provides examples of SL intervention activities for students with SRCD who are functioning at relatively early stages of reading, along with a basic intervention plan for these students. Like interventions for teaching foundational reading skills, these comprehension interventions address the core language content and exemplify the instructional features of SL, including explicit, systematic teaching; prompt, targeted feedback; and planned, purposeful choices of instructional examples, tasks, and texts.

About Early-Stage Readers with SRCD

Early-stage readers with SRCD all have the following in common: (1) a poor reader profile with difficulties centered on comprehension, usually oral language comprehension as well as reading comprehension; (2) word-reading skills in the average range or higher, including phonological skills and automaticity as well as accuracy of word reading; and (3) a need for intervention involving comprehension skills typically taught in the early to middle elementary grades. As with other poor reader profiles, early-stage readers with SRCD can vary substantially in age, with older students having more severe reading difficulties.

Many students with SRCD have underlying language weaknesses that do not affect their reading comprehension until they advance in school and are expected to read more challenging texts (Clarke et al., 2014). This was likely true for Mamie, and was probably the reason why teachers did not notice problems with her comprehension in earlier grades. Nathan's language comprehension difficulties were more obvious, affecting his reading comprehension almost from the start; therefore, his comprehension difficulties did not go unnoticed. Screening for language comprehension problems, as well as phonological and word-reading problems, in the first few grades of school could help identify children like Mamie earlier, and earlier intervention might prevent or lessen some of these children's reading difficulties (Clarke et al., 2014; Scarborough, 2005).

Given the many areas that underlie comprehension, the primary intervention needs of early-stage readers with SRCD can vary substantially. Some common needs include vocabulary, background knowledge, inferencing, understanding challenging syntax, understanding text structure, and comprehension monitoring. Also, some students with SRCD may read slowly because they are struggling to comprehend, or for other reasons not connected to problems in word reading, as was true for Nathan. These students are unlikely to benefit from the types of reading fluency interventions previously described for SWRD, such as timed repeated readings of text or flash card practice on common irregular words. Those interventions are aimed at increasing automaticity of word reading, and by definition, the problems of students with SRCD are based in comprehension, not word reading. Slow reading in students with SRCD is likely better addressed through interventions aimed at their specific comprehension needs. Improvements in comprehension may lead to increased rate of reading if students do not have to expend as much effort in struggling to understand a text.

Research on Interventions for Early-Stage Readers with SRCD

The Importance of Oral Language

Because the reading comprehension difficulties of students with SRCD are usually based in oral language weaknesses, addressing these weaknesses in intervention is vital. Interventions need to target the specific language weaknesses of individual students. Text reading should be part of intervention lessons, but text-reading activities must involve ample oral discussion, and including appropriate oral activities in lessons is very important.

In some cases, oral comprehension interventions can be even more effective than text comprehension interventions for students with SRCD. In a randomized controlled trial, the York Reading for Meaning project (Clarke et al., 2014) studied the impact of three 20-week interventions on a group of children who were 8–10 years old and had specific comprehension difficulties, with age-appropriate decoding and normal nonverbal reasoning, but significantly weaker listening and reading comprehension. The three interventions involved a text comprehension intervention, including teaching of metacognitive strategies for reading comprehension, inferencing, and written narratives; an oral comprehension intervention, including teaching of vocabulary, figurative language, and spoken narratives; and a combined intervention that put together specific components of the first two interventions. All three interventions benefited children's reading comprehension, and children in all three interventions maintained their gains when retested 11 months after the end of the intervention. However, only the oral language intervention group increased their gains in reading comprehension further at the 11-month follow-up. Clarke and colleagues attributed the advantage of the oral language intervention to its teaching of oral vocabulary, which was based on the multiple-context learning approach of Beck and colleagues (2002) and aims to foster a broad awareness of words, their connections to other words, and how new vocabulary can be learned.

Vocabulary

Vocabulary is a strong predictor of both oral and reading comprehension (Beck et al., 2002; NRP, 2000; RAND Reading Study Group, 2002), and limitations in vocabulary knowledge are common in poor readers with profiles of SRCD or MRD (Lesaux & Kieffer, 2010). Addressing vocabulary in intervention is therefore essential if a student has needs in this area.

Researchers interested in vocabulary (e.g., Beck et al., 2002; Biemiller, 2009; Coyne & Loftus-Rattan, 2022; Fisher & Blachowicz, 2005) have emphasized the importance of explicit teaching of academic words, words that students must know for success in school, with careful selection of words to be taught. As discussed in Chapter 2, Beck and colleagues (2002) distinguished different tiers of vocabulary words. Tier 1 involves words that would not usually need to be taught because they are common words most students would know (e.g., *house, boy, tree*). Tier 2 involves more unusual words, important for academic learning, and found in a wide range of texts (e.g., *forlornly, spectacular, delighted*). Tier 3 involves unusual or technical words from specialized content domains (e.g., *igneous, sedimentary,* and *metamorphic* types of rocks in earth science), which are important to success in their respective domains but do not generalize widely across texts. General vocabulary development should focus on the second tier of words, whereas the third tier is important to address as part of content learning in subjects like social studies and science. If schools developed specific vocabulary lists based on important words from the reading and other curricula in their schools, as suggested by Foorman and colleagues (2016), then that could be invaluable for interventionists seeking specific words to teach, as well as for general educators. In the absence of such a list, interventionists can try to develop their own, or consult a source for specific words, such as Gardner and Davies (2014).

Authorities such as Beck and colleagues (2002), Coyne and Loftus-Rattan (2022), and Clarke and colleagues (2014) have also highlighted the importance of introducing new vocabulary words in the context of sentences or passages; giving students multiple and frequent exposures to new words over time; providing student-friendly definitions of words rather than only formal dictionary definitions; and using visual representations such as word maps. Morphological interventions that teach students the meanings of word parts, such as common affixes, can also improve vocabulary knowledge and are especially effective for poor readers, including those with reading and language disabilities (Goodwin & Ahn, 2013).

In addition to explicit teaching of specific words and morphology, teaching students to infer word meanings from context can be effective (NRP, 2000). Using context to infer word meanings must be distinguished from using context cues to guess at words in decoding. The latter is problematic because it can lead students away from application of decoding skills and close attention to letter sequences in words. However, using context to infer word meanings is different. Consider a sentence such as *Alex told his little sister never to play with his airplane model, so when he saw that she had broken it, he was furious.* A teacher might encourage a student to use sentence or picture context, such as a picture of Alex looking furious, to infer that the word *furious* means *very angry.* Unlike using sentence or picture context to guess at words in decoding, teaching students to use context to infer word meanings is desirable, where the context enables doing so.

Sentences

Sentence-level interventions often focus on syntax, such as helping students understand the potentially confusing sentences discussed in Chapter 2. Whiteboard activities with visuals and marking, such as writing a sentence with center-embedded syntax and drawing a red arrow from the subject to its verb, can be effective in helping students to understand these kinds of sentences (Zipoli & Merritt, 2022). Sentence combining and sentence decomposition tasks also are effective (Saddler, 2012; Zipoli & Merritt, 2022). In sentence combining, students are given a set of kernel sentences to combine into a longer, syntactically correct sentence that includes the gist of all of the kernel sentences. In sentence decomposition, students do the opposite task, take a relatively complex sentence and break it down into simpler sentences. Both tasks can benefit students' writing as well as their reading comprehension (Smith & Haynes, 2022).

Sentence-level activities also can be used to develop many other comprehension-related abilities, including inferring word meanings from context, understanding figurative language, recognizing common signal words and how they affect the meaning of a sentence, and understanding anaphoric references such as pronouns. These activities may sometimes use two or three interrelated sentences rather than just a single sentence. The main goal of sentence-level activities is to develop comprehension abilities that will ultimately improve students' understanding of longer passages and texts. Oral discussion, with teacher explanation, questioning, and guided practice, should be a key part of these activities, especially when a new skill is introduced or when students are having difficulty with a skill. Because students with SRCD have grade-appropriate word reading, teachers can often take sentences directly from grade-level texts and curriculum materials, which can facilitate students' comprehension of these texts later on.

In intervention, students with SRCD do not usually require texts controlled to specific phonics patterns (i.e., decodable texts), but they do require texts at or near their instructional levels, which for some students may not be grade-level texts. Mamie, for instance, can read and understand most grade-level texts with some preteaching and scaffolding from her teacher, but Nathan's comprehension weaknesses are more severe, so reading grade-level texts is too difficult for him for now. He can read the words of these texts, but the comprehension demands are too overwhelming for instruction in these texts to be effective.

Discourse and Text Comprehension

An especially important aspect of discourse and text comprehension, one that is often problematic for students with SRCD (Clarke et al., 2014; Oakhill et al., 2015), is comprehension monitoring, monitoring one's own understanding during the act of reading (or listening) and recognizing when comprehension has broken down or something does not make sense. Poor comprehension monitoring may occur for many reasons, and students who fail to monitor their comprehension in a particular situation do not always have an underlying problem with comprehension itself. For example, if students with SWRD are reading difficult texts, well beyond their instructional levels, they might stop monitoring comprehension because they are overwhelmed by decoding demands and cannot continue to keep track of meaning. However, students with SRCD have core comprehension difficulties, which in some cases may directly affect their ability to monitor comprehension, even when they are reading texts they can decode well.

To convey the importance of actively thinking about meaning when reading, educators can begin with sentence-level activities such as asking students to identify sentences that do not make sense (e.g., *Last summer we took a vacation on the sun*). Students should be taught to apply strategies to try to repair comprehension breakdowns during text reading, for instance, rereading or looking up the meaning of an unknown word (Pressley & Afflerbach, 1995). Teaching students to summarize a text at specified points during reading also is helpful (Oakhill et al., 2015; Palincsar & Brown, 1984), since this kind of ongoing summarization requires comprehension monitoring and helps students identify a comprehension breakdown before completing an entire text.

Other discourse- and text-level comprehension activities benefit students with SRCD who are functioning at early stages of reading. Helpful activities include teaching students about narrative language, as well as about both narrative and informational text structure. Graphic organizers and other visual aids, such as story maps, are effective for this purpose (Hennessey, 2021; Zipoli & Merritt, 2022). The use of questioning also promotes comprehension (Cartwright, 2015; NRP, 2000), including both teachers' questioning of students and teaching students to generate their own questions. Questioning techniques can be implemented before, during, and after reading (Stevens & Austin, 2022). For instance, teachers can ask questions before students read to help provide a purpose for reading, as well as activate and identify gaps in students' background knowledge. Questioning during reading can encourage students to monitor comprehension and help them identify key ideas in a text. Questioning after reading can help students summarize an entire text and consolidate new learning, such as key vocabulary.

Inferencing is another common difficulty for students with SRCD (Clarke et al., 2014). Background knowledge plays an important role in inferencing (Elleman, 2017; Oakhill et al., 2015), so the most relevant background knowledge for understanding a text should be taught explicitly prior to reading. In addition, building students' background knowledge for specific topics (e.g., how scientists study past events) in a sustained way, across grades, can benefit their general reading comprehension as well as comprehension for those topics (Kim et al., 2023). Other effective activities to help students with inferencing include teaching them about different types of comprehension questions and how to answer them (e.g., by looking for explicit answers in the text vs. making connections to prior knowledge), as well as explicitly teaching and modeling how to look for relevant inference-related cues in a text (Elleman, 2017; Vaughn et al., 2022).

Some students have difficulties even with very basic types of inferences such as anaphoric references involving pronouns. Students with ASD sometimes have these difficulties and can benefit from anaphoric cueing techniques such as writing the referents of pronouns (e.g., the name of the character being referred to by *he* or *she*) above each pronoun (Whalon, Al Otaiba, & Delano, 2009). These techniques may also help other students with similar difficulties.

The Role of Writing

Graham and Hebert (2010) note the value of writing in developing students' reading. Reading and writing tap many of the same underlying abilities, so appropriate writing activities can develop important components of language that improve students' reading, as well as their writing. Intervention activities involving writing for students with SRCD should target individual students' underlying language weaknesses. For instance, students with syntactic weaknesses can benefit from sentence-combining and decomposition activities; those with vocabulary weaknesses can benefit from using new words in their writing. While oral activities and discussion are an essential part of interventions for SRCD, the use of writing activities in interventions can further develop and consolidate comprehension-related abilities.

Sample SL Intervention Activities

Explicit Teaching of Specific Vocabulary Words

Mamie's interventionist, Ms. Santiago, provides a good example of an SL approach to introducing new vocabulary words and teaching them explicitly. She works with Mamie in a small group of four children with similar comprehension needs. During a read-aloud of a children's book from the grade-3 curriculum, Ms. Santiago targets several words in the book for explicit instruction, including *astonished*. The words are all Tier 2 words, academic vocabulary that Ms. Santiago knows will be unfamiliar to the children.

- Ms. Santiago reads the sentence, *Lisa thought Mr. Edwards had moved far away, so she was* <u>astonished</u> *to see him at her front door.* She pauses and says, "*Astonished* is an unusual word. Does anyone know what this word means?" No hands go up.
- Ms. Santiago says, "First, let's all say the word together." The students repeat the word *astonished* in unison, while Ms. Santiago writes it on a small whiteboard for the students to see clearly.
- The teacher then says, "*Astonished* means 'very surprised.' Lisa was <u>very surprised</u> to see Mr. Edwards at her front door. What does *astonished* mean?" The students repeat in unison, "*Astonished* means 'very surprised.'" Ms. Santiago continues her reading.

Word Maps for Vocabulary

Ms. Santiago knows that a single explicit introduction of a new word is not sufficient for most students in her intervention group to retain it. For further practice on new words, she uses a number of activities, including word maps. Word maps, sometimes termed "semantic maps" or "mind maps," are a type of graphic organizer that can be very useful in vocabulary intervention (e.g., Clarke et al., 2014; Frayer, Frederick, &

Klausmeier, 1969; Hennessey, 2021). The specific details of word maps can differ. Figure 6.2 shows one sample word map for the word *astonished*. (For a template version of this activity optimized for student use, see Form 6.1 on page 152.)

Sometime after her initial introduction of the word, Ms. Santiago has the students complete the word map for *astonished*. She has included the context sentence from the read-aloud, as shown in the upper-left-hand corner of Figure 6.2. Various parts of the map require the students to fill in the definition of *astonished*, as well as synonyms and antonyms for it. Ms. Santiago helps the students to complete their maps, and she makes sure that they include any relevant, previously taught words, such as *amazed*. In the "other" section at the bottom of the map, students can fill in various options related to the target word. In the case of *astonished*, there is figurative language that students have learned, the expression *You could have knocked me over with a feather*, associated with being very surprised. In lieu of figurative language, in the "other" section, students could also write an additional sample sentence using the word *astonished*, or an example of a time when they themselves were astonished. Ms. Santiago has the students keep the word maps in a folder for occasional review or as a resource for other intervention activities, such as using new vocabulary words in their writing.

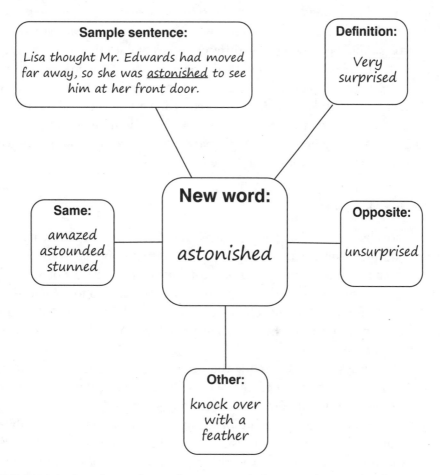

FIGURE 6.2. Sample word map for new vocabulary words (completed example).

Teaching Students to Infer Word Meanings from Context

Teaching students to infer word meanings from context is an important adjunct to explicit teaching of specific words because it can expand students' learning of new vocabulary, as well as help alert them to the ways that different words tend to be used. Students should be taught that figuring out word meanings from context involves looking for cues in the sentence or in surrounding sentences; occasionally, pictures that accompany a text may be helpful. Sometimes, however, there are no cues, and for these situations, students should rely on a different strategy, such as looking up the meaning of a word online or in a dictionary.

Table 6.1 displays some sample sentences that a teacher might use to teach students to infer word meanings from sentence context, with the target vocabulary word italicized. The students should first decide whether a sentence contains helpful context for determining the meaning of the target word. If not, the teacher can remind students that if the sentence were in a passage, other sentences around it might have helpful information for figuring out the meaning of the word; otherwise, a different strategy for determining the meaning must be employed.

For words with helpful context, Table 6.1 shows various cues that students can use to help infer word meanings, including definitions, synonyms, opposites, examples, and other cues. Teaching these specific terms to the students is not essential, but students' attention should be drawn to the different types of cues they may encounter. For instance, sometimes a sentence explicitly tells the meaning of a word (definition), gives its opposite, or gives examples that provide cues to the meaning of a word. At other times the reader has to think like a detective, reasoning about the specific situation and words that provide hints to meaning, as in the *concluded* item in the final row of Table 6.1. It is important to highlight the specific parts of the sentence that provide cues, as shown in the far right-hand column of Table 6.1.

Word Sorts for Morphology

Teaching of morphology is a key part of vocabulary intervention. Knowing the meanings of common morphemes can greatly expand children's vocabularies; for instance, with this understanding, students who learn *astonished* can also potentially understand *astonish, astonishing, astonishingly, astonishment,* and so forth. Word sorts are one useful activity for teaching morphology. After introducing several common morphemes and their meanings, teachers can have students sort and then discuss words containing the morphemes.

Figure 6.3 displays a word sort for the prefixes *un, re,* and *pre,* common morphemes taught in the primary grades, that Ms. Santiago has used with Mamie and her intervention group. The word cards are mixed together, and the students must sort them into separate categories for each morpheme. After children successfully sort the words, Ms. Santiago leads a brief discussion about the meaning of several words with each morpheme, highlighting how the morpheme affects the meaning of the base word (e.g., *unwise* means <u>not</u> wise, *preheat* means heating an oven to the right temperature <u>before</u> putting food in to cook).

TABLE 6.1. Sample Sentences with and without Context Cues for New Vocabulary Words

Sentence	Are there cues to word meaning?	Type of context cue	Parts of sentence providing cues
Lisa often misspells the word *astonished*.	No	Not applicable	
The *distaff*, or maternal, side of her family traced back to a small village in Greece.	Yes	Synonym	The phrase *or maternal* right after *distaff* tells you that *distaff* means *maternal*.
Mrs. Smith's favorite color is *mahogany*, a deep reddish brown.	Yes	Definition	The phrase *a deep reddish brown* gives you a definition of the color *mahogany*.
The stray cat was *feral*, unlike the many tame cats some people had as pets.	Yes	Opposite	The word *unlike* and the phrase *unlike the many tame cats most people had as pets* tells you that *feral* means the opposite of *tame* (wild).
The restaurant menu had a variety of *beverages*, such as soda, lemonade, coffee, and tea, as well as wine and beer.	Yes	Example	The examples after the words *such as* provide cues to the meaning of the word *beverages* and tell you that *beverages* are *drinks*.
The story *concluded* with a visit to the circus, with a show under the big top.	No	Not applicable	
Emma loves strawberry milk, but Willie *detests* it.	Yes	Opposite	*Emma loves strawberry milk* and the word *but* tell you that *detests* means the opposite of *loves* (hates).
The train schedule was highly *accurate*; it had no mistakes.	Yes	Definition	*It had no mistakes* provides a definition of the word *accurate*.
The story *concluded* with a happy ending in which John finally saw his friend again.	Yes	Other cues	*Happy ending* and *finally* are cues that *concluded* means *ended*.

An important point for students to understand is that simply containing a particular letter string is not sufficient for the letters in a word to be a morpheme; the letter sequence must also convey the appropriate meaning in the context of the word. For example, the *re* in *retell* is a morpheme, specifically, a prefix, but the *re* in *real* is not, because there is no base word, and *re* does not have a separate meaning in this word. Ms. Santiago makes this point in the initial introduction of the morphemes through examples and non-examples, such as *retell* versus *real*. In sorting tasks, including an "other" category, as shown on the right-hand side of Figure 6.3, reinforces this point.

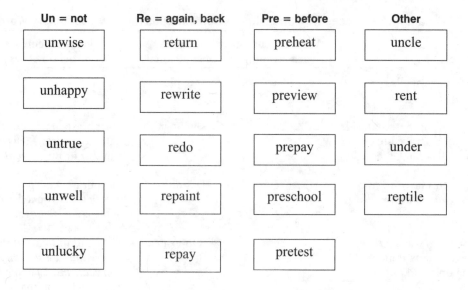

Un = not	Re = again, back	Pre = before	Other
unwise	return	preheat	uncle
unhappy	rewrite	preview	rent
untrue	redo	prepay	under
unwell	repaint	preschool	reptile
unlucky	repay	pretest	

FIGURE 6.3. Sample word sort for morphology.

Activities for Comprehension Monitoring

For students with significant difficulties in comprehension monitoring, such as Nathan, it can be helpful to start intervention at the sentence level. One useful initial activity is to give students a series of sentences that do and do not make sense (Vaughn et al., 2022). Students must identify the illogical sentences and tell why they do not make sense, as shown in Figure 6.4. (For a template version of this activity optimized for student use, see Form 6.2 on page 153.) Next, teachers can give students similar activities within paragraphs. For instance, an illogical sentence can be embedded in a paragraph, or a paragraph can contain a nonsense word like *grimp*. The ultimate goal of these activities is for students routinely to monitor their comprehension in everyday texts, such as instructional-level texts that they are reading in school.

Students need not only to identify their own comprehension breakdowns, but also to have strategies to use when something does not make sense, sometimes termed fix-up strategies (Pressley & Afflerbach, 1995). Examples of useful fix-up strategies to teach students include the following:

- Rereading a section of confusing text
- Reading beyond a section of confusing text to see if the confusing part is explained later
- Looking up an unfamiliar vocabulary word, term, or expression online or in a dictionary
- Using relevant signal words in a text to aid comprehension
- Using informational text features such as headings, graphs, charts, and glossaries

In these activities, teachers should model comprehension monitoring and use of strategies to repair comprehension, through oral text reading with think-alouds in which

Sentence	Makes sense? Yes or No	If no, what does not make sense?
Marvin was very hungry, so he did not want to eat.	*No*	*If Marvin is hungry, he should want to eat.*
Mr. Wheeler drives a flashy red car with square tires.	*No*	*Tires cannot be square.*
The doctor was a very tall woman in a white coat.	*Yes*	
The Johnsons traveled to Alaska for their summer vacation.	*Yes*	
Sarah smiled because she was very angry with her friend.	*No*	*People don't usually smile when they are angry.*
The twins were thrilled to get a new puppy as a birthday gift.	*Yes*	
The house on the corner has a long driveway made of jam.	*No*	*You can't make a driveway out of jam.*
When the stranger came to the door, the cat barked furiously at him.	*No*	*Cats don't bark.*

FIGURE 6.4. Comprehension monitoring activity with illogical sentences (completed example).

they make their own thinking processes explicit for students. Ensuring that reading materials are at an appropriate level of difficulty for individual students is also important because if the comprehension demands of a text are too overwhelming, students may stop monitoring comprehension.

Analyzing and Marking Sentence and Text Structure

Activities that involve analyzing and marking sentence structure, which can be extended beyond the sentence level, can also help students with SRCD (Zipoli, 2017; Zipoli & Merritt, 2022). Mr. Thorpe has used these activities with Nathan to improve his understanding of cause and effect through explicit teaching of signal words, sometimes called "connectives," in both narrative and informational texts. Teaching about signal words can help students understand the relationships among different events or statements in a text (Oakhill et al., 2015). The activities and sequence described below can easily be adapted for other types of signal words, such as those shown in Table 2.5 in Chapter 2.

Mr. Thorpe introduces cause and effect through several concrete examples that will be familiar to Nathan, for instance, turning on a faucet causes water to come out. He explains that certain words in a text provide cues to cause–effect relationships, focusing first on a few specific, commonly used words: *because, so, therefore*. He models identifying these words in several sentences, explaining the causal relationship between the two underlined parts of each sentence:

- *Kelly did not have a ride home,* **so** *she had to walk.*
- *Michael had to study for a test;* **therefore,** *he spent the evening working in his room.*
- **Because** *it had rained heavily for days, the dam broke.*

Mr. Thorpe then has Nathan identify signal words in additional sentences, with a brief discussion of the cause–effect relationship in each sentence.

In a subsequent lesson, Mr. Thorpe wants to convey that the underlying cause–effect relationship can be the same regardless of the surface wording of the sentence or the signal word in it (e.g., *therefore* vs. *so*). For this purpose, he uses multiple versions of the same sentence, as shown in Figure 6.5. For each version, he begins by asking Nathan to identify the signal word and circle it, then underline the two clauses in the sentence that have a causal relationship. Mr. Thorpe labels the cause (*Alex had a very long, difficult day at work*) and the effect (*he said no to his friend's invitation to go to the movies*), connecting the two with a solid line and arrow to show cause and effect. He includes a sentence in which the cause is stated <u>after</u> the effect—the last sentence containing *because*—to show that the cause is not always stated first.

Finally, Mr. Thorpe also wants Nathan to understand that there are not always signal words in a text on which to rely. Therefore, once Nathan can identify and analyze signal words as previously outlined, he introduces another type of example, the two sentences in Figure 6.6. These sentences convey the same cause–effect relationship about Alex, but the signal word is omitted, and Nathan must infer the causal

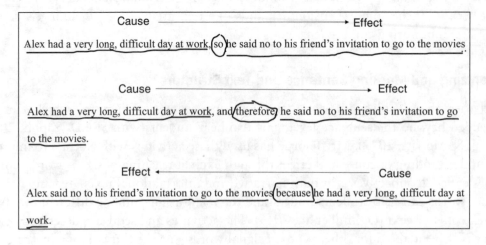

FIGURE 6.5. Sentences with cause-and-effect signal words.

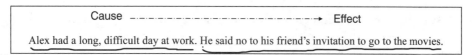

FIGURE 6.6. Sentences with cause-and-effect relationship but no signal words.

relationship. Mr. Thorpe uses the same marking activity with labeling of cause and effect, employing a dotted line to convey that Nathan has to make an inference. Eventually, as shown in Figure 6.7, Mr. Thorpe gives Nathan a short paragraph in which the cause itself must be inferred. Mr. Thorpe uses brackets to mark off the relevant sentences providing the cues for this inference, which describe Alex's workday without actually stating that Alex had a long, difficult day or that this is why he does not feel like going to the movies with his friend. Using questions and discussion, Mr. Thorpe helps Nathan make these inferences, labeling them as shown in Figure 6.7.

These activities can help Nathan and other students with similar comprehension difficulties become more sensitive to signal words in a text, as well as understand that they can infer cause–effect relationships even when these words are not explicitly stated. Teachers can adapt the activities as necessary for individual students. For a student such as Nathan, who has difficulties with pragmatic language and perspective taking, more time might need to be spent on inferring Alex's feelings by discussing how Nathan himself might feel if he were in the same situation. For practice items, teachers can use relevant sentences and passages from students' text reading, if appropriate.

The activities just described should be combined with teaching about broader text structure, such as the features of narrative and informational text shown in Table 2.4, as well as the passage structures in Table 2.5. Graphic organizers are very effective for teaching text and passage structure, and teachers can choose from a wide array of possible organizers (see, e.g., Hennessey, 2021; Oakhill et al., 2015). Some sample graphic organizers for text structure also are provided in later chapters of this book.

Using Questioning to Promote Inferencing

Several of the activities discussed so far promote certain types of inferences, such as the activities discussed previously for signal words and for inferring word meanings from context. Questioning is another way to promote inferencing. For early-stage readers with SRCD, questions should be asked frequently during students' reading, so that

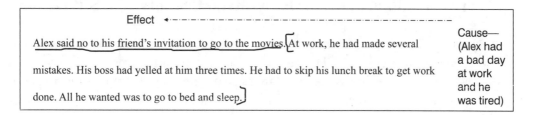

FIGURE 6.7. Sentences with cause-and-effect relationship in which cause must be inferred.

misunderstandings can be detected and addressed promptly. Questions need to target both explicitly stated information that is important to understanding a text, often termed "literal questions," as well as key inferences. Teaching students the distinction between literal and inferential questions, using student-friendly labels, promotes students' inferencing (Elleman, 2017; Vaughn et al., 2022). For students at early stages of reading, labels such as "right there" for literal questions (i.e., the information is right there in the text) and "between the lines" for inferential ones (i.e., the student must "read between the lines"), might be used.

Figure 6.8 displays some sample literal and inferential questions for the fiction book *Sarah, Plain and Tall* (MacLachlan, 1985), which is set on the American prairie in the 19th century. This book is part of the grade-3 curriculum in Mamie's school, and her interventionist, Ms. Santiago, uses it with Mamie's intervention group. The questions are aimed at text from the beginning of the book, just after an opening conversation between Anna, a young girl, and her little brother Caleb. In this conversation, Anna retells the story of the day Caleb was born, a story he has wanted to hear often. The text explicitly states that the children's mother died the day after Caleb's birth. It also describes the setting of the story on the prairie at the end of winter; the fact that Anna thought Caleb was ugly when he was first born; and the aftermath of Mama's death, when relatives came to visit. However, it requires the reader to infer *why* Mama died—that is, because of giving birth to Caleb—as well as the meaning of certain details, such as the fact that the children's father stopped singing after Mama died. There is a poignancy to the interchange between the siblings because Caleb is too young to remember or fully understand events that were devastatingly painful for his sister.

The questions in Figure 6.8 are ones that Ms. Santiago might ask during and after students' reading. In addition to using these kinds of questions to discuss particular texts, Ms. Santiago also explains the distinction between question types, specifically that the answers to "right there" questions can be found in the text itself, whereas for "between the lines" questions, students must use their background knowledge or cues in the text to provide answers. She models the process of answering questions for them. For instance, for the question about the prairie reaching out, students have to use background knowledge about what a prairie is. When students are having difficulty answering questions, she encourages them to think about these distinctions and decide on the type of question being asked.

SI Intervention Plans for Early-Stage Readers with SRCD

Table 6.2 shows a basic intervention plan that can be useful in intervention with students who have a profile of SRCD. The plan contains broad segments for five areas: vocabulary; sentence-level activities; oral language development; text reading and comprehension; and writing. For each lesson segment, the table includes a description, sample activities, and suggested time allocations, with a total lesson time of approximately 45–60 minutes. Depending on individual students' needs, the plan can be adapted in

Sample Literal Questions (Possible Answers):

1. What did Anna think of Caleb when he was born? (She thought he was ugly and smelled bad)

2. Where do Anna and Caleb live? (On the prairie; on the plains)

3. What is Anna remembering in this passage? (The morning that her mother died)

4. How do you know that Anna's conversation with Caleb takes place near the end of winter? (Because the passage says that "winter was nearly over")

5. Who came to the house after Anna's mother died? (Cousins and aunts and uncles)

Sample Inferential Questions (Possible Answers):

1. Why did Mama die? (She died because of giving birth to Caleb)

2. Does Anna tell Caleb how she really felt about him when he was born? Why or why not? (No, she doesn't tell him, because she doesn't want to hurt his feelings)

3. Why did the days "seem long and dark like winter days"? (Because the whole family was so sad about Mama's death)

4. The passage says that "the prairie reached out and touched the places where the sky came down." Can a prairie really reach out and touch something? What do you think this sentence is trying to describe? (No; the sentence is describing the way that the prairie is big and flat; the prairie is wide open, with no mountains and without many trees to block the view)

5. Why do you think Papa didn't sing anymore? (Because he was so sad about Mama's death)

FIGURE 6.8. Sample literal and inferential questions. (Source material for questions found in *Sarah, Plain and Tall*; MacLachlan, 1985.)

various ways, as described in previous chapters of this book. For instance, particularly for students with milder needs, different lesson segments might be alternated across days rather than being implemented every day, or less time might be spent on certain activities. Progress monitoring assessments should be used to inform these decisions and make any necessary adjustments on a continuing basis.

Some details of the plan in Table 6.2 should be noted. Vocabulary is addressed in two places, in the initial lesson segment and within the segment for text reading and comprehension. The former segment focuses on general vocabulary development and making connections among words, especially important for students like Mamie, who need intervention in this area. Vocabulary also is addressed in relation to text-specific vocabulary from the texts students are reading in intervention. Words for the former, general vocabulary development, generally are Tier 2 words, academic vocabulary that can be found across a wide range of texts, whereas words for the latter might sometimes include Tier 3 words, specialized content vocabulary.

The lesson segment for text reading and comprehension includes several other bulleted areas besides text-specific vocabulary: text structure, comprehension strategies (e.g., strategies for comprehension breakdowns), literal comprehension, and inferencing. These areas rarely are all addressed within a single lesson, but usually are all addressed over time. Individual students might also require more emphasis on some bulleted areas than others. Finally, similar to the intervention plan for SWRD, the intervention plan for SRCD includes a writing segment, but with a different focus. Whereas the plan for SWRD focuses on using writing activities to reinforce and further develop basic reading skills, the one for SRCD emphasizes developing specific

TABLE 6.2. Format for an Intervention Plan for Students with SRCD

Component(s)	Description	Sample activities
Vocabulary (~10 minutes)	General vocabulary development and making connections among words	Explicit teaching of specific words; teaching about morphology; word maps
Sentence-level activities (~5–10 minutes)	Understanding sentences (e.g., sentences with potentially challenging syntax, sentences with certain signal words, or sentences with an unfamiliar vocabulary word)	Analyzing and marking sentences on a whiteboard; identifying and discussing signal words in a sentence or pair of sentences; explicit teaching about how to infer word meanings from sentence context
Oral language development (~5–10 minutes)	Development of important areas of oral language relevant to reading comprehension (beyond the word/sentence level)	Teacher read-alouds of listening-level text with comprehension questions and discussion; student retellings; watching a short video to develop background knowledge and discussing it
Text reading and reading comprehension (~15–20 minutes) • Text-specific vocabulary • Text structure • Comprehension strategies • Literal comprehension • Inferencing	Reading text with comprehension	Explicit teaching of text-specific vocabulary; teaching about narrative and informational text structure; teaching students to monitor comprehension and apply fix-up strategies; comprehension questions and discussion of text students have read
Writing (~5–10 minutes)	Using writing to teach or reinforce vocabulary, background knowledge, syntax, inferencing, and other important areas relevant to reading comprehension	Answer in writing questions about texts that students have read or listened to; sentence combining activities; using new vocabulary words in written sentences; writing a summary of a text

areas relevant to reading comprehension. Neither plan, however, is intended to comprise a complete writing intervention.

A Sample Intervention Lesson for Mamie

Table 6.3 displays a sample 45-minute intervention lesson for Mamie and the three other students in her group, using the plan from Table 6.2. Vocabulary and background knowledge receive considerable emphasis in this lesson because all of the students have needs in these areas.

The interventionist, Ms. Santiago, begins with the word map activity for *astonished* that was previously described in this chapter. For a sentence-level activity, Ms. Santiago implements the activity for teaching students how to infer word meanings from context. Next, she shows the students a short video from the Web involving pioneer life on the prairie, followed by a few questions and brief discussion to ensure that students understood the key points from the video, such as what a *prairie* is. Students then read aloud from *Sarah, Plain and Tall*. Although all of the students can decode this text with instructional-level accuracy, it is a bit above students' instructional levels in relation to comprehension. However, Ms. Santiago thinks that with preteaching about background knowledge and vocabulary, as well as questioning during reading, the book will not be too difficult for any of them. Ms. Santiago's questions include both literal and inferential questions, such as those shown in Figure 6.8.

The lesson concludes with a short writing segment in which students write a few sentences describing their reading from the book thus far. The goal of this writing activity is simply to get students to process what they have read more deeply and retain it. In future lessons, Ms. Santiago will sometimes expand this segment of the lesson, focusing on specific comprehension abilities such as using new vocabulary words or summarizing key story events.

TABLE 6.3. Sample Intervention Lesson for Mamie (with Three Other Students)

Component(s)	Activity
Vocabulary (10 minutes)	Teacher presents the word map for *astonished* (previously introduced word during a read-aloud), with context sentence filled in; elicits definition, synonyms, and antonyms; helps students as needed to complete map, with questioning and discussion.
Sentence-level activities (10 minutes)	Teacher explains and models how to infer word meanings from context; notes that not all sentences have helpful context; students practice with several specific words and sentences.
Oral language development (5 minutes)	Students watch a 3-minute video from the Web about pioneer life on the prairie that provides helpful background information for their upcoming reading from *Sarah, Plain and Tall*; teacher leads a short discussion of the video to ensure students understood key background (e.g., what a prairie is).
Text reading and reading comprehension (15 minutes) • Comprehension strategy (apply background information to help comprehension) • Text-specific vocabulary • Literal and inferential comprehension	• Teacher explains that today students will start a new book, *Sarah, Plain and Tall*, set on the prairie in the 1800s; teacher notes importance of using background information to help understand the text. • Teacher displays and briefly explains two vocabulary words from the text, *homely* (not beautiful) and *wretched* (very bad). • Teacher asks several questions about the picture on the book cover (of a wagon on the prairie) involving what students think might happen in the book. • Students take turns reading aloud from Chapter 1 with frequent teacher questioning, including both literal and inferential questions.
Writing (5 minutes)	Students write two to three sentences describing what they have read so far.

Nathan's Intervention in Special Education

Intervention lessons for Nathan can also use the plan from Table 6.2. However, Nathan's specific intervention needs differ somewhat as compared to Mamie's, so Mr. Thorpe, Nathan's special education teacher, often needs to focus on skills other than the ones shown in Mamie's plan. As previously noted, grade-level texts are too difficult for Nathan for now. An important initial decision for Mr. Thorpe to make involves the texts he will use with Nathan in instruction. He decides on the texts first because he wants to coordinate other parts of Nathan's lessons, such as vocabulary and sentence-level activities, with Nathan's text reading.

Previous teachers have often found it very difficult to maintain Nathan's attention during lessons, including during text reading. However, like many students with ASD, Nathan has some passionate interests, and maintaining his attention for these interests is generally not a problem. Nathan also has accumulated a great deal of background knowledge about these topics, one of which involves shipwrecks. Mr. Thorpe has decided to capitalize on this interest and background knowledge by having Nathan read grade-2 and grade-3 level books about shipwrecks. He plans to use Nathan's interest as a springboard for teaching comprehension-related abilities such as inferencing. Later, he will try to expand Nathan's interests and text reading to a wider range of materials, including curriculum materials. Also, he continues to teach Nathan about certain curriculum-related areas such as important content vocabulary.

Here are some examples of areas on which initial lessons for Nathan might focus:

- Nathan had average-range vocabulary on standardized testing, but he does have difficulties with multiple meanings of words, such as *deck* of a ship versus a *deck* of cards. Teaching these multiple meanings explicitly would be helpful.
- Sentence-level activities for Nathan could address areas such as inferring word meanings from context, including multiple meanings of words; signal words, such as the activity for cause–effect signal words discussed previously; interpreting figurative language, which Nathan finds difficult; and comprehension monitoring, such as identifying and explaining illogical sentences. Sequencing of activities should be guided by the skills Nathan needs to comprehend the texts he is reading, as well as grade-level curriculum demands.
- In the area of oral language development, Nathan could particularly benefit from activities to promote pragmatic language and perspective taking, such as discussion of narratives and questioning about characters' feelings and motivations.
- For text reading, Mr. Thorpe plans to begin with a nonfiction book such as one about the *Titanic* or *Lusitania*; a little later, he will include books with a narrative focus (e.g., a character, real or fictional, who is on the *Titanic*), with questioning to promote comprehension monitoring, inferencing, and especially, perspective taking.
- Writing activities could reinforce areas such as multiple meanings of words (e.g., writing sentences that illustrate two different meanings of a word); answering

literal and inferential questions in writing; and using signal words in a written sentence about a text that Nathan has heard or read.

Additional Considerations for Written Expression

The underlying language difficulties of students with SRCD tend to manifest in their writing, as well as their reading. For example, students such as Mamie, who have weaknesses in vocabulary, usually display these vocabulary limitations in their writing, as well as their reading. Assuming appropriate Tier 1 instruction in writing, often these students will have grade-appropriate basic writing skills, especially in their ability to spell phonetically. Because English spelling requires other types of linguistic knowledge besides PA and phonics, some students with SRCD may have nonphonological spelling weaknesses, such as in morphological knowledge.

Many early-stage readers with SRCD are in the elementary grades. In these grades, when the writing demands of the curriculum are relatively low, writing difficulties may be overlooked or masked by students' strengths in basic writing. A modest amount of attention to providing writing interventions, in conjunction with the reading interventions discussed here, may help prevent more significant difficulties in writing later on. Furthermore, writing activities such as using new vocabulary words or signal words in their written expression, as mentioned earlier for Nathan, can benefit students' reading as well as their writing.

SUMMING UP: SL Interventions for Early-Stage Readers with SRCD

Here are key points from this chapter:

- Early-stage readers with SRCD require interventions focused on the kinds of comprehension skills typically taught in the early to middle elementary grades.

- Individual students' comprehension needs vary, but their difficulties often involve vocabulary, background knowledge, syntax, narrative language, comprehension monitoring, and/or inferencing—difficulties that affect students' writing as well as their reading.

- Early-stage readers with SRCD may be overlooked in the early to middle elementary grades due to their appropriate progress in developing foundational reading skills; screening for problems in language comprehension (along with screening for phonological and word-reading problems) could enable earlier identification of and intervention for these students in both reading and writing.

- Because their word-reading skills are grade-appropriate, these students usually do not require decodable texts in intervention, but they generally need to read texts at or at least near their instructional levels.

- Effective SL activities to improve students' vocabularies include explicit teaching of academic vocabulary words, morphology, and how to infer word meanings from context.

- Effective SL activities to improve text comprehension include explicit teaching of comprehension monitoring and strategies to repair comprehension breakdowns; explicit teaching of signal words and text structure; and activities to promote inferencing, such as teaching background knowledge and using questioning.

APPLIED EXERCISES

Exercise 1

Review the assessment information for Polly, the fifth grader with SRCD described in the applied exercises at the end of Chapter 3. Give at least three examples of SL activities from this chapter that would be likely to benefit Polly.

Answer

Polly's underlying comprehension weaknesses are similar to those of Mamie in this chapter—difficulties with vocabulary and background knowledge. SL activities for those areas—involving explicit teaching of academic vocabulary, morphology, how to infer word meanings from context, and background knowledge needed for the texts Polly is reading in school—should all be helpful.

Exercise 2

A fourth grader in an intervention group that has been learning about morphology shows frequent confusion when trying to identify prefixes. For instance, he identified *uniform* as having the prefix *un* and then became confused trying to use the prefix to figure out the meaning of the word. As another example, he identified the *mis* in *mission* as a prefix, with similar confusion. What kind of error is the student making, and what kind of teaching would be helpful?

Answer

The student does not seem to understand that a prefix must carry meaning in the context of a word; it is not just a sequence of letters at the beginning of a word. His teacher could help him by reviewing what a prefix is, with examples and nonexamples of prefixes, as well as sorting activities that include an "other" category. His teacher should also emphasize that when the prefix is separated from the remainder of the word, a base word should remain. The *sion* in *mission* is not a base word. *Uniform* has a base word, but it is *form*, not *iform*, and the prefix is *uni*, meaning one, not *un*.

Exercise 3

Mr. Davis, a seventh-grade special educator, has a student who is experiencing considerable difficulty with figurative language. Mr. Davis has explained this language explicitly to the student, but the student often does not retain these explanations. Mr. Davis thinks teaching him about using context to infer the meaning of expressions such as *raining cats and dogs* would be a helpful adjunct to explicit teaching of specific expressions. Discuss a sentence-level activity that Mr. Davis could use for this purpose.

Answer

One possible activity would be to use sentences similar to those in Table 6.1, with examples of figurative language that students need to learn and specific cues for students to identify in sentences. For instance, for an expression like *raining cats and dogs*, Mr. Davis could use a context sentence such as *Molly had to carry an umbrella because it was <u>raining cats and dogs</u>, and even then, she was soaked*. Phrases in the sentence, specifically *Molly had to carry an umbrella* and *she was soaked*, could be discussed as cues to the meaning of the figurative language *raining cats and dogs*.

Exercise 4

For students with problems in inferencing, why is it important to consider individual students' background knowledge for specific texts, and to explicitly teach background knowledge as needed?

Answer

Students' background knowledge matters for many reasons, but in relation to reading comprehension, it plays a key role in students' inferencing. It might appear that a student cannot make inferences when the true problem might be a lack of background knowledge, either a general lack of background knowledge or a lack of background knowledge related to specific texts. In either case, considering and addressing this area in intervention, as needed, is important.

Sample Word Map for New Vocabulary Words (Template Version)

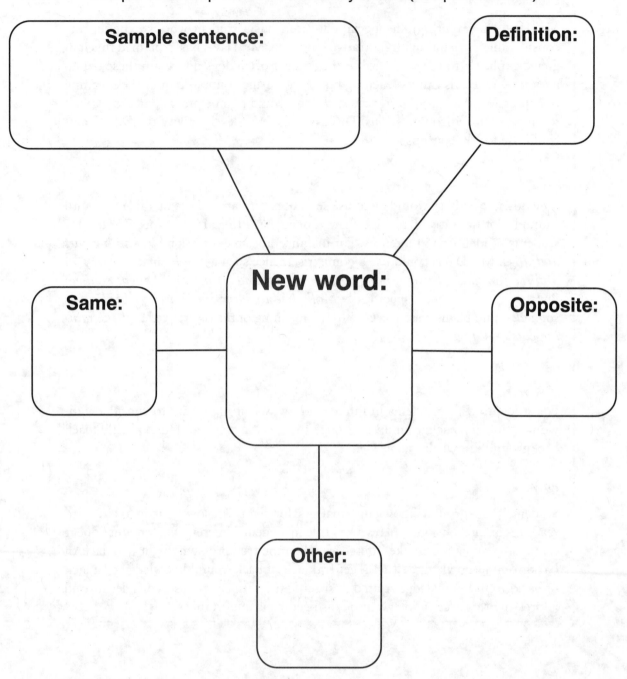

Sample sentence:

Definition:

New word:

Same:

Opposite:

Other:

Comprehension Monitoring Activity with Illogical Sentences (Template Version)

Sentence	Makes sense? Yes or No	If no, what does not make sense?
Marvin was very hungry, so he did not want to eat.		
Mr. Wheeler drives a flashy red car with square tires.		
The doctor was a very tall woman in a white coat.		
The Johnsons traveled to Alaska for their summer vacation.		
Sarah smiled because she was very angry with her friend.		
The twins were thrilled to get a new puppy as a birthday gift.		
The house on the corner has a long driveway made of jam.		
When the stranger came to the door, the cat barked furiously at him.		

CHAPTER 7

Structured Literacy Interventions for Specific Reading Comprehension Difficulties

Advanced Stages

Chapter 5 introduced Ms. Williams, a high school special educator in a suburban school district who was using SL interventions with a ninth grader named Conor. Conor had dyslexia and a profile of specific word recognition difficulties (SWRD). This chapter discusses a different ninth-grade student with whom Ms. Williams works, a student with a different reading disability and poor reader profile, named Gabe. Gabe has a profile of specific reading comprehension difficulties (SRCD). He was identified with a specific learning disability in the area of reading comprehension in grade 6, as well as with attention-deficit/hyperactivity disorder (ADHD) and problems in executive function (EF). Although Gabe's word reading is grade-appropriate, and although he was not seen as having any reading problems until fourth grade, he now experiences substantial difficulty comprehending grade-level texts. Gabe's reading difficulty centers on comprehension, not decoding, so he and Conor are not grouped together for their special education instruction. However, Ms. Williams recognizes that Gabe can also benefit from SL interventions, which she is using to address his comprehension difficulties.

Other advanced-stage readers with SRCD do not have disabilities, and they may be somewhat younger than Gabe. Hector, whose native language is Spanish, provides an example of this type of student. Hector is a sixth grader in a midsize school district serving a small number of English learners (ELs) with varied native languages. Hector's conversational English is excellent, but as he has advanced in school, he has struggled increasingly with meeting reading comprehension demands. Hector can read the words in grade-level texts, but understanding these texts is often a challenge.

This chapter addresses students with SRCD who are functioning at relatively advanced stages of reading, like Hector and Gabe. Advanced-stage readers with SRCD can vary in age, as well as in their specific comprehension weaknesses, but they all grapple with the sophisticated comprehension demands of the more complex texts used in the later grades. Like other poor readers discussed in this book, these students can be helped by SL interventions. Below is some additional detail about the history and specific reading difficulties of Hector and Gabe.

Hector

Hector was born in the United States, the third of four siblings. His parents immigrated from Guatemala the year before Hector's birth, and Spanish is the primary language spoken at home. In the past, the family moved often, but in recent years, Hector's parents have been settled in Hector's present school district. Because of the frequent moves in Hector's early schooling, however, his education was fragmented. In kindergarten and grade 1, he attended a school with a transitional bilingual education (TBE) program that emphasized developing literacy in both Spanish and English. Records of Hector's performance at this time are not available, but through an interpreter, Hector's parents stated that he did not have any early difficulties learning to read in either language. They also indicated that his early language development in Spanish was typical, similar to that of their other children, with no signs of speech–language problems. Hector's parents and their interpreter describe Hector as fully bilingual in both Spanish and English.

Hector moved to his present school district in grade 4. This school does not have a bilingual education program, and Hector had no further development of his Spanish literacy after grade 1, so his reading in Spanish is limited, much more so than his English reading. His school does have an English as a second language (ESL) program, but Hector's English is considered to be too good for him to be eligible for this program. Moreover, the English skills addressed in the program generally are quite basic and would not meet Hector's needs.

Hector's parents and teachers began having significant concerns about his reading last year, when Hector was in grade 5. They noticed that he had trouble with homework because he could not understand certain words in the texts he was expected to read. Although he struggled with both narrative and informational texts, Hector found the latter especially difficult because of their demands on specialized content vocabulary and background knowledge. Hector's teachers have also noticed that he sometimes struggles with understanding complex sentence structure, such as sentences with center-embedded syntax. These difficulties tend to manifest in Hector's writing, as well as his reading. For example, he sometimes employs incorrect or unusual sentence structure in his writing. Spanish has more flexible word order within sentences than English does (Swan & Smith, 2001), and Hector's word order in sentences sometimes mirrors word order that would be acceptable in Spanish but that is incorrect or sounds odd in English.

For middle school students, Hector's school district uses two measures in screening for reading problems, a spelling test and a reading comprehension measure. Although

Hector met grade expectations on the spelling test, his performance on the reading comprehension measure flagged him as being at risk, so the school reading interventionist, Mr. Morello, did some additional reading assessments. Mr. Morello gave Hector an oral reading inventory (ORI), as well as a criterion-referenced phonics measure similar to the ABC Test discussed in Chapter 3. Hector met mastery criteria on all sections of the phonics measure, including a section for multisyllabic words. On the ORI graded word lists, as well as the phonics test, he had a few mispronunciations involving unusual words that appeared unfamiliar to him. These were not decoding errors, but rather were based in not having heard the oral pronunciation of certain words. For example, he misread *preliminary* as pre-LIE-min-ary, with a long *i* in the second syllable, and *rigorous* as rig-OR-ous, placing the accent on the wrong syllable. Nevertheless, overall, Hector was at grade level in his performance on both the graded word lists and the criterion-referenced phonics measure.

However, in line with his teachers' feedback to the reading interventionist, Hector had trouble with comprehension. His performance on the ORI passages was at a fifth-grade level, about a year behind his grade placement, due entirely to problems with comprehension. Mr. Morello also administered both ORF and maze CBMs to Hector, the former as a check on his reading fluency and the latter as an additional indicator of his reading comprehension. Hector met grade benchmarks on the ORF CBM for both accuracy and rate of reading, but on the maze CBM, he made numerous errors, and his score was well below benchmark. Based on all of these results—the initial reading comprehension screening measure, maze CBM, ORI passages, and classroom performance—Hector has been selected for supplemental intervention in reading comprehension.

Hector's history and present level of conversational English are consistent with several findings from research on ELs. Authorities in this area (e.g., Baker et al., 2014; Cardenas-Hagan, 2020) have made a distinction between everyday conversational competence in English, sometimes termed basic interpersonal communication skills (Cummins, 1981), and higher-level academic functioning. The latter requires knowledge of English academic vocabulary, more formal academic language, and academic background knowledge (August, Carlo, Dressler, & Snow, 2005; Baker et al., 2014; Rivera, Moughamian, Lesaux, & Francis, 2008) that students may lack even when their everyday conversation in English is good. This pattern of stronger conversational ability than academic functioning in English fits Hector. Moreover, academic language and knowledge become increasingly important as students advance in school and are expected to understand more challenging texts. This might help to explain why, although both his parents and his teachers now have concerns about Hector's reading in English, he was not seen as having literacy difficulties in the primary grades.

ELs usually have one of two poor reader profiles: a profile of SRCD or of MRD (Baker et al., 2014). SWRD—a profile involving phonological and word-reading problems only, without accompanying language comprehension weaknesses—is unusual for this group of students. Currently, Hector's difficulties exemplify a profile of SRCD. All of his weaknesses on assessments involve reading comprehension, whereas his scores for word reading and spelling meet grade expectations. Also, feedback from his teachers and parents suggests that academic vocabulary is a significant need of Hector's, a pattern common in ELs (August et al., 2005; Baker et al., 2014) and an important clue to his reading comprehension problems. Nevertheless, as is true of other struggling readers, ELs can vary substantially in their specific weaknesses, and interventions must target individual students' needs (Baker et al., 2014). In Hector's case, for instance, complex syntax, as well as academic vocabulary is a weakness, so his intervention should target both of these areas.

Although formal data are limited, the available information about Hector's history to this point does not suggest a language or learning disability. Prior to beginning school, his oral language development in his native language was typical; he did not have initial difficulties learning to read in either Spanish or English; and his current difficulties appear to reflect limitations in exposure and/or confusions with his native language rather than a disability. However, his progress in intervention should be monitored, with adjustments to intervention as needed. If he does not show adequate growth in interventions that are generally effective for other ELs, a referral for comprehensive evaluation for special education should be considered.

Gabe

Early on, Gabe progressed normally in reading, although his mother says he was always an especially active child, unable to sit still for long periods. His mother began to have concerns about his reading comprehension when he was in grade 4. Like Mamie's school district, Gabe's district used an ORF measure in universal screening in the primary grades, and like Mamie, Gabe consistently met accuracy and rate benchmarks on this measure. Although his district did not screen for comprehension in these early grades, his teachers did not note comprehension as a concern.

In grade 5, Gabe's mother referred him for a comprehensive evaluation for special education. His school district determined that he did not meet eligibility criteria for special education at that time, but they did provide Gabe with intervention in reading comprehension through the school's reading specialist. Soon after beginning intervention, Gabe was identified by his physician as having ADHD, as well as difficulties in EF. Gabe's ADHD is being well managed medically. However, despite his treatment for ADHD and his school intervention, Gabe's mother continued to be concerned about his reading comprehension. The following year, in grade 6, he was referred for comprehensive evaluation again and was finally determined to be eligible as a student with a specific learning disability involving reading comprehension. He was also found eligible in written expression, math calculation, and math problem solving.

Figure 7.1 displays an assessment map with Gabe's standardized test scores in reading from a recent triennial evaluation, done at the beginning of the current school year, grade 9. The map also includes some scores from an independent evaluation that Gabe had in grade 8, as well as his performance on the state reading assessment, a reading comprehension test administered routinely to all eighth graders.

Student *Gabriel*   Grade *9*   Dates of Testing *Sept 10–Oct 1*

ORAL LANGUAGE COMPREHENSION

Oral Vocabulary (note receptive/expressive)
WIAT–4 Receptive Vocabulary *91*
WIAT–4 Expressive Vocabulary *92*
WJ–IV Picture Vocabulary *(exp; Grade 8) 93*

Oral Language (Listening) Comprehension (note format, e.g., cloze, maze, QA)
WIAT–4 Oral Discourse Comprehension *(QA) 90*
WJ–IV Oral Comprehension *(cloze; Grade 8) 91*

Other Oral Language
(All Grade 8)
WJ–IV Science *86*
WJ–IV Social Studies *92*
WJ–IV Humanities *84*

Real Words—Accuracy
WIAT–4 Word Reading *96*
WJ–IV Word Identification *(Grade 8) 101*

Nonsense Words—Accuracy
WIAT–4 Pseudoword Decoding *101*
WJ–IV Word Attack *(Grade 8) 103*

Word Reading—Automaticity
WIAT–4 Orthographic Fluency *95*
WIAT–4 Decoding Fluency *99*

WORD READING

Phonological/phonemic awareness

Oral Reading Fluency—Accuracy
GORT–5 Accuracy Scaled Score *9*

Oral Reading Fluency—Rate
GORT–5 Rate Scaled Score *9*
WIAT–4 ORF *92*

Silent Reading Fluency

Reading Comprehension (note test format, e.g., cloze, maze, QA, as well as other relevant features such as timing)
GORT–5 Comprehension *(timed; QA) 5*
WIAT–4 Reading Comprehension *(untimed; QA) 77*
WJ–IV Passage Comprehension *(untimed; cloze; Grade 8) 84*
State reading assessment *(untimed; QA; Grade 8) basic level*

Observations
On both the GORT and WIAT, student often missed key details and sometimes did not answer the question being asked

FIGURE 7.1. Assessment map for Gabe.

The map shows that, consistent with a profile of SRCD, Gabe's scores for word reading are all well within average range. Most of his oral language scores hover at the low end of average range; his only below-average scores in this area were on two tests of academic background knowledge: WJ-IV Science and WJ-IV Humanities. His standard scores for these subtests were in the mid-80s, below-average range but not extremely low. Also, Gabe's scores for accuracy and rate of text reading were all within average range.

Nevertheless, Gabe's reading comprehension was substantially lower than one would expect from his oral language, in line with research on SRCD (Spencer & Wagner, 2018). He did best on WJ-IV Passage Comprehension, a test with a cloze format and sentence-length passages that tends to tap word reading—a strength for Gabe—relatively more than language comprehension (Keenan et al., 2008). However, his score on this test was still below average, and all of his other reading comprehension scores suggested even weaker performance. On WIAT-4 Reading Comprehension, an untimed test in which the student has access to passages in answering open-ended questions presented orally by the examiner, Gabe had a standard score of 77. This score is around the 6th percentile and substantially below his score on an oral measure of his comprehension from the same test battery, WIAT-4 Oral Discourse Comprehension (standard score = 90, percentile rank = 25). Since word reading and reading fluency do not appear to account for this disparity, what else might?

One factor that could explain this pattern involves differences between oral and reading comprehension, such as the fact that texts for reading comprehension tend to involve more difficult academic vocabulary, syntax, and background knowledge than do many oral comprehension measures (Spencer & Wagner, 2018). Gabe's history also suggests another possible explanation, his difficulties with EF. As discussed in Chapter 1, EF involves a set of cognitive processes deployed in reading comprehension, as well as many other tasks, such as cognitive flexibility, working memory, inhibition, and higher-level planning and monitoring skills (Cartwright, 2015). Although EF and oral language abilities are interconnected, EF is generally conceptualized as involving a distinct set of cognitive processes.

Many researchers (e.g., Duke & Pearson, 2002; Oakhill et al., 2015; RAND Reading Study Group, 2002) have emphasized the idea that good reading comprehension involves an active effort to make meaning from text. This idea is helpful in understanding the role of EF in reading comprehension. A student could have good, or at least adequate, word reading and oral language comprehension, but without an active effort to understand (i.e., consistently thinking about meaning during reading and using strategies to repair comprehension when something does not make sense), reading comprehension will suffer, particularly in challenging texts. Gabe often does not demonstrate an active approach to reading comprehension.

For example, when Gabe has a reading assignment, he tends to immediately plunge into the text without any of the planning processes that many good readers use, such as reading the required comprehension questions first, before reading the text. He does not attend to informational text features that can aid comprehension, such as emboldening of important vocabulary words or accompanying charts and tables. Interestingly,

Gabe does seem to monitor comprehension when reading, but he does not appear to use fix-up strategies. For instance, when reading texts aloud, he sometimes comments about a difficult section of text ("Hmm, I have no idea what that means"), but he does not actively employ strategies to repair comprehension, such as looking up an unfamiliar vocabulary word or term online.

On a recent ORI, Gabe performed at grade level on graded word lists, but at about a sixth-grade level, 3 years below grade placement, on graded passages—due to difficulties with comprehension, not word reading. His most frequent difficulties involved vocabulary questions, despite his average-range vocabulary on standardized testing, as well as questions about key details. Vocabulary weaknesses and overlooking key details sometimes caused him to misunderstand important points in the text. In the relatively short, 200-word passages found on the ORI, some of his EF-related difficulties, such as lack of planning or inattention to informational text features, were less evident, but these difficulties are very apparent in his day-to-day classroom performance.

About Advanced-Stage Readers with SRCD

Advanced-stage readers with a profile of SRCD all have the following in common: (1) a poor reader profile with difficulties centered on comprehension, often including oral language comprehension as well as reading comprehension; (2) word-reading skills in average range or higher, including phonological skills and automaticity as well as accuracy of word reading; and (3) a need for intervention involving comprehension skills typically taught in the upper elementary grades and beyond. At these grade levels, although comprehension of narratives remains important, informational texts tend to receive particular emphasis because students must read to learn in multiple content areas such as social studies and science (Chall, 1983). The comprehension demands are also much more complex than in earlier grades. For example, students are expected to read significantly longer texts with a greater degree of independence; to integrate information across multiple texts and sources, as opposed to one or two; and to find evidence in the text as well as evaluate the quality of that evidence (Common Core State Standards Initiative, 2023).

Many students with SRCD at this level have weaknesses in EF as well as oral language comprehension (Cartwright, 2015; Cutting et al., 2009). Just as oral language weaknesses in certain areas (e.g., vocabulary) may have a bigger impact as students advance in school and the reading comprehension demands increase, certain EF weaknesses also may have a bigger impact as students move into the upper elementary grades and middle school (Eason, Goldberg, Young, Geist, & Cutting, 2012). For instance, while planning, organization, and monitoring processes can impact reading comprehension at any grade level, their impact is likely greater for more complex texts and reading demands. Gabe may have always had EF difficulties, but these difficulties probably had a smaller impact on his comprehension of the easier texts of the early grades than they had later, when he had to use reading as a tool to gain information in multiple content areas.

While the specific intervention needs of individual advanced-stage readers with SRCD vary, these needs often include the language areas discussed in Chapter 6, such as vocabulary, sentence structure, background knowledge, and inferencing. Advanced-stage readers with SRCD require a focus on application of these language skills to the more complex texts and comprehension demands of the later grades, as well as to writing. In addition, because comprehension of informational texts becomes increasingly prominent at advanced grade levels, advanced-stage readers with SRCD may need relatively more emphasis on specialized content vocabulary (i.e., Tier 3 words) as compared to early-stage poor readers. If a student has weaknesses in EF, then addressing those weaknesses in the context of reading comprehension and writing also is important.

As noted in Chapter 6, for early-stage readers with SRCD, advanced-stage readers with SRCD may sometimes read slowly because they are struggling to comprehend. However, these students' slow reading is not based in word reading problems. Therefore, SL interventions focused on their comprehension needs are more likely to benefit their rate and ease of reading than are interventions aimed at accuracy or automaticity of word reading.

Research on Reading Interventions for ELs

For ELs of all poor reader profiles and stages of reading, research supports interventions involving both the content and features of SL (Tridas, 2020). ELs require an emphasis on oral language development in general and vocabulary in particular (August et al., 2005; Baker et al., 2014; Cardenas-Hagan, 2020), making the language content of SL approaches especially valuable for them. Like other at-risk and struggling readers, ELs also benefit from features of SL such as explicit, systematic teaching; prompt, targeted feedback; data-based decision making; and planned, purposeful selections of instructional examples, tasks, and texts (Baker et al., 2014; Tridas, 2020). Many interventions that are effective for other struggling readers, including interventions involving foundational skills if a student has needs in that area, are also effective for ELs.

However, ELs do have some particular needs relative to struggling readers who are not ELs. While ELs benefit from multiple approaches to vocabulary instruction involving explicit teaching of specific words, morphology, and inferring word meanings from context (Baker et al., 2014), some ELs may require more attention to basic words (August et al., 2005), words that might be considered Tier 1 vocabulary for other students. As compared to other at-risk or struggling readers, ELs may also have greater, or different, gaps in background knowledge that stem from having different past experiences.

ELs can benefit from teaching about cognates, especially if the students' native language is one that has many cognate words in English, such as Spanish. *Cognates* are words that are similar in both meaning and spelling across the native language and English, words such as *television*, *honor*, *normal*, and *clasico* for Spanish and English. There is a continuum of similarity, with some words being slightly less obvious cognates—for example, *maravilloso* in Spanish and *marvelous* in English—and some words are false or misleading cognates. *Embarazada* is a Spanish word that seems as though it should mean "embarrassed," but it actually means "pregnant"; *carpeta* seems like it must mean "carpet," but it actually means "folder." Overall, however, teaching about cognates can help ELs expand their English vocabulary knowledge (August et al., 2005; Pollard-Durodola, 2020).

Grouping recommendations for poor readers' interventions have typically emphasized homogeneous groups of students with similar needs and levels of functioning. However, some authorities have highlighted the value of more heterogeneous groups for ELs (e.g., Baker et al., 2014), especially for students with a profile of SRCD. Intervention groups that include students with varied levels of English language functioning may benefit students who are at earlier stages of language learning in English. These experiences can also be provided through peer or partner activities that pair ELs with more proficient English speakers (Cardenas-Hagan, 2020; Rivera et al., 2008).

For students such as Hector, who have a profile of SRCD but are functioning at more advanced stages of reading, teaching about academic vocabulary and language is especially important. Cognate instruction can continue to help students at this stage in learning specialized content words in math, science, and social studies, for which there are many Spanish–English cognates (Pollard-Durodola, 2020). Many ELs also benefit from teaching of academic background knowledge needed to understand the texts they are reading in school, especially complex informational texts.

Other Research Relevant to Advanced-Stage Readers with SRCD

Advanced-stage readers with SRCD—including those who are ELs—can profit from many of the intervention activities discussed in Chapter 6, but these activities will be applied to more advanced texts and tasks. Consider the questioning activity to promote inferencing in Figure 6.8 involving *Sarah, Plain and Tall*, a typical text for early grade levels. In contrast, one of the example texts from the Common Core State Standards Initiative (2023) for the beginning of high school is Shakespeare's play *The Tragedy of Macbeth*. To make inferences involving the latter text, the same types of questioning techniques, including organizing questions into before, during, and after reading activities, can be effective. However, students require (among other skills), far more sophisticated vocabulary and background knowledge for inferential comprehension of *The Tragedy of Macbeth* than *Sarah, Plain and Tall*.

Research on reading comprehension interventions with older poor readers is very informative for advanced-stage readers with SRCD, even though many of these studies involved poor comprehenders who also had mild word-reading weaknesses. In recent years, researchers have emphasized the importance of teaching background knowledge and inferencing to improve comprehension (e.g., Compton et al., 2014; Elleman, 2017). Barth and Elleman (2017) implemented a small-group intervention for inferencing with a group of sixth to eighth graders who had reading comprehension difficulties as well as mild word-reading weaknesses. This short-term intervention involved only ten days of instruction. Interventionists employed both narrative and informational texts, which were carefully chosen and sequenced to help students build a knowledge base to facilitate inferencing. Four main inference strategies were taught: using text cues to clarify unknown vocabulary or ideas, activating and applying background knowledge, answering inferential types of questions, and for narratives, understanding characters' perspectives and the author's purpose.

Despite the brief time span of the intervention, results showed that the intervention group made significant reading comprehension gains relative to a comparison group, including on a standardized measure, the WIAT-3. These results suggest that inferencing can be explicitly taught. They also indicate that although older poor readers with severe, persistent reading problems frequently require much more intensive and longer-term interventions in order to progress in reading (Vaughn, Denton, & Fletcher, 2010), struggling readers with milder difficulties may benefit from short-term interventions.

Explicit teaching of certain EF skills to promote reading comprehension can also help many adolescents with SRCD, such as Gabe. Although not originally conceptualized in terms of EF, research supports teaching of certain EF skills to improve reading comprehension (Cartwright, 2015). This research includes instruction in specific reading comprehension strategies, many of which involve EF types of skills. For example, explicit teaching of comprehension monitoring and inferring word meanings from context, as well as summarization—for typical, at-risk, and struggling readers—is very well supported by research (NRP, 2000; Vaughn et al., 2022). Teaching students about both informational and narrative text structure to improve comprehension is also effective (Hennessey, 2021; NRP, 2000).

A meta-analysis of reading comprehension interventions for struggling readers in third through 12th grades (Filderman, Austin, Boucher, O'Donnell, & Swanson, 2022) supports the value of teaching both background knowledge and specific reading comprehension strategies such as comprehension monitoring and summarization. The meta-analysis found significantly higher effects for background knowledge instruction and comprehension strategy instruction, as compared to instructional enhancements, such as the use of technology to enhance comprehension. These positive effects were not moderated by grade level, suggesting that these interventions can benefit older as well as younger students. Other evidence (e.g., Fletcher et al., 2019; Vaughn et al., 2022) also strongly supports teaching of vocabulary, background knowledge, summarization, questioning, and comprehension monitoring for older struggling readers with reading comprehension difficulties. Taken together, these research findings show that appropriate interventions can make a substantial impact, even for older poor comprehenders.

Sample SL Intervention Activities

Explicit Teaching of Morphology for Academic Vocabulary

Mr. Morello is delivering SL reading intervention to Hector in a small group of five students, all sixth and seventh graders. Only one of these students is an EL like Hector, and the students' oral English skills vary, but all of the students can benefit from teaching of advanced morphology. The students are already familiar with easier affixes such as *un-*, *-ly*, and *-er*, as well as with terms for parts of speech (e.g., noun, adjective). Mr. Morello is now emphasizing roots and affixes that students need in order to understand, as well as spell and read, more difficult academic vocabulary words from content areas such as social studies and science. He has selected for explicit teaching some common Latin and Greek roots that he knows students will encounter in these content subjects. He has also chosen to begin with roots that have similar meanings and spellings in Spanish and English. The roots he currently is teaching are shown in the far left column of Table 7.1, which displays a grid he will use in today's activity, and which is partially based on an activity in Baker and colleagues (2014).

Students have previously learned affixes such as *-ology* and *-ist* and, in an earlier lesson, Mr. Morello has already introduced the roots shown in Table 7.1. In that earlier lesson, he explained the meaning of these roots, provided examples and non-examples of words containing each root, and emphasized the idea that the root, like any morpheme, must carry meaning in the context of a word (e.g., the *geo* in *surgeon* is not a morpheme and does not refer to the earth). In today's lesson, he wants to help students generalize the root across a family of semantically interrelated words: those for an area of study, the word for someone who studies it, and adjectives and adverbs based on those words. The grid also includes a column for examples of additional words containing each root.

TABLE 7.1. Sample Grid for Academic Words with Greek and Latin Roots

English root (Spanish equivalent)	Meaning	Noun: Area of study	Noun: Person who studies it	Adjective (describing word for a noun)	Adverb (describing word for a verb or adjective)	Additional words
arche (arque)	very old	archeology	archeologist	archeological	archeologically	archaic
astro (astro)	star	astronomy	astronomer	astronomical	astronomically	astrophysics
aud (aud)	hear	audiology	audiologist	audiological, audible	audiologically, audibly	inaudible, auditorium, audience
bio (bio)	life	biology	biologist	biological	biologically	biography, biographer, autobiography
geo (geo)	earth	geology	geologist	geological	geologically	geography, geographer, geographical
psych (psic)	mind	psychology	psychologist	psychological	psychologically	psychiatry, psychiatrist, psychopath

Mr. Morello begins by distributing the blank grid to the students, with only the far-left column of roots filled in. Monitoring students' work and providing help as needed, he then encourages students to complete the rest of the grid by asking questions (e.g., "What does the root *astro* mean? What is the word for the area of scientific study involving the stars, the word with *astro* in it? How about the word for the person who studies it?") As the students fill in different words, Mr. Morello draws their attention both to the patterns in the grid (e.g., most, but not all, of the areas of study end in *-ology*; all of the adverbs end in *-ly*) and to potentially confusing words. For instance, the area of scientific study involving the stars is *astronomy*, not *astrology*. Similarly, the adjective *astronomical* can be used in the context of astronomy (e.g., *astronomical observations detected a previously unknown star*), but it is often used in everyday language to mean extremely large, as in the sentence, *Joe spent money constantly, so his debts were astronomical*. Mr. Morello also briefly discusses other words in the far-right column of the grid.

In a subsequent lesson, Mr. Morello has students do a follow-up activity to help ensure deeper understanding of the words and their correct use, as well as to help students retain the meaning and spelling of the roots. This activity is shown in Form 7.1 (page 179).

In the follow-up activity, students read a series of sentences with blanks in them and fill the appropriate word from the grid into the blank. Then, in several open-ended items, they write sentences using words with the various roots and involving different parts of speech. They are expected both to spell words correctly and use the correct word; if a word is misspelled, Mr. Morello has students refer back to the grid to correct it. In future lessons, Mr. Morello will continue to review these roots in additional reading and writing activities.

Sentence Combining and Sentence Decomposition

Another SL activity that Mr. Morello uses with Hector's intervention group involves sentence-combining and sentence decomposition tasks (Saddler, 2012; Zipoli & Merritt, 2022). These tasks are especially helpful for Hector's confusions with English syntax, but all of the students can benefit from them in some way, in relation to their written expression or reading comprehension. Mr. Morello has emphasized sentence combining first. He gives the students sets of interrelated kernel sentences that must be combined into a grammatically correct, longer sentence (see Table 7.2). The students can already do easier levels of sentence combining, such as those involving adjectives, adverbs, and compound sentences, and they are familiar with the terms *clause* and *phrase*. In today's lesson, Mr. Morello focuses on combinations involving center-embedded syntax, such as relative clauses.

• Mr. Morello tells the students, "You already know how sentence-combining activities can help you improve both your reading and writing, and you are doing a great job with the sentence combining activities we have done so far. Today we are

TABLE 7.2. Sample Items for Sentence Combining Task Involving Center-Embedded Syntax

Kernel sentences	Sample correct combination(s)	Sample incorrect response	Sample teacher feedback
• The story was recently published online. • Laura wrote the story.	• The story that Laura wrote was recently published online. • The story that was recently published online was written by Laura.	Laura wrote the story that was recently published online.	"This is a clear, grammatically correct sentence that includes both of the kernel sentences. It's a very good sentence. However, right now, we are working on sentences with center-embedded clauses or phrases. This sentence doesn't embed one kernel sentence into the middle of the other sentence. One way you could do that is to start the combined sentence this way: 'The story that Laura wrote . . .' Can you finish the sentence?"
• Fossils are the traces of living things from long ago. • Fossils show how these past living things looked.	• Fossils, which are the traces of living things from long ago, show how these past living things looked. • Fossils, which show how past living things looked, are the traces of living things from long ago.	Fossils are the traces of living things from long ago and they show how these past living things looked.	"You included both kernel sentences— good. But you just connected both sentences with the word *and*, instead of making one kernel sentence into a clause and embedding it into the other sentence. You could use the word *which* to do this, for example, 'Fossils, which . . .' What should come next? Can you complete the sentence?"
• My Aunt Sadie used to be a champion gymnast. • Aunt Sadie is eighty years old. • Aunt Sadie demonstrated several cartwheels for us at the party.	• My Aunt Sadie, who is 80 years old and who used to be a champion gymnast, demonstrated several cartwheels for us at the party. • My 80-year-old Aunt Sadie, who used to be a champion gymnast, demonstrated several cartwheels for us at the party.	My Aunt Sadie, who used to be a champion gymnast, demonstrated several cartwheels for us at the party.	"This is very much on the right track, but you left out one of the kernel sentences. Can you find it? Yes, the one about Aunt Sadie's age. Try to find a way to include that idea in the sentence you have already written."

going to learn to combine sentences in a way that is a little more difficult because it involves embedding, or inserting, a clause or phrase based on one kernel sentence into another one."

- Mr. Morello displays the kernel sentences shown in the first row of Table 7.2 to the students, and he asks one of the students to read the sentences aloud. Then he says, "Now, there are lots of ways you could put these sentences together to make a good, grammatically correct sentence, but today we are going to focus on one particular way to do it, with an embedded clause or phrase. Some of the more difficult sentences in your reading use this kind of structure, and sometimes you will want to use this type of sentence in your own writing. Here is one way these kernel sentences could be combined using an embedded clause. [Mr. Morello displays the first combination from Table 7.2.]

- Then Mr. Morello asks the students if they can come up with another good combination. If a student comes up with the second correct combination shown in Table 7.2, or another correct one, he affirms the response. If a student gives an incorrect answer, he provides feedback and coaching, as shown in the far-right column of Table 7.2 for one possible incorrect response.

- Mr. Morello is also alert to Hector's occasional confusions based on Spanish syntax, and if Hector gives this kind of response, he provides feedback such as, "I think you could say it that way in Spanish, but in English, say it this way. . . . "

- Mr. Morello continues with multiple sentence-combining items involving embedded clauses and phrases, as shown in Table 7.2, followed by additional practice activities.

In a later lesson, Mr. Morello introduces the intervention group to sentence decomposition tasks with center-embedded syntax involving clauses or phrases. He presents these tasks as involving the opposite of what students have already learned to do in sentence combining, that is, breaking a longer, more complex sentence into individual, shorter ones. He begins with one of the combinations in Table 7.2 to illustrate how students can break long sentences apart as well as combine short sentences. For most of his work on sentence decomposition, however, he uses sentences selected from students' content-area reading, including both narrative and informational texts. He emphasizes how a better understanding of individual sentences can help improve students' overall reading comprehension.

Two examples of sentences with center-embedded syntax, some correct ways of breaking down (decomposing) each sentence, possible incorrect responses from students, and sample teacher feedback to those errors, is displayed in Table 7.3. In addition, Figure 7.2 shows how Mr. Morello marks up the first sentence from Table 7.3 on a whiteboard to help a student who is having particular difficulty decomposing the sentence.

TABLE 7.3. Sample Items for Sentence Decomposition Task Involving Center-Embedded Syntax

Sentence	Sample correct response	Sample incorrect response	Sample teacher feedback to incorrect response
Space weather scales that are similar to those for hurricanes can convey the strength of solar storms.	• Space weather scales are similar to those for hurricanes. • Space weather scales can convey the strength of solar storms.	Hurricanes can convey the strength of solar storms.	"You need at least two shorter sentences to break down the original sentence. Here is one good way to do it." Teacher writes original sentence on a whiteboard and says, "Notice that there is an embedded clause right after 'space weather scales.' The embedded clause is 'that are similar to those for hurricanes.' [Teacher puts brackets around the embedded clause.] The embedded clause describes the space weather scales. So the noun phrase that goes with the verb 'can convey' is 'space weather scales.' [Teacher underlines noun phrase and verb, then draws arrow.] What can convey the strength of solar storms? Right, space weather scales, not hurricanes. So, here is an example of how you could break down the original sentence into two shorter sentences . . ."
The famous photograph of a migrant woman from Oklahoma was the photographer's most important work.	• The famous photograph was of a migrant woman. • The migrant woman was from Oklahoma. • The famous photograph was the photographer's most important work.	• The famous photograph was of Oklahoma. • The photograph was important.	"This sentence has an embedded phrase right after the word *photograph.* What is it? Yes, the phrase 'of a migrant woman' is on the right track, but the whole phrase is even longer. Where was the woman from? Right, Oklahoma. The whole phrase 'a migrant woman from Oklahoma' describes the famous photograph, which is a photograph of a migrant woman, not a photograph of Oklahoma. What does the rest of the sentence say about the famous photograph? Correct, the photograph was the photographer's most important work. Good. So here is one way you could break down the original sentence . . ."

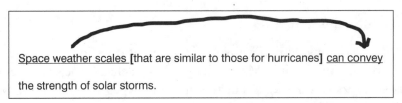

FIGURE 7.2. Sentence markup to help a student understand center-embedded syntax.

A Routine for Comprehension Monitoring with Strategies to Repair Comprehension

Gabe's special education teacher, Ms. Williams, is seeing him for his reading intervention in a small group with two other students. These students have comprehension needs similar to Gabe's. One weakness that all of the students have is in comprehension monitoring and especially in using strategies to repair comprehension. Ms. Williams has developed a routine for the students to use for these difficulties during their text reading, modeled after an activity in Vaughn and colleagues (2022). The routine is shown in Form 7.2 (page 180).

Ms. Williams has taught the students to apply the steps in the routine after approximately every page of reading—more frequently if necessary, as when the students are reading text they find especially challenging. Using the steps shown in Figure 7.2, they do the following:

1. Ask themselves if they understand the section of text they have just read; if so, they repeat the key points to themselves and continue reading.
2. If not, they identify the confusing part of the text—a word, phrase, sentence, or paragraph—by underlining or highlighting it. If they are not reading a copy of a text that can be marked, they write down the page number, paragraph number, and confusing part in a notebook kept for this purpose.
3. They try to repair their confusions using one of the strategies shown in Form 7.2, third step. Using students' class readings, Ms. Williams has modeled using each of these ways to repair comprehension breakdowns. Information about text structure and signal words has also been previously taught, so students were familiar with it before implementing the routine.
4. Students then ask themselves whether the strategy worked for them. If so, they repeat the key ideas to themselves, and keep reading. If not, they try another strategy, discuss their confusion with a classmate, or talk to the teacher.

While the routine was somewhat laborious the first few times that Ms. Williams tried it, the students are now much more accustomed to it. They are able to use it independently in homework, and Ms. Williams gives them time in class to ask questions about and discuss any lingering confusions that they have recorded in their notebooks. Overall, they now have a much more active approach to reading comprehension.

Questioning Activities

In Chapter 6, questioning activities involving different question types were discussed as a way to promote inferencing. Ms. Williams also teaches Gabe's intervention group about different types of questions, but the question types she uses are a little different from the ones in Chapter 6. Ms. Williams's question types are based in part on Raphael and Au (2005) and Vaughn and colleagues (2022; see also Stevens & Austin, 2022). These question types are as follows:

- **Right-there questions:** The answer is stated right in the text, often in a single sentence similar to the question. For example, the text states that Mary had bright red hair and the question is, *What color was Mary's hair?*
- **Think-and-search questions:** The answer is stated in the text, but in multiple places, not in a single sentence. For example, the text states three reasons why Abraham Lincoln is widely regarded as our greatest president, in different paragraphs, and the question is, *Name three reasons why Abraham Lincoln is thought to be our greatest president.*
- **Inference questions:** The answer is not stated in the text, and the student has to make an inference based on information or clues that are stated in the text; or on information from class or previous readings; or on their own experience. For example, a text about the 2004 Indonesian tsunami states that shortly before the tsunami hit, some beachgoers ran away when they saw the water receding far from the shore; the question is, *Why did some beachgoers run away?* Students must use background information they have learned about tsunamis to infer that these people understood that the drawback of the water was a sign of an approaching tsunami.

Currently Gabe and his intervention group are reading a series of articles on basic genetics, to help them with their science class reading, which involves this topic. The texts for the general education science class are extremely difficult for these students; Ms. Williams has tried to use them, but even with teacher scaffolding and preteaching, the texts are much too dense for the students to comprehend well. So instead, Ms. Williams is using Web articles on basic genetics—let's call the website Louise Spear-Swerling's *Lessons in Genetics*—which covers content similar to the science curriculum at Ms. Williams's school. The general education science program at Ms. Williams's school involves a great deal of hands-on inquiry learning, and many students find the class texts difficult, so the science teacher does extensive oral discussion. Ms. Williams has found that Gabe and the other students in his group can generally be successful in the class by learning similar content from the Web-based texts. By using the Web-based texts, as opposed to simply teaching content orally, she can cover key content vocabulary and content knowledge, while still teaching the students important reading skills such as those involving text structure, comprehension monitoring, and the use of fix-up strategies.

Figure 7.3 shows the opening sections of the text *DNA, Genes, and Chromosomes*, with some sample questions involving the three question types. Ms. Williams displays the Web-based text using a computer, and students take turns reading from hard copies

DNA, Genes, and Chromosomes

What is a Gene?

Deoxyribonucleic acid, or DNA, is a self-reproducing molecule found in almost all living things. DNA contains the necessary information for an organism's functioning and development. The DNA molecule is similar to a twisted ladder in appearance, with two linked, winding strands. Because of this shape, DNA is sometimes referred to as a double helix.

Genes, which are considered the basic unit of inheritance, are segments of DNA. They provide the information needed to construct specific proteins or RNA molecules involved in various biological functions. These genes are passed from parent to child and influence a wide range of inherited traits. Genes are located on chromosomes in the nucleus of a cell.

Chromosomes in Humans

Chromosomes are threadlike, linear structures composed of a single molecule of DNA, along with proteins. Humans have 23 sets of chromosomes, two in each set; there are 46 altogether. Chromosomes are numbered by size, beginning with the largest, Chromosome 1. The genes for each chromosome occur in a particular order. For example, a gene found in a certain place on Chromosome 5 in one person will be found in that same place in other people.

In humans, Chromosome 23 is a sex chromosome that differs depending on whether the individual is male or female. Males generally have an X and a Y chromosome (XY) and females two X chromosomes (XX). Each parent contributes one of these chromosomes to a child. The other 22 pairs of chromosomes, which are not sex chromosomes, are termed *autosomes*.

Chromosomes in Other Species

While other species have chromosomes, theirs often vary in number and shape from those of humans. For instance, many bacteria only have one chromosome in the shape of a circle. Different species also vary in the number of sets of chromosomes that they have. Some types of plants have four copies of each chromosome—four in each set—or even more.

However, within a species the number of chromosomes, the number of sets of chromosomes, and the shape are constant. For example, all dogs have 39 pairs of rod-shaped chromosomes, with two in each set for a total of 78, regardless of the breed of dog.

Noncoding DNA

Although genes are extremely important, they make up only a small percentage of human DNA. DNA that does not code for a product is called noncoding DNA. Scientists know that some noncoding DNA serves key purposes such as helping to regulate the production of proteins. Other noncoding DNA might have been left by viruses that infected our ancestors long ago, and our ancestors then passed this DNA down to us. The purpose of some noncoding DNA is currently unknown. Other species also have noncoding DNA, with some species, such as certain plants and protists, having even more noncoding DNA than humans do.

An old term for noncoding DNA is "junk DNA." Many contemporary scientists think this outdated term is a bad one, however. Non-coding DNA may have important functions that have yet to be determined and that science may reveal in the future.

Sample Right-There Questions (Possible Answers)

1. How are chromosomes numbered? (According to their size, starting with the largest, Chromosome 1)
2. How many sets of chromosomes do people have? (23 sets)
3. What is a gene? (A gene is a segment of DNA that provides the information for building specific proteins or RNA molecules involved in various biological functions; also, genes are considered the basic unit of inheritance)

(continued)

FIGURE 7.3. Text and sample questions on basic genetics.

4. What are autosomes? (The first 22 sets of chromosomes that are not sex chromosomes)
5. In humans, how do the sex chromosomes differ between males and females? (Most females have two X chromosomes [XX] whereas most males have an X and a Y chromosome [XY]).

Sample Think-and-Search Questions (Possible Answers)

1. Explain how chromosomes, genes, and DNA relate to each other. (A chromosome is a single molecule of DNA, and genes are segments of DNA on a chromosome that provide information for constructing specific proteins or RNA molecules involved in various biological functions. However, chromosomes also include a lot of noncoding DNA.)
2. Describe two ways that other species can vary from humans in the number of chromosomes they have. Give examples. (Other species often have pairs of chromosomes, but not the same number of pairs as humans do. For example, humans have 23 pairs, but dogs have 39 pairs. Also, some species do not have pairs of chromosomes. For instance, some species of plants have four or more copies of each chromosome instead of two like humans; many bacteria have only one chromosome.)

Sample Inference Questions (Possible Answers)

1. Why can each of our genes be mapped to a specific location on a particular chromosome? (Because genes that code for a given trait are always found on the same chromosome and in the same location on that chromosome, for everyone.)
2. Why is it true that, in humans, the father and not the mother determines the sex of a child? (Because most human females have two X chromosomes, so they always contribute an X chromosome to a child. But most human males have an X and a Y chromosome, so they can contribute either one to a child, which will determine whether the child will be male or female.)
3. Explain why noncoding DNA is important. (Noncoding DNA is known to have some important functions, such as containing information that is needed to regulate the production of proteins. There is also some DNA whose function is currently unknown but that is still believed to be significant by scientists. Even though we do not yet know what the purpose of this DNA is, it may be shown to have an important purpose in the future.)

FIGURE 7.3. *(continued)*

of the text. Ms. Williams asks questions after each section of text. The Web-based text is accompanied by multiple charts, diagrams, and pictures; Ms. Williams draws students' attention to these both before the reading and, if relevant, when students are answering questions.

In addition to asking students her own questions, Ms. Williams encourages students to ask themselves questions based on the three question types. One way she does this is to incorporate asking questions into students' classwork and homework. For tonight's homework, students will read another Web article involving basic genetics. Students will be asked to use the comprehension-monitoring routine from Form 7.2 in their reading, as well as to generate and write down at least four right-there questions, with answers. (Later, Ms. Williams will include the other question types.) She will provide a few minutes in the next class to discuss students' questions, to address any confusions, and to review key content from the article.

Independent Pleasure Reading for Students with SRCD

As discussed in Chapter 5, appropriately structured voluntary pleasure reading activities, when used in conjunction with effective SL interventions, have the potential to benefit a range of struggling readers (Mol & Bus, 2011; Wei et al., 2021). Developing habits of reading for enjoyment, using the kinds of steps discussed in that chapter, is important for students with SRCD, as well as those with other poor reader profiles. Ms. Williams has involved both Gabe and Conor in these kinds of groups.

While being able to decode grade-appropriate texts is not an issue for students with SRCD, these students may still require easier texts for pleasure reading due to their difficulties with comprehension. If texts are too difficult for students in terms of comprehension, reading may feel laborious, and students will not want to read. For students with SRCD, one potentially fruitful avenue for choosing books involves books matched to individual students' interests and background knowledge. For instance, students like Gabe and Hector, who have general weaknesses in academic background knowledge, might still have a strong knowledge base for a specific topic that interests them, such as music, art, or a sport. Teachers can try to broaden students' interests over time, so that they are exposed to a wider range of background knowledge and vocabulary. Nontraditional reading materials, such as magazines, comics, or manga, also can be good sources for exposure to new vocabulary because they often use relatively sophisticated vocabulary (Hayes & Ahrens, 1988), coupled with drawings or pictures that can enhance comprehension.

SL Intervention Plans for Advanced-Stage Readers with SRCD

The lesson format from Chapter 6, shown in Table 6.2, can be used for advanced-stage readers with SRCD. The same broad lesson segments apply to both advanced-stage readers with SRCD and early-stage readers, although for the former, the focus will be on more advanced literacy skills. Lessons can be further adapted to suit individual students' needs, such as spending more or less time on a particular area, or to meet other constraints, such as scheduling of instructional blocks at upper grade levels.

A Sample Intervention Lesson for Gabe

Table 7.4 displays a sample, 50-minute intervention lesson for Gabe and his intervention group. The lesson begins with a quick review of previously taught Tier 2 vocabulary words selected from the novel the students are reading for their English class. However, most of the lesson focuses on the basic genetics text shown in Figure 7.3. For the sentence-level activities, Ms. Williams selects two specific sentences from the text that she thinks students may find confusing, based on their previous difficulties in text reading. These two sentences involve ellipsis: *Humans have 23 sets of chromosomes, two in each set; there are 46 altogether* and *For example, all dogs have 39 pairs of rod-shaped chromosomes, with two in each set for a total of 78, regardless of the breed of dog.* For these sentences, she elicits from students, or explains as needed, that the word *chromosome* is understood in the latter part of each sentence—that is, *46 chromosomes altogether* and *a total of 78 chromosomes*. Next, the students watch a short video that provides background information related to today's reading, with Ms.

TABLE 7.4. Sample Intervention Lesson for Gabe (with Two Other Students)

Component(s)	Activity
Vocabulary (5 minutes)	Teacher briefly reviews 10 previously taught vocabulary words (Tier 2 words from students' English novel) by displaying printed words and asking for definitions or synonyms.
Sentence-level activities (5 minutes)	Teacher presents and discusses two potentially confusing sentences, involving ellipsis, from today's science reading.
Oral language development (5 minutes)	Students watch a 2-minute video from the Web that reviews background knowledge on DNA relevant to today's reading; teacher leads brief discussion of the video's key points and previews the purpose of today's reading (learning about cell structures called chromosomes and their relationship to DNA).
Text reading and reading comprehension (25 minutes) • Text-specific vocabulary • Text structure and comprehension strategies • Literal and inferential comprehension	• Teacher reviews previously taught content vocabulary important to understanding text (*DNA, RNA, molecule, nucleus*) by stating a definition and asking students to tell the correct word that goes with it. • Teacher displays and briefly explains one new content vocabulary word, *chromosome* (structures in a cell nucleus made of one molecule of DNA); students repeat word and definition. • Teacher displays text and draws students' attention to important text features (e.g., headings, charts) by asking students why they should pay attention to these features when reading this kind of text. • Students take turns reading text aloud with frequent teacher questioning, using the three types of questions in Figure 7.3. • Teacher assigns related article for homework; reviews use of comprehension monitoring routine and briefly explains writing of right-there questions.
Writing (10 minutes)	Students write a short paragraph summarizing what they learned about chromosomes and which questions they still have.

Williams leading a brief discussion to ensure students recall key points from it. She also presents a purpose for today's reading, which is to learn about chromosomes and their relationship to DNA.

Ms. Williams begins the text comprehension segment of the lesson by reviewing key content vocabulary, as well as teaching one new word, *chromosome*, using a student-friendly definition, shown in Table 7.4. She asks students to repeat both this word and its definition. She also briefly explains the meaning of another new word, *protist*—a type of microscopic organism—in the context of the reading. She does not place much emphasis on teaching this word because it is not important to understanding this text or the topic of basic genetics. In addition, she implements the rest of the questioning activity that has been previously discussed, as shown in Figure 7.3 and Table 7.4. The lesson concludes with a writing activity in which students summarize what they learned about chromosomes, as well as any questions they have about what they read. If necessary, sentence stems ("In today's reading I learned that chromosomes . . ." and "One thing I still have questions about is . . .") can be used to help with the writing task.

Hector's Intervention

Hector's intervention can use the same lesson format as Gabe's, and he and Gabe can benefit from many of the same intervention activities. For instance, both students (and their intervention groups) can profit from activities for morphology, explicit teaching of academic vocabulary, and explicit teaching of background knowledge for the texts they are reading in school. Although Hector has not been identified specifically with EF weaknesses, activities such as the comprehension monitoring routine and other comprehension strategies (e.g., teaching about text structure) would likely be helpful for Hector as well as Gabe.

Here are three specific needs of Hector's that differ from Gabe's:

1. Hector can benefit from teaching about Spanish–English cognates, whereas this is not relevant for Gabe.
2. Sentence-level activities to teach sentence comprehension and sentence writing can help both students, but might need to be focused a bit differently. For example, Hector's sentence-level difficulties appear to relate at least partly to syntax confusions involving his native language, whereas this is not true for Gabe.
3. Hector is not as far behind in reading as Gabe is. Therefore, Hector could probably comprehend reasonably well in grade-level texts, with some preteaching and scaffolding from his interventionist.

Additional Considerations for Written Expression

Underlying weaknesses in language or EF typically impact the written expression of advanced-stage readers with SRCD, most of whom are in middle or high school. Like reading demands, written expression demands become much more challenging at advanced grade levels, and students who were not previously seen as having serious difficulties with writing may begin to struggle more in this area. Application of their developing language skills in writing, as well as reading, is valuable for these students. Teaching of EF types of strategies in writing, such as planning, goal setting, organization, revision, and editing processes (e.g., Graham et al., 2016) benefits most students but may require particular emphasis for students such as Gabe, who have been identified with EF weaknesses.

Some older students require assistive technology to meet grade-level challenges in literacy, but the most helpful assistive technology usually differs for students with SRCD as compared to SWRD (Erickson, 2013). Assistive technology that involves extended oral presentation of content, such as reading of text aloud, can be very helpful for students with SWRD; however, it may be less helpful for students with SRCD, since many of these students' reading difficulties are based in language comprehension.

In writing, technological aids for basic writing skills such as spelling can benefit students with SWRD, but students with SRCD may benefit more from other kinds of technology, such as aids to help with choosing effective vocabulary words or organizing a piece of writing.

SUMMING UP:
SL Interventions for Advanced-Stage Readers with SRCD

Here are key points from this chapter:

- Advanced-stage readers with SRCD require interventions focused on the kinds of comprehension skills typically taught in the upper elementary grades and beyond, often involving informational texts, although teaching of narrative texts remains important.

- These readers benefit from many of the kinds of activities discussed in Chapter 6, but applied to more challenging texts.

- SL activities can be as effective for ELs as for other struggling readers, but ELs typically require additional emphasis on academic vocabulary, academic language, and background knowledge; they also often benefit from teaching of cognates.

- Many advanced-stage readers with SRCD have problems in EF in addition to problems with language comprehension, and both areas may have a greater impact on reading comprehension as students advance in school.

- Students with problems in EF can be helped by explicit teaching of EF strategies such as comprehension monitoring and using strategies to repair comprehension, as well as learning strategies for planning, organizing, and revising their writing.

APPLIED EXERCISES

Exercise 1

Ms. Smith is a middle school teacher who works in a school that serves a high proportion of ELs. Many of these students struggle in reading. What are the most common poor reader profiles (SWRD, SRCD, MRD) that Ms. Smith is likely to find among these struggling readers? Why might this be the case?

Answer

The most common poor reader profiles among ELs involve SRCD and MRD. These profiles are common in this subgroup of students because many ELs have difficulties with English vocabulary and language comprehension, due to limited experiences with English. This background tends to lead to either an SRCD profile, or MRD, if the student also has problems with word reading. As with all poor readers, however, individual ELs' difficulties can vary, so Ms. Smith should use assessments to determine students' specific intervention needs.

Exercise 2

Leo, a fifth grader, is doing a sentence decomposition activity in his intervention group. The sentence is, *The scout who traveled in advance of the enemy troops approached the border at dawn.* Leo's response is *The scout traveled in advance of the enemy troops* and *The enemy troops approached the border at dawn.* What kind of mistake is Leo making? What specific teacher feedback would be helpful?

Answer

The first part of Leo's decomposition is correct, but the second sentence is not. Leo has probably become confused by the fact that the words *enemy troops* and *approached* are adjacent to each other in the sentence. His teacher should first acknowledge the correct part of his answer. She can help him understand the rest of the sentence correctly by noting that there is an embedded clause, *who traveled in advance of the enemy troops*, in the original sentence, and that the embedded clause separates the noun *scout* from its verb *approached*. Therefore, it is the scout who approached the border at dawn, not the enemy troops, and the second sentence should be *The scout approached the border at dawn.* A visual markup of the sentence similar to the one in Figure 7.2 could also be helpful.

Exercise 3

Dinah is a seventh grader who has been identified with problems in EF. Although Dinah met grade expectations in reading in the primary grades, in recent years, she has had increasing difficulties with reading comprehension. This year, her problems are especially serious, and she is also having problems with writing assignments. Her most significant writing weakness involves a lack of organization in writing. Her most significant reading weakness involves difficulties with summarization and determining the gist or main idea of a passage. Dinah does not have problems with word reading, rate of reading, or spelling. Dinah's parents do not understand why her EF problems are creating so many more literacy difficulties for her now than they did in earlier grades. How would you explain this to them?

Answer

Dinah's increasing difficulties probably reflect increased expectations for literacy, including writing as well as reading, in the upper elementary grades and middle school. For example, students have to comprehend longer, more complex texts, and they are expected to produce longer, more complex texts in their writing. Problems with specific EF skills such as planning and monitoring one's work would have a bigger impact on these more complex tasks than on the simpler literacy tasks of the early grades.

Exercise 4

What kinds of steps should be taken to help Dinah?

Answer

To obtain a fuller picture of Dinah's skills, diagnostic assessments of specific components of reading and language, such as vocabulary, would be very helpful. Weaknesses in these areas should be addressed in intervention. With regard to EF, explicit teaching about comprehension monitoring, fix-up strategies, text structure, and summarization should help improve Dinah's reading comprehension. In writing, Dinah would benefit from explicit teaching of writing processes such as planning, organization, revision, and editing. EF strategies should be taught in the context of specific reading and writing tasks, as was done for Gabe.

Follow-Up Practice Activity with Sentences for Academic Vocabulary

Part I. Directions: Fill in the blanks with the appropriate word from the grid involving the roots *arche, astro, aud, bio, geo,* and *psych.*

1. Rita has always been interested in earth science, so it makes sense that she decided to study _____ in college. (geology)

2. Tom was having trouble with his hearing, so he decided to go to an _____ for a hearing test. (audiologist)

3. The results of Tom's _____ exam were encouraging, because they showed that he did not have a serious hearing problem. (audiological)

4. In my psychology class, we study learning, emotions, motivation, and many other _____ topics. (psychological)

5. The _____ looked through his telescope at a distant star. (astronomer)

6. The radio was turned down so low that the music was barely _____. (audible)

7. The _____ went to a place in Greece, where there were signs of a very old city that they wanted to dig up. (archeologists)

8. An _____ dig is an area being studied, where archeologists carefully remove layers of earth to find out what is underneath. (archeological)

9. The study of _____ includes many aspects of plant, animal, and human life. (biology)

10. The governor tried to reassure everyone that the chemicals spilled in the train accident were not _____ harmful to humans. (biologically)

11. Many _____ have written books about the life of Abraham Lincoln. (biographers)

12. If someone writes a book about his or her own life, that is called an _____. (autobiography)

Part II. Write an example of a complete, correct sentence that shows the meaning of each of the words below:

a. A noun with the root *geo.*

b. An adjective with the root *bio.*

c. An adverb with the root *psych.*

Routine for Comprehension Monitoring with Strategies to Repair Comprehension

1. Did I understand what I just read? If so, what are the key points?

2. If not, what don't I understand? Highlight or write down the confusing part.

3. Try a strategy to repair confusions, such as:

   - Rereading carefully

   - Applying background knowledge

   - Looking up a confusing word or term (e.g., in glossary or online thesaurus/dictionary)

   - Using text structure and features (e.g., headings, subheadings, pictures, figures, graphs, charts)

   - Using signal words (e.g., cause–effect, summary, example, continuation, contrast)

4. Did that help? If yes, what are the key points? If not:

   - Try another strategy

   - Discuss with a classmate

   - Get help from a teacher

CHAPTER 8

Structured Literacy Interventions for Mixed Reading Difficulties

Early Stages

Emily Odesky, the reading interventionist mentioned in Chapter 4 for her SL intervention with a group of first graders, has a new student named Dashawn. He is a second grader, a recent transfer to Ms. Odesky's school. Dashawn's reading problems quickly became evident in his new school, due to his difficulties reading second-grade text. When Ms. Odesky observed Dashawn in his classroom, she could tell that he had poor decoding, but she had the sense that his difficulties went beyond word reading. For instance, even when the teacher read a popular children's book aloud to the class, so that no reading was required of him, Dashawn had some trouble understanding the vocabulary of the book and answering comprehension questions.

This chapter describes students with broader intervention needs than those described in previous chapters because their difficulties encompass both word reading and language comprehension. These students have a profile of mixed reading difficulties (MRD). Like students with other poor reader profiles, those with MRD can vary in age, as can the severity of their reading problems, and they may include students with and without disabilities.

Ellie, a seventh grader, provides an example of an older student with MRD, as well as one with severe reading problems related to a disability. As a preschooler, Ellie was identified with a specific language impairment (SLI), sometimes termed developmental language disorder. She has received both speech–language and special education services throughout her schooling. Nevertheless, Ellie's language problems have seriously impacted her literacy achievement, and the gap between Ellie and her age peers appears to be widening. A recent triennial evaluation found Ellie's scores in numerous components of literacy—word reading, oral language comprehension, reading comprehension, and fluency—to have declined considerably relative to her previous triennial in grade 4. At a recent PPT meeting, it was agreed that Ellie's program would be substantially revised to use SL.

This chapter addresses poor readers with MRD who are at early stages of reading, like Dashawn and Ellie. After reviewing some key issues in teaching students with this profile, as well as research on interventions for them, the chapter provides examples of specific SL intervention activities that can be valuable for these students. The chapter also introduces a new intervention plan for students with MRD, as well as sample intervention lessons. Let's begin by considering some additional information about both Dashawn and Ellie.

Dashawn

Dashawn attended kindergarten and first grade in a school strongly oriented toward discovery learning. The core general education program provided little explicit, systematic teaching of foundational literacy skills, vocabulary, or comprehension. Although some children did learn to read well with this approach, many did not, and Dashawn was one of the latter. Furthermore, the school had a very unstructured approach to behavior and classroom management. Dashawn was often in trouble behaviorally, usually in relation to reading—for example, refusing to attempt reading passages and being off-task when children were expected to read silently during the long sustained silent reading block.

Ms. Odesky's school has a much more structured core general education curriculum both with regard to literacy instruction and behavioral expectations. Dashawn has made a good adjustment to his new school, and he is doing better behaviorally. However, when Ms. Odesky administered some reading assessments to Dashawn, the results showed that her intuitions about Dashawn's reading during her initial classroom observations were correct. Dashawn not only had significant difficulties in decoding, but he also had weaknesses in language comprehension. Table 8.1 summarizes the results of Ms. Odesky's assessments.

On a criterion-referenced phonics measure similar to the ABC Test discussed in Chapter 3, Dashawn knew all single-consonant sounds, as well as all short- and long-vowel sounds except for *y*; for *y*, he knew only the consonant sound, /y/ as in *yellow*. He also confused the consonant digraphs *sh* and *ch*, and he knew few other sounds for letter patterns. These weaknesses were reflected in his decoding and spelling of short-vowel words. For example, he read *mush* as *much* and misspelled *fish* as *fich*. Another common error pattern involved words with consonant blends. Dashawn decoded and spelled some of these words correctly, but especially in words with five or more phonemes (e.g., *trust*, *clamp*), he sometimes dropped one of the interior phonemes of the word, reading *trust* as *tust* and spelling *clamp* as *clap*. After testing was completed, Ms. Odesky had Dashawn try some of these words again, pointing to each word and

TABLE 8.1. Assessment Data for Dashawn (Grade 2)

Assessment	Dashawn's data
Criterion-referenced phonics test	
• Sounds for letters/letter patterns	• Mastered: Single consonant sounds; short and long vowels except *y*; *th*, *wh*, *ck*. Confused *sh*, *ch*; knows very few VR or VT patterns.
• Decoding	• Mastered: CVC words; some skills for closed with blends/digraphs (60%) but not mastered; other categories well below mastery (< 40%).
• Spelling	• Spelling skills align with decoding skills.
CBM—winter of grade 2	
• ORF accuracy	• Well below benchmark
• ORF rate	• Well below benchmark
Oral reading inventory (ORI)	
• Graded word lists	• Independent level: preprimer; instructional level: end of grade 1
• Graded passages	• No independent level; instructional level: primer (middle of grade 1)
Informal listening comp measures	
• Oral vocabulary	• Below grade expectations
• Listening passages from alternative form of ORI	• Below grade expectations

encouraging him to look more carefully at all the letters in the word, but not providing any other cues. Under these conditions, Dashawn was able to self-correct several of the words. His errors on these words did not seem due to an inability to blend phonemes or lack of letter-sound knowledge, but rather to a failure to look carefully at letters within words, especially in a longer word. Still, he clearly needed more practice reading, as well as spelling, these words.

Ms. Odesky also administered a benchmark CBM for oral reading fluency, using the assessment for winter of grade 2, because it was the middle of the school year. On this measure, Dashawn scored well below benchmark for both accuracy and rate of oral reading in grade-2 text. On an untimed oral reading inventory (ORI), Dashawn had some sight word knowledge, as shown by his performance on the graded word lists (see Table 8.1); however, on the graded passages, his performance was poorer, with difficulties involving both comprehension and word reading.

Dashawn's comprehension weaknesses were also evident in two informal measures of language comprehension that Ms. Odesky administered, a vocabulary assessment and a listening comprehension assessment. The listening comprehension assessment used an alternate form of the ORI, in which Ms. Odesky read passages aloud to Dashawn and asked him comprehension questions. Similar to his performance when reading, Dashawn sometimes made errors that appeared to reflect lack of background and vocabulary knowledge, as well as difficulties with inferencing. For example, one passage involved a child whose cat was missing. The cat was hiding in an attic, and Dashawn did not know what an attic was, so he was unable to answer an inferential question about why the child's search of the main part of the house did not lead to her finding the cat.

The assessments established that Dashawn required intervention. Ms. Odesky sees him in a small group with two other students, second graders whose literacy needs are similar to Dashawn's. All of the students can benefit from SL interventions for vocabulary and background knowledge, as well as for word reading and spelling skills involving one-syllable, short-vowel words.

Ellie

Ellie, a hardworking, focused seventh grader, is well liked by teachers and other students. Her middle school employs a collaborative model of service delivery for most students with disabilities, in which these students are placed in general education classes, and the special educator works with them in those classes, collaborating with the general educator to meet students' needs. The general education curriculum emphasizes the use of cooperative group activities and inquiry learning. For instance, in science, students work together in small groups on various laboratory tasks related to the specific science topic being studied.

Ellie has done reasonably well in her classes. Support from her special education teacher, Mr. Murphy, as well as accommodations and Ellie's consistently strong effort, have helped her to pass class requirements, often with grades of B or higher. Although all of Ellie's teachers recognized that she had significant difficulties with comprehension and written expression, they viewed her word-reading problems as minor. They were stunned by her performance in her most recent triennial evaluation. Figure 8.1 displays an assessment map with Ellie's most recent standardized test scores.

Ellie's standard scores for reading and oral language comprehension were all low, with standard scores in the 70s or lower on all subtests. These scores showed weaknesses in multiple component areas of word reading, including phonological skills, real-word reading, and automaticity of word reading, as well as in multiple component areas of language comprehension, such as vocabulary and syntax. Ellie's lowest scores were on measures of oral reading fluency and reading comprehension—not surprising because in these areas, problems in word reading and language comprehension have a dual impact.

Mr. Murphy administered a criterion-referenced phonics measure to obtain more detail about Ellie's specific phonics skills. Ellie had received substantial phonics intervention in the primary grades, and Mr. Murphy anticipated that Ellie would be able to master many word categories on the phonics test, except perhaps for multisyllabic words. Unfortunately, however, the test showed that Ellie had much weaker phonics skills than Mr. Murphy expected. She mastered phonics categories for decoding some, but not all, one-syllable words. Although she could successfully decode short-vowel,

Student *Ellie*   Grade 7   Dates of Testing *Jan 9–22*

ORAL LANGUAGE COMPREHENSION

**Oral Vocabulary
(note receptive/expressive)**

PPVT-5 (receptive) **78**

WJ-IV Picture Vocab (exp) **75**

**Oral Language
(Listening) Comprehension
(note format, e.g., cloze,
maze, QA)**

WJ-IV Oral Comprehension **74** (cloze)

Other Oral Language

CELF-5 Receptive Language Index, **76**

CELF-5 Expressive Language Index, **74**

WORD READING

Real Words—Accuracy

WJ-IV Word Identification **78**

**Nonsense Words—
Accuracy**

WJ-IV Word Attack **74**

**Word Reading—
Automaticity**

TOWRE-2 Sight Word Efficiency **70**

TOWRE-2 Phonetic Decoding Efficiency **63**

**Phonological/phonemic
awareness**

CTOPP-2 Phonological Awareness Composite **72**

**Oral Reading Fluency—
Accuracy**

DIBELS 8 ORF *intensive level/at risk*

**Oral Reading Fluency—
Rate**

DIBELS 8 ORF *intensive level/at risk*

Silent Reading Fluency

WJ-IV Sentence Reading Fluency **62**

**Reading Comprehension
(note test format, e.g.,
cloze, maze, QA, as well as
other relevant features
such as timing)**

WJ-IV Passage Comprehension **63** (untimed; cloze)

DIBELS 8 Maze *intensive level/at risk* (timed CBM; maze)

Test of Reading Comprehension (TORC-4) Index **65**, individual subtests all ≤ **70** (silent reading, varied tasks)

Observations

Many errors on DIBELS Maze; very low score

Student showed excellent effort and persistence on all testing

FIGURE 8.1. Assessment map for Ellie.

SE, and open-syllable patterns, including with common suffixes (e.g., -s, -ing, -ed) and in nonsense words, she did not master one-syllable VR or VT word patterns.

On an ORI, Ellie had the ability to read many words by sight, including some multisyllabic words; her highest instructional level on graded word lists was grade 4. This sight-word knowledge, combined with Ellie's consistently strong effort and good ability to function in group activities with other students, might explain why her severe decoding weaknesses were not more apparent to her teachers. In line with other testing, on the ORI graded passages, Ellie's highest instructional level was about grade 2 to grade 3, with problems involving both word reading and language comprehension.

In her previous triennial as a fourth grader, Ellie's performance on standardized testing was notably better, with some standard scores in the mid-80s. Ellie's current scores suggest that the gap between Ellie and her age peers is widening, and she is falling further behind. Moreover, her performance in basic reading, reading fluency, and reading comprehension raised concerns about her attainment of functional literacy, that is, the literacy skills required to function in everyday life. Ellie's parents were understandably upset, and the PPT made the decision to substantially revise Ellie's program. The school has provided Mr. Murphy with professional development in SL. Although Ellie still participates in general education classes, her revised program prioritizes providing explicit teaching in the key literacy skills that Ellie needs, in both word reading and comprehension. It also increases collaboration between Ellie's speech–language teacher and her special education teacher.

About Early-Stage Readers with MRD

Early-stage readers with MRD all have the following in common: (1) reading difficulties based in both word reading and language comprehension and (2) a need for intervention in basic word-reading and spelling skills at the one-syllable level. Regardless of a student's level of oral language comprehension, significant limitations in word reading greatly impair reading comprehension; thus, word reading is the primary consideration in deciding whether the student is an early-stage or advanced-stage reader with MRD. Also, as discussed in Chapter 7 in relation to students with specific reading comprehension difficulties (SRCD), problems with executive function may play a role in poor reading comprehension for students with MRD, although this was not the case for Dashawn or Ellie.

As with other poor reader profiles, interventions for MRD must be targeted to individual students' weaknesses. One student with MRD might have language-comprehension weaknesses that primarily involve vocabulary, whereas another student might have a much broader range of language needs. In addition, for individual students, the severity of word-reading weaknesses as compared to language-comprehension weaknesses may differ. Consider a student with dyslexia, who also has had limited exposure to academic vocabulary and language. This student might have severe difficulties with word reading, coupled with milder language-comprehension weaknesses that are more experientially based. The relative severity of weaknesses in the two areas matters in intervention planning because educators usually want to allocate more time and emphasis to the weaker area, especially if the disparity between the two is pronounced.

Many, though not all, early-stage readers with MRD require decodable texts for their reading intervention. Whether or not a student requires decodable texts, all students generally need to read texts at their instructional levels. In addition, distinguishing between texts used for students' reading and for their listening comprehension (e.g., in oral activities such as teacher read-alouds) is essential. Typically, the oral language comprehension of students with MRD is better than their reading comprehension, due to the impact of poor word reading on the latter. Therefore, teachers can use higher-level texts for students' listening than for their reading, which can provide more opportunities for comprehension development, such as exposure to more sophisticated vocabulary, background knowledge, and figurative language. If students' language-comprehension weaknesses are mild, teachers may be able to use grade-appropriate texts for listening activities, with some preteaching and scaffolding.

Given the range of needs of many students with MRD, internal integration of interventions is particularly important for these students, to help make interventions more efficient. Internal integration is characteristic of SL approaches. For instance, instructional tasks, examples, and texts are purposely chosen to reinforce previously taught skills and provide opportunities for practice. Certain types of instructional activities can also enhance integration and efficiency of teaching. Teaching students about morphology can help improve not only their word reading but also their spelling and vocabulary knowledge (Carlisle, 2010; Goodwin & Ahn, 2013). Spelling activities can enhance students' PA and phonics skills; these activities may even serve as a more effective way to develop beginning decoding skills than traditional phonics instruction (Herron & Gillis, 2020). Integration of interventions with core general education instruction is also highly desirable and increases the effectiveness of interventions (Fletcher et al., 2019).

Research on Interventions for Early-Stage Readers with MRD

The Importance of Multicomponent Interventions

A profile of MRD is very common among poor readers, especially among students with relatively severe reading comprehension difficulties, students from low-socioeconomic status (low-SES) backgrounds, and ELs (Capin et al., 2021; Lesaux & Kieffer, 2010). Although students with MRD typically have language weaknesses, many do not meet criteria for speech–language services (Nation, 2005). For instance, a student's oral language weaknesses may be considered primarily experiential in nature, not the result of a disability, or their language scores may not be low enough for eligibility for services. Nevertheless, even mild language weaknesses may cause problems with literacy learning, especially when coupled with poor word reading and as students advance in school.

Students with MRD require multicomponent interventions, interventions that address both word reading and language comprehension. Research suggests that multicomponent interventions can be very effective, especially if they have the key features of SL, such as being highly explicit and systematic, targeting students' specific needs, and monitoring progress, as well as adjusting interventions as needed (Fletcher et al., 2019; Foorman, Herrera, Dombek, Schatschneider, & Petscher, 2017; Wanzek et al., 2020). Many intervention studies involving at-risk children in the primary grades have emphasized foundational reading skills, with significant positive effects on multiple areas of reading, including reading comprehension (Gersten, Haymond, Newman-Gonchar, Dimino, & Jayanthi, 2020). More recently, some studies have incorporated additional intervention components focused on oral language comprehension, which is particularly relevant for students with MRD.

Foorman and colleagues (2017) studied the effectiveness of two small-group literacy interventions implemented with at-risk readers in grades K–2. At-risk readers were from schools classified as low performing in their state, and they included a high proportion of low-SES students and ELs. The two interventions addressed not only foundational reading skills such as PA and phonics but also language skills such as vocabulary and syntax. The interventions differed mainly in relation to whether they were embedded in the core general education literacy program or were stand-alone interventions. Both interventions were effective, with relatively minor outcome differences between them. Most important, although the interventions spanned only 27 weeks, they impacted many students' performance on a variety of outcome measures that included language as well as foundational skills. Across grades K–2 and both interventions, at-risk students improved, on average, 13–25 percentile points in basic reading skills and 6–25 points on language measures.

Interventions for Students with Speech-Language Disabilities

Students with speech–language disabilities are often at risk in reading, both early on and in the later grades. Moreover, even when a child's early speech–language problems appear to have resolved and the student is no longer eligible for speech–language services, he or she may still be at increased risk of reading problems (Zipoli & Merritt, 2017). Therefore, a student's speech–language history should be considered when determining risk for reading difficulties, even if the student currently does not receive speech–language services.

Students with SLI, Ellie's primary disability, are at especially high risk of reading disorders (Adlof, 2020; Zipoli & Merritt, 2017). In the absence of effective intervention, the language and literacy problems of these students often persist into adulthood (Whitehouse, Line, Watt, & Bishop, 2009). SLI involves language difficulties that are not mainly attributable to other known causes of language problems such as intellectual disabilities, hearing impairment, autism, or experiential factors, such as limited exposure to English. Most children with SLI have weaknesses in oral language comprehension, but they vary in the extent to which they have poor word reading (Adlof, 2020). Some authorities (e.g., Adlof, 2020; Catts, Adlof, Hogan, & Weismer, 2005) view a student such as Ellie—who has severe phonological and word-reading difficulties coupled with significant broad language comprehension weaknesses—as having co-occurring SLI and dyslexia.

In relation to phonological skills, word reading, and spelling, students like Ellie can benefit from the same types of interventions that are effective for students with dyslexia, such as those discussed in Chapter 4. However, Ellie's intervention needs are significantly more complex than Ruben's or Shakira's, the students discussed in that chapter. In addition to addressing foundational skills, Ellie's intervention must address multiple areas of language comprehension, using activities such as those described in Chapters 6 and 7. These activities should target Ellie's specific needs in both word reading and language comprehension.

Research supports the value of explicit, systematic teaching of reading and reading-related language abilities for students with SLI and other language disorders. For example, a systematic review of literacy interventions for school-age students with developmental language disorders (Coleman, Venediktov, Troia, & Wang, 2013) found benefits for phonics instruction, with strength of evidence ratings strongest for synthetic-phonics approaches. With regard to language comprehension, explicit teaching about sentences with potentially confusing syntax can benefit sentence comprehension and writing, including for students with language impairments and learning disabilities (Saddler, 2012; Westby, 2012; Zipoli, 2017). Narrative language interventions that use oral storytelling, often with visual representations such as icons, manipulatives, or story maps, also can improve students' reading comprehension and writing (Spencer & Petersen, 2020; Zipoli & Merritt, 2022).

Gillon, McNeill, Denston, Scott, and MacFarlane (2020) implemented a classwide intervention called the Better Start Literacy Approach with kindergartners in New Zealand. Researchers conducted the study in a low-income, diverse community that had been severely impacted by a series of destructive earthquakes. The participants included children with identified speech-sound disorders and broader oral language weaknesses. The intervention used evidence-based principles and explicit teaching aimed at improving students' phonological awareness, letter knowledge, vocabulary, and word reading, embedded in the general education curriculum. Results showed that children with oral language weaknesses only, as compared to those with dual weaknesses in speech and language, had better literacy outcomes. Children with dual weaknesses had a strong response to PA and vocabulary instruction, but needed additional support to transfer these skills to reading and spelling. Both language groups, however, had improved literacy outcomes when they received the intervention earlier in the school year.

Overall, the findings reviewed in this section suggest that multicomponent interventions with the features of SL, aimed at both word reading and language comprehension, can benefit many poor readers with MRD, including those with speech/language disabilities.

Sample SL Intervention Activities

This section provides examples of SL intervention activities that can help early-stage readers with MRD. These students can also benefit from intervention activities discussed in previous chapters, as long as the activities are appropriate to students' specific needs in word reading or language comprehension, and are combined in an intervention that addresses both areas. Furthermore—again, if chosen to match individual students' needs—the word reading activities described in this section can also benefit early-stage readers with specific word recognition difficulties (SWRD), such as those discussed in Chapter 4, and the comprehension activities can benefit students with SRCD, such as those discussed in Chapter 6.

A Beginning Word Sort for Teaching Syllable Types

Word sorts for teaching syllable types were discussed in Chapter 4, using a word sort appropriate for Ruben, who was ready to learn the SE syllable type. However, Dashawn is at a somewhat earlier stage of decoding than Ruben, and he does not know any syllable types yet. Here is how Ms. Odesky introduces syllable types to Dashawn and his intervention group.

1. She reviews which letters are vowels (*a, e, i, o, u*) and which are consonants (all the other letters), a distinction that has been previously taught. (She leaves out *y* for now because that letter can be either a vowel or a consonant.) Dashawn's group knows this information well, so Ms. Odesky reviews it simply by eliciting it from the students. When this distinction was first taught, she had students sort single letters on letter cards into separate piles labeled <u>V</u> and <u>C</u>, or mark vowels and consonants in a random list of letters, using the letters *v* and *c*.

2. Ms. Odesky reminds the students that although they know both long- and short-vowel sounds, most of the words they have learned to read so far have short vowels. Soon they are going to learn how to read many read new words, and they will need to know whether to make the vowel short or long. Knowing about syllable types can help them decide the vowel sound. The first syllable type to learn is closed. That is what they will learn today.

3. Using the same general procedure described in Chapter 4, in the section on "Word Sorts for Syllable Types," Ms. Odesky explains the closed-syllable type. (See Table 2.1: A closed word has only one vowel and ends in a consonant; the vowel will be short.) She notes that the term *closed* comes from the idea that the consonant(s) at the end of the word close up the vowel. Then she shows various examples of closed and not-closed, one-syllable words, modeling how to decide whether the word is a closed syllable. She does not employ potentially confusing words such as those with a vowel *r* (e.g., *corn, star*) or those that are irregular (e.g., *what*). The children will learn VR and additional word patterns later, after they have mastered reading closed and SE syllables; they learn irregular words in a different part of the lesson.

4. With teacher guidance, students practice classifying several examples of words as closed or not closed. Ms. Odesky then follows up with a sorting task in which students are given words on index cards to sort into two piles (see Figure 8.2). In the sorting task, as well as her initial introduction of closed syllables, Ms. Odesky does not distinguish different short-vowel patterns, such as CVC words and short-vowel words with blends or digraphs because those distinctions are not relevant to the vowel sound. She wants the students to grasp this last point, so she uses a range of short-vowel patterns. She also avoids words that students are likely to know by sight (e.g., *cat*) because she wants them to focus on the letter pattern in the word rather than determine the vowel sound by reading the word first.

5. Once students have sorted the words, Ms. Odesky has students take turns reading the closed-syllable pile, first giving the vowel sound, then reading the word (e.g., "/o/, drop"). If students have difficulty blending a more difficult word (e.g., *spend*, *thrill*), Ms. Odesky provides appropriate scaffolding and feedback.

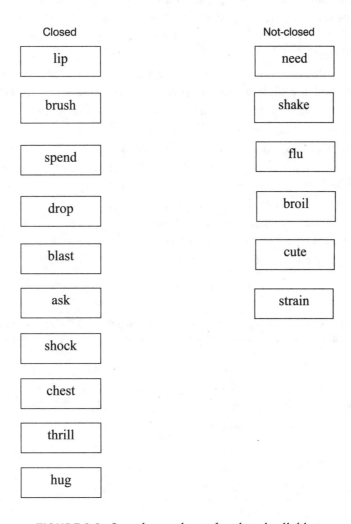

FIGURE 8.2. Sample word sort for closed syllables.

SL Activities for Vowel Team Words

Mr. Murphy has been working with Ellie for several weeks, and he has had the opportunity to teach her numerous VR and VT patterns that she did not know, using flash cards with the patterns on them (e.g., *ir*, *or*, *ai*, *ay*). However, he has found that Ellie still has some difficulties decoding these patterns within words (e.g., *chirp*, *storm*, *paid*, *clay*). She does not always look carefully at letter sequences within words, especially in the middle of words. He has designed an SL activity, shown in Figure 8.3, to help Ellie with this problem. (For a template version of this figure optimized for student use, see Form 8.1 on page 206.)

In the activity, Ellie is given a list of words with VR or VT patterns that she has learned. The activity shown in Figure 8.3 focuses on three vowel teams—words with *ai*, *ay*, and *aw*. The activity requires Ellie to underline the patterns in words, give the sound of the pattern, then read the word. Once Ellie becomes consistently successful with this task, Mr. Murphy will gradually drop the steps of underlining and then saying the VT sound, and Ellie will simply read the word. Moreover, because Mr. Murphy wants Ellie to look closely at each word, he has included some non-examples—words that do not have any of the VTs in them. Ellie can skip over these words and is not expected to read them.

Ellie also practices spelling some of these words using a column activity similar to the one described for Destiny in Chapter 5. Ellie's activity contrasts one-syllable words with *ay* (e.g., *pray*, *stay*, *clay*, *tray*) and *aw* (*draw*, *claw*, *law*, *straw*), using two columns labeled <u>ay</u> and <u>aw</u>. Before Ellie tries this activity, Mr. Murphy teaches her two helpful generalizations for spelling: A long /a/ sound at the end of a one-syllable word is spelled with *ay*, and the sound /aw/ at the end of a one-syllable word is usually spelled with *aw*. Similar to Destiny's activity, Mr. Murphy dictates multiple words that randomly alternate between the two columns (e.g., *pray*, *draw*, *claw*, *clay*, *straw*, *tray*). Ellie first decides on the correct column—that is, the correct vowel team to use—and then she writes the whole word using the correct spelling. If she has difficulty, Mr. Murphy encourages her to watch his mouth as he slowly articulates the

---

Directions: Underline the vowel teams in the words below. Not every word has a vowel team. If a word contains a vowel team, give its sound, then read the word.

str<u>ay</u>	cl<u>aw</u>	m<u>ai</u>d
gr<u>ai</u>n	yam	w<u>ai</u>st
dr<u>aw</u>n	<u>ai</u>m	b<u>ay</u>
dial	branch	<u>ai</u>l
l<u>aw</u>	cl<u>ay</u>	trial
b<u>ai</u>t	st<u>ai</u>n	l<u>aw</u>n
marsh	h<u>aw</u>k	flake

FIGURE 8.3. Vowel-team activity (completed example).

word and stretches the vowel sound, then pair the sound he is making with the correct letter pattern, *ay* or *aw*.

A Map for Narrative Text Structure

Graphic organizers are commonly used to enhance students' comprehension of a variety of text and paragraph structures (see, e.g., Hennessey, 2021; Oakhill et al., 2015; Westby, 2012; Zipoli & Merritt, 2022). Ms. Odesky uses one type of graphic organizer, a map of story elements, to teach Dashawn's group about narrative text structure. This map is shown in Form 8.2 (page 207).

The far left side of the map displays the important story elements of setting (i.e., where and when a story took place) and characters. The plot of a story usually involves a sequence of events, shown in the central part of the map, with a starter event—sometimes termed an initiating event—that kicks off the plot. The starter event can also involve a problem or conflict in a story. A narrative usually ends with some kind of resolution of the plotline, problem, or conflict, shown in the ending box on the far-right side of Form 8.2. Stories also may have a theme or moral, as in Aesop's fables.

Ms. Odesky deliberately uses straightforward language in her narrative map, but she does teach the students the vocabulary words *setting* (where and when a story happens); *characters* (who is in a story, people or animals); and *event* (something important that happens in a story). She introduces the map in relation to a previous read-aloud, a story that students already know well, eliciting various story elements from this story (e.g., "Who were the important characters in _____?"). She explains that most stories are organized a certain way, with key parts in common, and knowing this organization can help students better understand a story.

Because the students in Dashawn's group can currently read only very basic decodable texts, Ms. Odesky does not use these in teaching the narrative map. Rather, she uses the map in conjunction with read-alouds of children's literature appropriate to the students' listening level. For example, after she reads a story aloud to them, she sometimes does a subsequent reading, during which she and the students fill in the parts of the map together. She also elicits inferences from the students, which she explains to them as things that are not actually stated in the story, but that they can figure out based on clues in the story or based on what they already know. She fills in important inferences using dotted lines. Figure 8.4 shows an example of a completed narrative map for a read-aloud of the classic children's book *Strega Nona* (dePaola, 1975).

Maps can be completed in more than one way, to distinguish or highlight somewhat different events within a story. Similarly, many inferences about a story can be made, and which inferences teachers or students choose to show on a map can differ. For *Strega Nona*, Ms. Odesky chose to highlight an inference about Anthony's stomachache that is based both on information in the text and a drawing of Anthony looking queasy on the final page of the book. She knew that the children had the knowledge to make this inference, which provides an amusing conclusion to the story. Many other inferences could also be included. In her future work with Dashawn's group, Ms. Odesky will place increased emphasis on inferencing because this is an area of difficulty for all of the children.

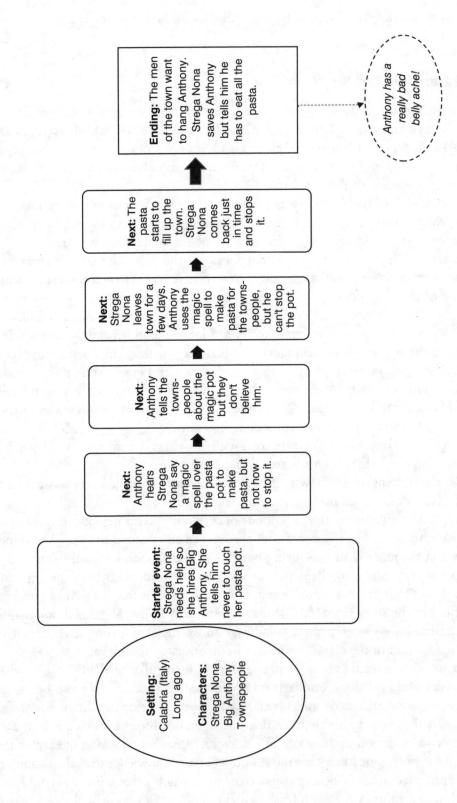

Setting: Calabria (Italy) Long ago

Characters: Strega Nona Big Anthony Townspeople

Starter event: Strega Nona needs help so she hires Big Anthony. She tells him never to touch her pasta pot.

Next: Anthony hears Strega Nona say a magic spell over the pasta pot to make pasta, but not how to stop it.

Next: Anthony tells the townspeople about the magic pot but they don't believe him.

Next: Strega Nona leaves town for a few days. Anthony uses the magic spell to make pasta for the townspeople, but he can't stop the pot.

Next: The pasta starts to fill up the town. Strega Nona comes back just in time and stops it.

Ending: The men of the town want to hang Anthony. Strega Nona saves Anthony but tells him he has to eat all the pasta.

Anthony has a really bad belly ache!

FIGURE 8.4. Example of narrative map for *Strega Nona* (dePaola, 1975).

194

Sentence-Level Activities

Numerous sentence-level activities can benefit both Dashawn and Ellie, although they must be targeted to each student's skills level and specific needs. Due to each student's difficulties with decoding, sentence-level activities should be done orally for now, unless they are written using words the student can decode.

Mr. Murphy is teaching Ellie about common signal words involving continuation (e.g., *also, furthermore, in addition*) and contrast (e.g., *but, however, nevertheless*). (See Chapter 2, Table 2.5.) He begins with sentence-level activities to highlight how these words link clauses within a sentence, or sometimes link a pair of sentences in a longer text. He starts with a subset of the most common signal words for continuation and contrast.

1. First, Mr. Murphy emphasizes that paying attention to signal words can improve one's understanding of a text, as well as improve one's writing. He explains that words involving *continuation* continue a similar idea, whereas those involving *contrast* tell a contrasting, or different, idea. Then he shows and models several examples of these words in sentences, similar to the initial items shown in Form 8.3 (page 208).

2. Next, he follows up with the activity displayed in Form 8.3. Ellie is shown a sentence or pair of sentences containing a blank, as well as three options involving signal words in parentheses at the end. Ellie has to choose the best word out of the three options to fit in the blank. To highlight the ideas of continuation and contrast, Mr. Murphy uses some similarly worded sets of items that exemplify each idea, such as items 1 and 2 in Form 8.3.

3. Because of Ellie's decoding problems, Mr. Murphy reads all sentences and answer options aloud to her, multiple times if needed. He also notes the importance of listening to the entire item, as well as all answer options, before choosing the correct signal word.

4. If Ellie has difficulty determining the correct answer to fill in a blank, Mr. Murphy explains the item in relation to signal words for continuation and contrast. For instance, in the first sentence, the appropriate choice is the word *but*, because the second part of the sentence (*her parents would not let her*) is saying something that differs from, rather than continues, the idea in the first part (*Lucy really wanted to go to the concert*).

5. As Ellie's reading improves and she can read less controlled texts successfully, Mr. Murphy plans to choose sentences from these texts for sentence-level activities, which Ellie will be able to read. He also will encourage Ellie to apply her knowledge of signal words when reading and trying to understand texts.

In addition, Mr. Murphy employs a writing activity that reinforces Ellie's understanding of signal words and can help her use them in her writing. As with the previous activity, for now, he provides help reading and spelling words. In the writing activity, he gives Ellie sentences like the ones below, which include signal words Ellie has been taught, and which require Ellie to complete each sentence in a way that makes sense:

- Jim was very hungry, but _____.
- The day had been very hot. Furthermore, _____.
- Molly dropped a glass while she did the dishes. However, _____.

Comprehension Monitoring

Like many poor readers, Ellie has significant difficulties with comprehension monitoring in reading. In the past, she tended to read texts too quickly, making frequent word-reading errors and rarely stopping to try to self-correct. Since receiving professional development in SL, Mr. Murphy has been using texts more appropriate to Ellie's skills level, as well as encouraging her to think about meaning as she reads. He knows that this advice will not be successful if the texts are too difficult for her, so for now, he has been having her read decodable texts with multiple word patterns (closed, SE, open, some VR and VTs) that she can decode with only occasional support from him. He expects to transition Ellie to less controlled texts, but still ones at her instructional level, in a few weeks.

To improve Ellie's comprehension monitoring, Mr. Murphy began with activities involving illogical sentences such as those shown in Chapter 6 (Figure 6.4). Initially, he read these sentences aloud to Ellie because of her decoding difficulties, with modeling and explanation of what was or was not illogical in each sentence, followed by practice items with oral discussion and questioning. Ellie now does very well with these.

Next, Mr. Murphy has decided to use passages taken from Ellie's current decodable text, with illogical, inconsistent, or unclear sentences inserted in different paragraphs. He also includes non-examples, that is, paragraphs not containing a problematic sentence. Ellie has to locate the problematic sentences within each paragraph, highlight them, and then explain what is illogical, inconsistent, or unclear, with Mr. Murphy providing coaching as needed. Figure 8.5 displays an example of this activity. (For a template version of this figure optimized for student use, see Form 8.4 on page 209.)

In the first two paragraphs in Figure 8.5, each of the highlighted sentences is illogical. It does not make sense that Jake and his father would return the fish to the lake after Jake's mother had baked it for dinner, and it does not make sense that the truck would go faster after Jake's dad slammed on the brakes. The third paragraph is a non-example, one without a problematic sentence, to help ensure that Ellie reads carefully and monitors comprehension. The last paragraph has a sentence that is problematic in two ways. The description of the kitten as big and red is not consistent with the previous information that it was small and black, with white markings on its legs. Also, Mr. Murphy knows that Ellie is unlikely to be able to decode the word *feline* or to know what the word means. He plans to use this word as a way to begin teaching fix-up strategies, such as looking up an unfamiliar word in an online resource.

Directions: Find the sentence in each paragraph that does not make sense and highlight it. Not every paragraph has this kind of sentence.

1. On Saturdays, Jake and his dad go to the lake. They can hike in the hills. They can also go fishing in the lake. Jake and his dad really like to fish a lot. If they catch a fish, they bring it home and Jake's mom bakes it for dinner. ==Then Jake and his dad bring the fish back to the lake.==

2. One Saturday, Jake is in the truck with his dad. As they drive down the street, a cat jumps in front of them. Jake's dad slams on the brakes and turns the wheel to the left. ==The truck goes faster and faster.== Jake's belt pulls snug across his chest and lap. The truck quickly comes to a stop. Jake is very glad to see that the truck missed the cat, who runs back to the sidewalk and up a tree.

3. Now Jake can see that the cat is really a kitten. It has black fluffy fur with white markings on its legs. It clings to a branch and makes a sad meow. Jake jumps out of the truck. He wants to save the kitten, but his dad does not want him to go after it. He thinks that Jake could fall and get hurt.

4. So Jake's dad goes after the kitten himself. After some time, he gets it and brings it to Jake. ==The feline is big and red.== Jake pets the kitten for a while and wants to take it home, but Jake's dad says no. They must check that the kitten is not someone's pet.

FIGURE 8.5. Sample comprehension monitoring activity in a decodable text (completed example).

SL Intervention Plans for Early-Stage Readers with MRD

Table 8.2 displays an intervention plan that may be useful in interventions with early-stage readers with MRD. The plan is adapted from Spear-Swerling (2022a) and addresses both word reading and language comprehension. It involves broad segments for four areas: word recognition and spelling; fluency; language comprehension, text reading and reading comprehension; and writing to reinforce or develop important components of reading.

Table 8.2 includes a description, sample activities, and suggested time allocations for each lesson segment, with a total lesson time of 45–60 minutes. However, as with other intervention plans in this book, the plan for students with MRD can be adapted in many ways. For instance, for students like Ellie who are far behind, the full intervention time is likely required, although it could be delivered in two sessions a day rather than in one long block, if necessary. For students with milder needs, less time in intervention may be required. For all students, time allocations for the various lesson segments may be adjusted to reflect individual students' needs.

As discussed in Chapter 4, the first lesson segment, word recognition and spelling, involves multiple bulleted areas. Not every bulleted area will necessarily be covered

TABLE 8.2. Format for a Multicomponent Intervention Plan for Students with MRD

Component(s)	Description	Sample activities
Word recognition and spelling (~15–20 minutes) • Phonemic awareness (PA) • Phoneme–grapheme, grapheme–phoneme, and morphological relationships • Generalizations (rules) • Decoding unfamiliar words • Spelling words • Irregular (exception) words	Skills for reading and spelling printed words • Key PA skills such as phoneme blending and segmentation • Correspondences for single letters, letter patterns (e.g., *sh, ch, ay*), and morphemes (e.g., *-ed, -ing, -ful, un-, re-*) • Generalizations for decoding (e.g., -VCe) and spelling (e.g., adding suffixes to a -VCe base word) • Apply above skills to decode unfamiliar printed words. • Apply above skills to spell printed words. • Read and spell words that are exceptions to common phonics relationships.	• Oral practice with teacher modeling and counters • Explicit teaching with letter cards; multisensory activities • Explicit teaching of generalizations; word sorts; flexibility training • Word-building activities with letter tiles; decoding a set of sorted words on index cards • Word-building activities with letter tiles; writing words; column activities • Multisensory activities; highlight regularities as well as irregularities in words; mnemonics
Fluency (~5 minutes)	Practice reading words automatically and reading text fluently.	Timed flash card practice on irregular words; repeated reading of familiar text, timed or untimed; purposeful fluency activities
Language comprehension, text reading, and reading comprehension (~15–25 minutes)	Developing important areas of oral language comprehension relevant to reading, including vocabulary; *and* application of decoding and language comprehension skills to accurate reading of an unfamiliar text with comprehension	Teacher read-alouds of listening-level text with comprehension questions and discussion; word maps for vocabulary; explicit teaching of text-specific vocabulary; sentence-level activities, done orally or with sentences selected from texts students are reading; guided oral reading with teacher feedback to decoding errors, and with discussion and questions about texts students have read
Writing (~10 minutes)	Using writing to teach or reinforce important components of reading, both foundational skills (e.g., phonemic awareness, decoding, spelling) and higher-level skills (e.g., reading comprehension, text composition)	Write and spell dictated sentences; answer in writing questions about text that students have read or listened to; sentence-combining activities

Note. From Spear-Swerling (2022a). Copyright © 2022 The Guilford Press. Reprinted by permission.

in every session, and some students may not need work in every area. As an example, although in the primary grades Ellie had significant needs in PA, currently she has the phoneme segmentation and blending skills she needs to decode one-syllable words. Phoneme blending and segmentation may need some additional attention as Ellie progresses to multisyllabic words; if so, this teaching can be done in conjunction with her decoding and spelling intervention, as described for Conor in Chapter 5 (see, e.g., Figure 5.7).

In the intervention plan, language comprehension, text reading, and reading comprehension are combined in one segment because students with MRD typically need intervention in all of these areas. Also, the activities for these areas are often highly interrelated and sometimes done concurrently. For example, as students read a text aloud, the teacher usually asks comprehension questions and discusses the text, and may also draw students' attention to text structure or new vocabulary. This segment may also include sentence-level activities such as those aimed at challenging syntax and inferring word meanings from context.

Many comprehension activities that may be included in this lesson segment—such as those involving vocabulary, syntax, text structure, and inferencing—can be done either orally or in conjunction with students' text reading. For early-stage readers with MRD, usually these areas are initially best taught in the context of oral activities and teacher read-alouds because the texts that students can read are too basic to adequately address these areas. Knowledge and skills developed orally can positively impact students' reading comprehension (Clarke et al., 2014), and, for those with MRD, should transfer to students' reading comprehension as their decoding abilities improve. Of course, even if students can only read very simple decodable texts, it is still important to ensure that they are comprehending and monitoring comprehension as they read. However, for students at these early stages of word reading, oral language activities can be especially valuable in improving comprehension because in these activities, the students are not hampered by their limitations in decoding.

As part of this third segment, it is essential to include oral, not silent, text reading as part of lessons for early-stage readers with MRD. Like students with SWRD, students with MRD need practice applying their decoding skills in text reading with guidance from a teacher and appropriate teacher feedback to errors. Oral text reading is also important to the teacher's ability to monitor students' accuracy of word reading in passages. Within this segment of the lesson, the amount of time that teachers spend on oral language, text reading, and reading comprehension activities—as well as the sequencing of these activities—may vary depending on individual students' needs, and the skills the teacher plans to address in a given lesson.

Progress monitoring assessments should be used to decide whether time allocations for any part of the lesson require adjustment. Suppose, for instance, that progress monitoring assessments show that students are progressing in their phonics skills for single words but are not consistently applying those skills in text reading (e.g., because they often guess at words based on context). This suggests that more time needs to be spent on text reading, with teacher feedback that encourages application of decoding skills rather than guessing.

A Sample Intervention Lesson for Ellie

Table 8.3 displays a sample 60-minute intervention lesson for Ellie, delivered one-to-one, using the plan from Table 8.2.

The lesson segment for word reading and spelling focuses on teaching one-syllable VR and VT words, the phonics skills that Ellie needs to master next. Previously learned letter sounds and word patterns are also briefly reviewed in this section, as well as practiced in the context of Ellie's text reading and writing. In addition to other activities, this segment uses the underlining activity shown in Figure 8.3.

Ellie's text reading is in a decodable chapter book, and for fluency practice, Ellie does a brief reread—a few minutes' worth—at the end of the chapter she read in the last lesson. This also serves as a reminder of what was happening in the book when Ellie last read it. Mr. Murphy does not use timing of repeated reading with Ellie, although he has used timing successfully with several of his other students. In Ellie's case, though, he is concerned that timing might worsen Ellie's tendency to read too quickly, without attending to meaning as she reads. Instead, he emphasizes accurate reading with attention to meaning, as well as appropriate prosody.

For the third lesson segment, Ellie begins with the comprehension monitoring activity shown in Form 8.3 and described in that part of the chapter. She does her first reading of the new text silently, looking for the illogical sentences. After she and Mr. Murphy discuss those sentences, she reads the text again, this time orally. Mr. Murphy asks both literal and inferential questions as she reads and provides appropriate feedback to any decoding errors that Ellie makes. At the end of this lesson segment, Mr. Murphy teaches three new content-vocabulary words—*architecture, currency,* and *famine*—that Ellie needs to learn for her social studies class. Even though the words are well beyond Ellie's present level of decoding, Mr. Murphy writes them on a whiteboard as he discusses them. He has Ellie repeat each word, then, when he orally gives the definition of each word in an unpredictable order, Ellie has to tell which word goes with the definition (e.g., "Which new word is another word for money? Is it *famine, architecture,* or *currency*?").

For the final writing segment of the lesson, Ellie uses each new content-vocabulary word in a sentence illustrating its meaning. She is expected to apply previously taught spelling and basic writing skills correctly, but Mr. Murphy helps with harder words that she has not yet learned to spell. The point of this activity is mainly to help Ellie remember the new words, but for other lessons, Mr. Murphy will use different writing activities, such as the one described for signal words involving continuation and contrast. He also will teach a broader range of vocabulary (i.e., Tier 2 as well as Tier 3 words) as he transitions Ellie to less controlled text.

Mr. Murphy and Ellie's speech–language teacher now collaborate much more closely than they did before the changes to Ellie's reading program. The two teachers work on many of the same language areas—such as vocabulary, sentence structure, and listening comprehension—but they now better coordinate their work to provide greater intensity for Ellie. For example, in their teaching of vocabulary, both teachers address morphology, and they include the same roots and affixes in instruction. School administrators have supported these efforts by providing some additional planning and collaboration time for both teachers.

TABLE 8.3. Sample Intervention Lesson for Ellie

Component(s)	Activity
Word recognition and spelling (20 minutes) • Review of previously learned sounds for letters and letter patterns, especially short vowels, long vowels, common consonant digraphs, previously taught VR patterns (e.g., *ar, or, ur, ir, er*) and VT patterns (e.g., *ai, ay, aw*) • Decode words with new/review VR and VT patterns, as well as previously mastered word patterns (e.g., closed, SE) • Generalizations for spelling: at the end of a short word, use *ay* to spell long /a/ and *aw* to spell /aw/ • Spell one-syllable VT words with *ay* and *aw*	• Teacher uses flash cards to quickly review previously learned sounds (timed, 1 minute); teacher does a second review of any missed sounds (1 minute). • Teacher emphasizes importance of attending to letter patterns within words. • Ellie completes underlining activity involving *ai, ay, aw* within words and reads the words. • Teacher reviews six to eight additional words that include previously taught patterns (e.g., *turn, far, brake, stem*) by writing words for Ellie to read. • Teacher explains spelling generalization about using *ay* and *aw* at the end of a short word, pointing out examples of words from the underlining activity. • Ellie completes column activity involving spelling of words with *ay* and *aw*, writing several dictated words in each column.
Fluency (5 minutes)	Ellie rereads end of last chapter from a decodable text, with a focus on accuracy, prosody, and reading with attention to meaning.
Language comprehension, text reading, and reading comprehension (25 minutes)	• Ellie completes comprehension monitoring activity from the next chapter of her decodable text, first reading the text silently; teacher discusses with Ellie, focusing on any errors in finding illogical sentences and introducing the idea of fix-up strategies, to be explicitly taught in a subsequent lesson. • Ellie reads the same text orally (without the illogical sentences); teacher provides feedback to any decoding errors and asks literal and inferential questions as Ellie reads. • Teacher explicitly and orally teaches three new content-vocabulary words from Ellie's social studies class: *architecture* (the design of buildings); *currency* (money); *famine* (severe lack of food that causes people to starve). • Ellie repeats each word and says the word when the teacher gives its definition orally.
Writing (10 minutes)	Using a written model of the new vocabulary words, Ellie writes each of the new words in a sentence that shows its meaning; she is expected to apply previously learned spelling and basic writing skills correctly, but teacher helps with words she has not yet learned to spell.

Additional Considerations for Written Expression

Just as in reading, in interventions for written expression, students with MRD require multicomponent interventions. These interventions should include both basic writing skills, especially spelling, and higher-level text-generation abilities that involve translating one's thoughts into language. Students' specific writing needs tend to reflect their underlying language problems. Dashawn, whose language weaknesses include vocabulary and background knowledge, displays those weaknesses in his writing, as well as his reading. Similarly, Ellie's difficulties with syntax and other language areas are evident in her writing, not just her reading. Individual students' language weaknesses should be addressed in both reading and writing, and doing so can facilitate students' learning in both areas.

For most early-stage readers with MRD, and similar to those with SWRD, spelling is an especially important area to address in writing interventions. Many early-stage readers with MRD require intervention in the phonological aspects of spelling, since their difficulties with word reading tend to involve underlying phonological weaknesses. Spelling activities such as those focused on phoneme segmentation and phoneme–grapheme relationships can also be a very effective way to build word-reading skills (Herron & Gillis, 2020; Moats, 2020, 2022).

SUMMING UP: SL Interventions for Early-Stage Readers with MRD

Here are key points from this chapter:

- All students with MRD require multicomponent interventions that address both word reading and language comprehension.

- Early-stage readers with MRD require interventions focused on both basic word-reading and spelling skills at the one-syllable stage and on the specific areas of language comprehension in which they are weak.

- Examples of intervention activities that can benefit these students include underlining or circling common letter patterns within words to facilitate decoding words with those patterns; narrative maps to enhance comprehension of narratives; sentence-level activities, such as those involving signal words; and comprehension monitoring activities, such as those involving illogical sentences embedded within passages for students to identify.

- Early-stage readers with MRD can benefit from many of the intervention activities discussed in previous chapters, especially in Chapters 4 and 6, if activities are selected to suit individual students' needs.

- In written expression, these students require multicomponent interventions that address both basic writing skills such as spelling and higher-level text generation abilities; these interventions should be targeted to individual students' specific writing difficulties, which often reflect their underlying language weaknesses.

APPLIED EXERCISES

Exercise 1

Consider the assessment data (e.g., Table 8.1) and other information provided about Dashawn in this chapter, as well as the intervention plan in Table 8.2. Which specific letter sounds (grapheme–phoneme relationships) would you want to address in the first segment of the lesson? Which specific word patterns (e.g., CVC, closed with digraphs, SE, VR) would be most important to address in word decoding and spelling?

Answer

Dashawn and his intervention group need to master decoding one-syllable, short-vowel (i.e., closed syllable) words with consonant digraphs and blends. The most important letter sounds they must know to decode these words successfully are sounds for short vowels and common consonant digraphs (e.g., *sh, ch, th, wh*), so these should be reviewed, with special attention to *sh* and *ch*, because Dashawn confuses these. Sounds for blends do not need to be learned as separate patterns because children can decode blends by sounding out the individual letters in the blend.

For word reading, the most important patterns to include are closed syllables with digraphs and blends. Children's difficulties with blends can be addressed in decoding these words. The same word patterns should also be addressed in spelling, using different examples of words than the ones used for decoding, to help promote generalization of phonics skills. Previously learned sounds (e.g., single consonants) and word patterns (e.g., CVC words) should also be included as a review. However, unless children are having difficulty with a previously learned skill, the review should be fast paced, to allow more time for developing new skills.

Exercise 2

Why do Dashawn and the other children in his group need to read decodable text in their intervention? Which specific word patterns should Dashawn be able to read in this text?

Answer

Dashawn and his group are still at an early stage of decoding, and a decodable text provides them with more practice applying decoding skills to text reading. Also, an uncontrolled text will likely contain many words they cannot decode, potentially leading to maladaptive strategies such as guessing. Dashawn should be able to read a decodable text with CVC words, as well as some short-vowel words with digraphs and blends. The teacher can start with a decodable text that seems to be a reasonable match to the children's decoding skills, then use progress monitoring assessments of children's word accuracy and comprehension in that text, adjusting to a more or less advanced text as needed. For example, if children's word accuracy often drops below 90% in a text, then an easier text should be tried.

Exercise 3

For Dashawn's language comprehension development, would you use a decodable? If so, explain why; if not, say why not, and provide an example of the type of text you would use.

Answer

Decodables are not the best type of text to use for language comprehension development because they are highly constrained to specific word patterns, which tends to limit the vocabulary, rich language, and background knowledge they contain. For language comprehension, read-alouds of children's literature would be most appropriate for Dashawn and his group. Because Dashawn's language comprehension weaknesses do not appear to be severe, read-alouds can probably employ age- and grade-appropriate texts, with some scaffolding from the teacher. Other comprehension activities, such as teaching about narrative text structure and new vocabulary, can be combined with the read-aloud.

Exercise 4

What would be an example of an appropriate vocabulary intervention activity for Dashawn and his group? An appropriate writing activity? Consider relevant activities from previous chapters, as well as those in the current chapter.

Answer

Any of the vocabulary activities discussed in Chapter 6—explicit teaching of specific words, word maps, teaching about how to infer word meanings from context, and teaching about basic morphology (e.g., *un* as in *unhappy* means *not*)—could benefit Dashawn's group. Writing activities could focus on basic writing skills, especially spelling, such as sentence dictation that incorporates spelling and other basic writing skills (e.g., ending punctuation) that Dashawn has been taught. Writing activities can also focus on text-generation skills, such as using new vocabulary words in a sentence, but in that case would have to be designed in a way that enables Dashawn to complete the writing task despite his limited spelling skills (e.g., by using technology).

If you have completed previous exercises 1 through 4, you have addressed most of an intervention lesson for Dashawn. Please see Table 8.4 for a sample

45-minute intervention lesson for Dashawn and his group. This sample uses the word sort shown in Figure 8.2 and the narrative map shown in Form 8.2. Other sample lessons, using other activities, could also be appropriate. For instance, the fluency segment could use the timed repeated reading activity described in Chapter 4, in an appropriate decodable text, in lieu of the untimed activity shown in the sample lesson.

TABLE 8.4. Sample Intervention Lesson for Dashawn (with Two Other Students)

Component(s)	Activity
Word recognition and spelling (15 minutes)	
• Review of single consonants, short vowels (all but *y*), long vowels (all but *y*), and *sh, ch, th, wh, ck*	• Teacher uses flash cards to quickly review previously learned sounds for letters/letter patterns (timed, 1 minute); teacher does a second review of any missed sounds (1 minute).
• Closed-syllable type	• Teacher briefly reviews which letters are vowels and which are consonants (omitting *y*) by eliciting from students.
	• Teacher explains closed syllables with multiple examples and non-examples; students sort closed and not-closed syllables.
• Decode and spell words (CVC, closed syllables with blends and digraphs)	• Students take turns reading sorted closed syllables.
	• Students spell five closed syllables with blends and digraphs dictated orally by the teacher (e.g., *mash, flip, ramp*); teacher provides scaffolding and feedback as needed.
• Review previously taught irregular words	• Teacher does flash card review of previously taught irregular words (timed, 1 minute).
Fluency (5 minutes)	Students take turns rereading from a familiar (previously read) decodable text with short vowel words, with an emphasis on accuracy, prosody, and fluency of reading.
Language comprehension, text reading, and reading comprehension (20 minutes)	• Text reading and reading comprehension: Students take turns reading from an unfamiliar (new) decodable text with short vowel words; teacher provides feedback to decoding errors and also asks literal and inferential questions to ensure students understand text.
	• Review of previously introduced narrative map (done orally): Teacher shows map, reviews its parts, and elicits relevant vocabulary meanings from students (e.g., *setting, characters*); tells students that next time they will complete a map for a new story, *Strega Nona*.
	• Teacher read-aloud of *Strega Nona*, with literal and inferential questions and discussion.
	• During read-aloud, teacher introduces two Tier 2 vocabulary words (e.g., *valuable, steaming*).
Writing (5 minutes)	Teacher dictates three sentences for students to write, with closed syllables, previously taught irregular words, and learned conventions for basic writing (e.g., ending punctuation, capitalization of the word *I* and names).

Vowel Team Activity (Template Version)

Directions: Underline the vowel teams in the words below. Not every word has a vowel team. If a word contains a vowel team, give its sound, then read the word.

stray	claw	maid
grain	yam	waist
drawn	aim	bay
dial	branch	ail
law	clay	trial
bait	stain	lawn
marsh	hawk	flake

Map for Narrative Text (Template Version)

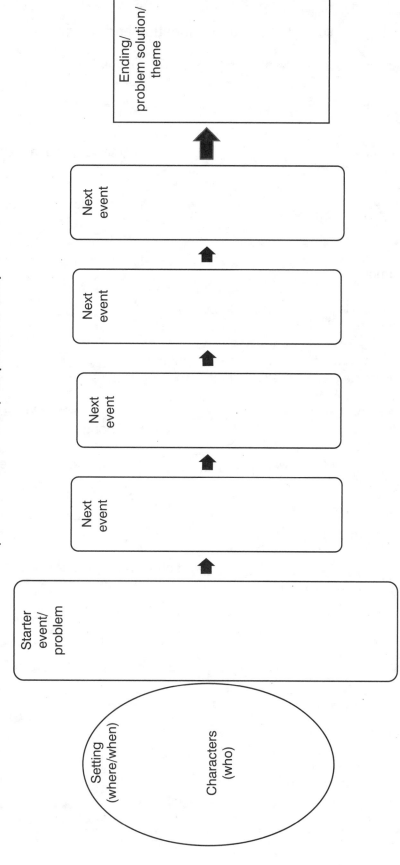

Sentences for Signal Words Involving Continuation and Contrast

Directions: Decide which word or phrase in parentheses fits best in the blank.

1. Lucy really wanted to go to the concert, _____ her parents would not let her. (also, but, furthermore)

2. Angie planned to go to the movies, _____ her parents agreed that she could go.   (and, although, however)

3. Jim tripped and cut his knee; _____, he twisted his ankle. (but, also, however)

4. Tom fell and banged his head, _____ luckily he was not badly hurt. (in addition, although, furthermore)

5. While Mary was cooking, a dish towel next to the stove caught fire. _____, Mary had a fire extinguisher and quickly put it out. (and, also, however)

6. While Rick was cooking, a dish towel next to the stove caught fire. _____, the fire started to spread to some paper towels. (furthermore, nevertheless, but)

7. Mrs. Jones gave the students piles of homework; _____, she told them there would be a quiz at the end of the week.   (however, in addition, although)

8. Mr. Smith gave the students piles of homework, _____ afterward, he cancelled some of it. (furthermore, and, but)

9. The snowstorm lasted all night. _____, it kept snowing the next day. (nevertheless, however, furthermore)

10. The snowstorm lasted all night. _____, school was not cancelled the next day. (in addition, furthermore, nevertheless)

Sample Comprehension Monitoring Activity in a Decodable Text (Template Version)

Directions: Find the sentence in each paragraph that does not make sense and highlight it. Not every paragraph has this kind of sentence.

1. On Saturdays, Jake and his dad go to the lake. They can hike in the hills. They can also go fishing in the lake. Jake and his dad really like to fish a lot. If they catch a fish, they bring it home and Jake's mom bakes it for dinner. Then Jake and his dad bring the fish back to the lake.

2. One Saturday, Jake is in the truck with his dad. As they drive down the street, a cat jumps in front of them. Jake's dad slams on the brakes and turns the wheel to the left. The truck goes faster and faster. Jake's belt pulls snug across his chest and lap. The truck quickly comes to a stop. Jake is very glad to see that the truck missed the cat, who runs back to the sidewalk and up a tree.

3. Now Jake can see that the cat is really a kitten. It has black fluffy fur with white markings on its legs. It clings to a branch and makes a sad meow. Jake jumps out of the truck. He wants to save the kitten, but his dad does not want him to go after it. He thinks that Jake could fall and get hurt.

4. So Jake's dad goes after the kitten himself. After some time, he gets it and brings it to Jake. The feline is big and red. Jake pets the kitten for a while and wants to take it home, but Jake's dad says no. They must check that the kitten is not someone's pet.

CHAPTER 9

Structured Literacy Interventions for Mixed Reading Difficulties

Advanced Stages

Chapter 3 described detailed assessment data for Lucas, an eighth grader with mixed reading difficulties (MRD) based in language comprehension, as well as reading multisyllabic words. While Chapter 3 described some broad recommendations for Lucas's intervention, this chapter provides more detailed examples of specific SL activities that could help him. Tanya, a fifth grader identified with dyslexia who also has executive function (EF) difficulties associated with ADHD, is another example of an advanced-stage reader with a profile of MRD. Like Lucas, Tanya's intervention needs include reading of long words, as well as comprehension.

This chapter focuses on SL interventions for students with MRD who are functioning at relatively advanced stages of reading. Similar to those discussed in previous chapters, these students can vary in age, the severity of their reading difficulties, and the underlying causes of their poor reading, which may or may not involve a disability. The chapter begins with some additional information about both Tanya and Lucas. Next, it summarizes some issues in teaching advanced-stage readers with MRD, as well as intervention research relevant to them. Finally, the chapter describes specific SL intervention activities that are effective for these students, with applied practice activities and sample intervention plans.

Tanya

Tanya's reading difficulties became apparent early in first grade, when she struggled with phoneme blending, phoneme segmentation, and decoding and spelling of simple

CVC words. However, at this early grade level, her comprehension was seen as a strength. Tanya's father had a history of problems in learning to read, and when Tanya failed to progress in the literacy intervention her district provided, her parents referred her for a comprehensive evaluation. As a result of this evaluation, in the middle of grade 2, Tanya was identified with dyslexia.

Tanya's special education instruction has used an intensive SL intervention that emphasizes PA, word reading, spelling, and reading fluency—similar to the types of SL interventions described for students with specific word recognition difficulties (SWRD) in Chapter 4. In her SL intervention, Tanya made very good progress in her ability to read one- and two-syllable words, as well as transfer these skills to the reading of text. There was also clear progress in her rate and fluency of reading, although progress in this area went more slowly than her progress in accuracy. Unfortunately, however, in grade 4, a new problem emerged involving reading comprehension. This new problem was not simply a secondary consequence of Tanya's decoding difficulties, which had been greatly improved but not completely eliminated by her SL intervention, because difficulties with reading comprehension were now evident even when Tanya was reading texts at her instructional level, texts she could decode well. Around this time, Tanya was also diagnosed with ADHD and difficulties with EF.

Teachers have noted that Tanya does not consistently monitor comprehension, in either listening or reading; furthermore, when her comprehension breaks down, she does not use strategies to repair comprehension, such as asking questions or rereading. She has particular difficulty with the more challenging informational texts of the middle elementary grades, such as determining the main points of the text. On the state reading assessment, she sometimes answered questions incorrectly that teachers thought she probably knew because she appeared to skip over some questions and multiple-choice answer options. On the positive side, teachers view Tanya's background knowledge and vocabulary as strengths.

Recently Tanya had a triennial evaluation to determine whether her reading or other special education needs had changed, as well as whether she continued to be eligible for services. Figure 9.1 displays an assessment map with Tanya's standardized reading and language scores from this evaluation.

The map shows that Tanya's vocabulary is solidly average, and her broad oral language comprehension is only slightly below average range (standard score [SS] = 88). Also, a speech–language screening did not suggest any disabilities in this area. However, Tanya continues to demonstrate some weaknesses in both real-word and nonsense-word reading, involving accuracy as well as automaticity, as well as some weaknesses in PA. Furthermore, as anticipated based on her word-reading problems, Tanya's accuracy of text reading, as well as her rate and fluency of text reading, are below average. Although these data do show improvement from Tanya's earlier evaluation for special education, it is clear that she still requires intervention in the areas of word reading and reading fluency.

Tanya's reading comprehension scores, shown on the right-hand side of Figure 9.1, suggest that reading comprehension is a significant area of need. These scores are substantially lower than one would predict based on her oral language comprehension

Student *Tanya*   Grade *5*   Dates of Testing *Dec 12–Jan 25*

ORAL LANGUAGE COMPREHENSION

Oral Vocabulary (note receptive/expressive)

WIAT–4 Receptive Vocabulary 98

WIAT–4 Expressive Vocabulary 101

Oral Language (Listening) Comprehension (note format, e.g., cloze, maze, QA)

WIAT–4 Oral Discourse Comprehension (QA) **88**

Other Oral Language

Oral Reading Fluency— Accuracy

GORT–5 Accuracy Scaled Score **7**

Oral Reading Fluency— Rate

GORT–5 Rate Scaled Score **6**

WIAT–4 ORF **81**

Silent Reading Fluency

Reading Comprehension (note test format, e.g., cloze, maze, QA, as well as other relevant features such as timing)

GORT–5 Comprehension (timed; QA) **4**

WIAT–4 Reading Comprehension (untimed; QA) **80**

State reading assessment (untimed; QA; Grade 4) **below basic level**

Observations

Student's vocabulary and background knowledge met grade expectations; sometimes had trouble recognizing main points of a text; on the state assessment, sometimes overlooked items or did not consider all answer options

WORD READING

Real Words—Accuracy

WIAT–4 Word Reading **85**

Nonsense Words— Accuracy

WIAT–4 Pseudoword Decoding **88**

Word Reading— Automaticity

WIAT–4 Orthographic Fluency **82**

WIAT–4 Decoding Fluency **84**

Phonological/phonemic awareness

WIAT–4 Phonemic Proficiency **86**

CTOPP Phonological Awareness Composite **88**

FIGURE 9.1. Assessment map for Tanya.

and vocabulary knowledge. Tanya's difficulties with word reading and reading fluency undoubtedly impact her reading comprehension negatively in some texts, partially accounting for her reading comprehension problems. However, the observations in the lower right corner of Figure 9.1, as well as her teachers' observations of Tanya's classroom performance in reading, suggest that problems with EF also play a role in her comprehension difficulties.

Moreover, unlike Tanya's word reading, her reading comprehension problems appear to be worsening. In her previous evaluation, Tanya's reading comprehension scores were higher, and comprehension was not seen as a problem. At least in part, this pattern may reflect increases in expectations for reading comprehension as Tanya has advanced in school. When she first began receiving special education services in grade 2, Tanya was only able to read very basic decodable texts that did not make heavy demands on her comprehension, whereas in grade 5, her decoding has improved to the point that she can read more challenging texts. Grade expectations for comprehension have also increased greatly from grade 2 to 5.

Diagnostic assessments provide further detail about Tanya's intervention needs and are consistent with the standardized testing shown in the map. A criterion-referenced phonics assessment indicated that Tanya's current difficulties in word reading revolve almost entirely around reading long words, mostly words of three or more syllables. A frequent error pattern in Tanya's word reading is that she does not know sounds for many morphemes, especially more advanced roots, prefixes, and suffixes used in academic words. On an ORI, Tanya's highest instructional level on graded word lists was grade 4, slightly below grade placement, but her highest instructional level in passages was grade 3, reflecting difficulties in comprehension, as well as word reading.

In spelling, Tanya's skills lag significantly behind her word-reading skills. She can spell one-syllable words with short vowels correctly, including those with consonant blends and digraphs. She also knows some basic spelling rules, such as the floss rule, which have been taught in her SL intervention program. However, her performance is still very variable for one-syllable, regular words with alternative spellings (e.g., *chain* vs. *chane*, *skirt* vs. *skert*); and on long words, she sometimes omits phonemes or sequences them incorrectly (e.g., *govermint* for *government*). Tanya's typical spelling errors, taken from informal spelling assessments and writing samples, are shown on the left-hand side of Table 9.1.

Tanya's triennial evaluation determined that she continued to be eligible for special education, but that she did have some additional instructional needs. Her special education teacher, Jen Rosen, is planning to adjust Tanya's reading program to include SL interventions in comprehension, as well as word reading, spelling, and fluency.

Lucas

Assessment data for Lucas are detailed in Chapter 3. These data show that Lucas's reading intervention needs involved instruction in decoding long words, including flexibility training and sounds for letter patterns common in long words (e.g., *ph*, *ps* in

TABLE 9.1. Sample Spelling Errors for Tanya and Lucas

Spelling word—Tanya	Tanya's spelling	Spelling word—Lucas	Lucas's spelling
chain	chane	*treatment*	treatmint
crowd	croud	*tallest*	tallist
jeans	jeens	*artist*	artest
skate	scait	*painful*	painfull
purse	perse	*wonderful*	wonderfull
skirt	skert	*gravity*	gravaty
president	prezdent	*widen*	widin
government	govermint	*statement*	statemint
wonderful	wondeful	*manager*	maniger
paragraph	paragaff	*customary*	custimarry
hospital	hopittal	*prosperous*	prospirous

a word of Greek origin); reading fluency; and comprehension, especially vocabulary and background knowledge. Lucas's highest instructional level on ORI graded word lists was grade 7, about a year below his grade placement, and in passages was grade 6, with both word reading and comprehension problems having an impact on Lucas's passage reading.

Additional assessment data involving Lucas's spelling are on the right-hand side of Table 9.1, which shows some of Lucas's typical error patterns in spelling. Lucas's spelling is more advanced than Tanya's, and he can spell most one-syllable words correctly. Also, some of his error patterns differ from Tanya's. In particular, Lucas is less prone to making phonological errors, even in long words. He does, however, show a pattern of frequent morphological types of errors, sometimes misspelling common affixes (e.g., *treatmint* for *treatment*), and failing to use morphemic information to aid in spelling of words, even though he can read many of these words. For instance, Lucas is able to read and spell the word *manage*, but he did not apply that knowledge in spelling *manager*; he made a similar error in spelling *prosperous* despite being able to spell *prosper*; and he appears confused about when to use *-ist* (a suffix meaning a person who does something) as compared to *-est* (the superlative, as in *biggest, tallest*, etc.).

Lucas's educational history provides further insights into his literacy difficulties. From early childhood, Lucas's family situation was unstable, and he has lived with a variety of relatives, as well as in one foster placement. Due to this instability, he has attended many different schools, often with quite varied approaches to reading instruction and with little continuity of instruction. These factors had a negative impact on Lucas's reading achievement, with his reading problems first becoming apparent in the middle elementary grades. Furthermore, Lucas's school attendance was sometimes poor, which did not help matters.

Lucas's family situation has finally stabilized, and for about the past year he has been attending the same school consistently, one that provides SL interventions to struggling readers. His attendance has been good, and he has shown substantial progress in intervention. In addition to the assessments described in Chapter 3, Lucas also had a speech–language evaluation. This evaluation concluded that although Lucas did have some problems with vocabulary and morphology, he did not have a speech–language disability. He was also found not to be eligible as a student with a specific learning disability, dyslexia, or other disability. Nevertheless, it is clear that Lucas does require continued reading intervention. This intervention is being provided by Mr. Morello, the reading interventionist from Chapter 7.

About Advanced-Stage Readers with MRD

Advanced-stage readers with MRD all have the following in common: (1) reading difficulties based in both word reading and comprehension and (2) a need for intervention in more advanced word-reading skills, beyond the one-syllable level. In word reading, these students often require flexibility training and teaching of advanced morphology—that is, word parts common in relatively sophisticated academic vocabulary, such as multisyllabic words of Greek and Latin origin. As is true for other poor readers, and particularly those with a comprehension component to their reading difficulties, problems with EF play a role in poor reading comprehension for some advanced-stage readers with MRD, such as Tanya.

Teachers should target interventions to students' specific needs, with consideration of the severity of weaknesses in word reading and language comprehension, and with good integration of interventions, as discussed in Chapter 8. Many older students with a profile of MRD have moderate weaknesses in both word reading and comprehension (Capin et al., 2021), with similar needs in areas such as multisyllabic word reading, reading fluency, vocabulary, comprehension monitoring, and inferencing, so grouping of these students for intervention is often feasible.

Unlike early-stage readers, advanced-stage readers with MRD do not usually require decodable texts, but teachers might consider using a range of text difficulty levels with these students. For homework and situations in which students are expected to function entirely on their own, texts should be at an independent level, or assistive technology may be required. For classroom situations in which students have the support of a teacher, and particularly in intervention, they can read somewhat more difficult texts at their instructional levels. Furthermore, texts might occasionally include relatively challenging grade-level texts, with appropriate teacher and technological supports. Sometimes termed *stretch texts* (Vaughn et al. 2022), these more challenging texts can provide students with greater exposure to the vocabulary, language, and concepts of advanced reading materials, as well as facilitate students' participation in the general education curriculum.

Advanced-stage readers with MRD can continue to benefit from oral activities—read-alouds, short videos, oral discussion, and so on—as an avenue for building comprehension. Oral activities can use more challenging texts than reading activities, since in the former, students are not hindered by their difficulties in decoding or reading fluency.

Research on Interventions
for Advanced-Stage Readers with MRD

Chapters 5, 6, and 7 reviewed the value of SL interventions for reading long words and for key components of comprehension such as vocabulary, syntax, morphology, background knowledge, and inferencing, as well as for literacy-related EF processes such as comprehension monitoring. If selected and adapted to suit students' specific needs, these same intervention activities can benefit advanced-stage readers with MRD. However, they must be combined in a multicomponent intervention that addresses both word reading and comprehension, as discussed in Chapter 8 for early-stage readers with MRD.

Writing activities are beneficial in all reading interventions and can help develop both word reading and language comprehension abilities, as well as EF processes. For example, spelling activities that enhance students' understanding of morphology can improve not only students' spelling but also their vocabulary and word-reading (Carlisle, 2010; Goodwin & Ahn, 2013) skills. Writing activities involving summarization of a text that students have read or heard can enhance their comprehension (Graham & Hebert, 2010). Teaching students about different passage structures common to informational texts in reading, then having them apply these structures in their writing, benefits students' learning in both areas (Graham et al., 2016).

Spelling is especially challenging for poor readers (Moats, 2022), particularly those with SWRD or MRD. As noted in previous chapters, good spelling in English requires many types of linguistic knowledge beyond basic PA and phonics, including knowledge of morphology; common orthographic patterns and conventions (e.g., the fact that English words do not start with doubled letters or end in a *v*); spelling rules (e.g., rules for adding suffixes to a base word); and knowledge of alternative spellings and word-specific spellings (Apel, Masterson, & Brimo, 2012; Moats, 2020, 2022; Treiman, 2017). To put it another way, good phonics skills are necessary, but not sufficient, for good spelling in English. Given their relatively broad language weaknesses, students with MRD are especially likely to have poor spelling. Advanced-stage readers with MRD frequently need intervention in aspects of spelling beyond basic phonics skills, such as explicit teaching of morphology, spelling rules, and word-specific spellings.

It is sometimes believed that the wide availability of computer spell-checkers renders spelling instruction obsolete. However, while spell-checkers and other assistive technology in writing are valuable tools, they do not make spelling intervention unnecessary. First, spell-checkers do not catch many spelling errors, even for students who can spell reasonably well phonetically (Joshi et al., 2008). Furthermore, the need for frequent use of spell-checkers may create a drain on mental resources for higher-level aspects of writing, such as text generation (Apel et al., 2012). Perhaps most important, correct spelling of words is strongly connected to the ability to read words, including the ability to read words automatically (Apel et al., 2012; Ehri, 2005; Treiman, 2017). Improving spelling can lead to increases in word-reading speed (Ouellette et al., 2017), facilitating fluent text reading.

In addition to continued intervention in word reading and spelling, intervention activities for fluency can benefit advanced-stage readers with MRD. Timed repeated readings of passages, which are often effective for students with SWRD (Stevens et al., 2017; Wexler et al., 2008), should be used judiciously for advanced-stage readers with MRD. Because students with MRD have weaknesses in comprehension, as well as word reading, timing of text reading may result in a negative trade-off with comprehension or lead students away from the close reading that is frequently important for advanced types of texts. Moreover, older students may find timed readings of text boring and unengaging. For these students, purposeful fluency activities (Vaughn et al., 2022), such as those described in Chapter 5, or a prosodic approach that involves reading text aloud with expression, such as reading a play aloud with parts assigned to different students, may be more effective.

As an adjunct to SL interventions, and as is true for other poor readers, encouraging advanced-stage readers with MRD to read for enjoyment is important. Most of these students read well enough to find materials that are of interest to them, especially with the help of a teacher or other adult. Activities such as book groups, assigning independent reading as homework with some student choice of reading materials, and using a topic interest inventory or reading motivation plan (Wei et al., 2021), can help promote reading fluency, as well as many other reading-related abilities, even in struggling readers (Mol & Bus, 2011).

In their multicomponent interventions, different subgroups of advanced-stage readers with MRD may have some specific needs. For instance, as compared to other advanced-stage readers with MRD, ELs with this profile may require a relatively greater emphasis on English academic language and vocabulary, and they may benefit from teaching about cognates (Cardenas-Hagan, 2020). Students with ASD can have a profile of MRD (Norbury & Nation, 2011; Whalon, 2018), with problems in word reading, as well as comprehension; some of these students may benefit from intervention activities focused on pragmatic language and perspective taking (e.g., Dodd et al., 2011), combined with other comprehension activities and appropriate word-reading intervention. Multicomponent SL interventions can help all of these students but may require some adjustments in content and emphasis to be most effective. As for any student receiving intervention, progress monitoring assessments should be used to decide whether an intervention is working, and whether further adjustments are needed.

Sample SL Intervention Activities

This section provides examples of SL intervention activities effective for advanced-stage readers with MRD. These readers can also benefit from appropriately chosen intervention activities discussed in previous chapters. Moreover, if selected to match individual students' needs, the activities described in this chapter can sometimes benefit students with other poor reader profiles. For example, the spelling activities discussed in this section can benefit students with SWRD, and the comprehension activities can benefit those with specific reading comprehension difficulties (SRCD).

An Instructional Routine for Words with Alternative Spellings

In the earliest stages of spelling, when students are learning how to spell one-syllable, short-vowel words, most words have only one plausible spelling based on phoneme–grapheme relationships, and sometimes, knowledge of a spelling rule. For example, the only plausible spellings for *man* and *ship* are *m–a–n* and *s–h–i–p*. The words *smell* and *brass* require knowledge of the floss rule in spelling, involving doubling the spelling of *l* and *s* at the end of a one-syllable short-vowel word; otherwise, they can be spelled similarly to *man* and *ship*, simply by listening for and transcribing the sounds of the word in sequence.

However, as students advance beyond the earliest stages of spelling, they must learn words that can have alternative spellings, and for many of these words, there are no spelling rules. Sometimes morphology provides a helpful clue; for example, the *hear* in *heard* is a morphological clue to its spelling. When morphological or other clues are available for words, teachers should certainly encourage students to use them. Nevertheless, to spell many of these words correctly, the student must either be familiar with the printed word or study specific words to learn their spellings. Tanya has a need for SL instruction in spelling involving these kinds of words. Furthermore, improving Tanya's ability to spell these words may improve her ability to read them automatically (Ouellette et al., 2017).

Like all students, Tanya makes varied types of spelling errors. As shown in Table 9.1, her errors include some phonologically based errors, mostly on long words, such as *govermint* for *government*. Ms. Rosen will address these types of errors when Tanya begins to work on spelling long words, such as through the activity shown in Figure 5.7 and described in Chapter 5. For now, however, Ms. Rosen focuses on Tanya's spelling of common one-syllable words, which often involve a different type of error, her limited knowledge of specific word spellings. When Tanya misspells *chain* as *chane* or *crowd* as *croud*, she is not making errors in phonics. Rather, she doesn't know the spelling of long /a/ or /ow/ used in these particular words. There is no rule or morphological clue that Ms. Rosen can teach her for these words; Tanya has to learn them through explicit teaching about alternative spellings, practice activities, and studying them.

Here is how Ms. Rosen uses SL to teach these kinds of words to Tanya and Jelani, the other student grouped with Tanya for her special education instruction. The general approach, involving teaching of common alternative spellings of the same sound, is modeled after Gillingham and Stillman (1997). Ms. Rosen's instructional routine includes having students study words and take regular spelling tests, an approach that has not always met with resounding success (Apel et al., 2012). However, as illustrated further below, Ms. Rosen's routine differs in important ways from traditional spelling tests with random words that students are simply expected to memorize. Ms. Rosen currently is teaching common one-syllable words with different spellings of /er/, shown in Table 9.2.

1. First, Ms. Rosen explicitly teaches different spellings of the same sound, in this case /er/. She focuses on no more than three different spellings, beginning with the most

TABLE 9.2. Examples of Common One-Syllable Words with Different Spellings of /er/

er	*ir*	*ur*	*ear*	*wor*
her	sir	fur	earn	work
herd	fir	burn	learn	word
germ	stir	turn	heard	worse
term	bird	hurt	earth	worst
fern	third	curl	pearl	worm
serve	shirt	purse		worth
nerve	dirt	nurse		
	skirt	curve		
	first	church		
	girl	curb		
	birth			

common ones: *er*, *ir*, and *ur*. She places multiple letter cards in front of the students and asks them to point to the ones that say /er/; the students have to point to *er*, *ir*, and *ur*.

2. Ms. Rosen always contrasts at least two different spellings of a sound, to help students attend to different ways that the same sound may be spelled. The students already know these letter–sound relationships in relation to reading, and they can read these kinds of words easily. However, Ms. Rosen explains that in spelling, they have to turn this process around, and go from sounds to letters. Furthermore, for words with /er/, there is no rule to know which spelling to use; students have to practice and study the words.

3. At the beginning of each week, Ms. Rosen gives the students a brief initial assessment to determine which words they do not know how to spell. This past week, she used the words from the three left-hand columns of Table 9.2 on the initial assessment. She then developed a spelling list for the students to study, based on the words with *er*, *ir*, and *ur* that they did not know, involving about a dozen specific words. Other words with /er/, as well as other alternative spellings of sounds (e.g., spellings of long /a/, spellings of /ow/) will be taught in subsequent weeks. When relevant, she will also draw students' attention to other information that is important to spelling certain words (e.g., spell a word using the *wor* pattern only when you hear /w/ before the /er/, or use word meaning to spell homonyms such as *fir* and *fur*).

4. Ms. Rosen reminds the students that they will have a spelling test at the end of the week on these words, and that the best way to learn them is to practice spelling them for a little bit of time each day. Ms. Rosen also will include a few "surprise words"—that is, previously taught words—on the postassessment to help monitor whether the students are retaining spellings of words over time. These assessments provide informal data that can be used to help determine students' progress in spelling and adjust the spelling intervention as needed.

5. During the week, Ms. Rosen includes numerous practice activities to help students learn the words on the weekly word list. Early in the week, she puts the *er*, *ir*, and *ur* headings on a whiteboard and asks students to take turns pointing to the correct spelling of /er/ when she says a word from the weekly list (e.g., "Which spelling is used in the word *curve*?"). A bit later in the week, she includes practice activities such as the one shown in Form 9.1 (page 232). In this activity, students have to select the correct spelling of /er/ for one of the spelling words given a sentence that provides context, then write the whole word.

6. If a student has continuing difficulties learning a word, Ms. Rosen tries a version of the Picture This strategy (see Apel et al., 2012), which is introduced by asking the student to picture a familiar room, such as his or her bedroom, recalling as many items in the room as possible. Students are asked to mentally scan the room from left to right, then right to left, with the teacher pointing out how a well-formed mental image can help the student remember many details of the image. The strategy is then applied to the problematic spelling word, with the teacher showing the word and describing various details of it, such as the number of letters in the word, the number of vowels and consonants, and so on. Both teacher and student take turns spelling the word orally while looking at it, then the student tries to write it from memory. If the student spells the word correctly from memory, he or she is asked to try to spell it backward. Success on this last step suggests that the student has formed a good mental representation of the word (Apel et al., 2012).

7. Ms. Rosen regularly has the students use their spelling words in dictated sentences, as well as other written expression activities, and she monitors the students' spelling of these words. If she notices that they are making repeated errors on words they were previously taught, she includes these words for further review in lessons. She has also found games helpful in providing ongoing review of spelling words, such as a simple board game in which students roll a die to advance but must write a previously learned spelling word correctly first.

Teaching Morphology to Improve Spelling and Vocabulary

Mr. Morello is providing intervention to Lucas in a group of six seventh- and eighth-grade students, all of whom need to work on reading and spelling of multisyllabic words, fluency, and comprehension. All of the students can benefit from teaching of specific affixes, as well as other aspects of morphology, in both spelling and reading. In spelling, Mr. Morello has been working on the suffixes *-ist*, *-est*, *-en*, *-ful*, *-ity*, and *-ment* because all of the students have difficulty with spelling at least some of them. He has included some suffixes that students usually learn early in intervention, such as *-est*, because of the confusions that Lucas and several other students are having in spelling these suffixes (e.g., *-est* vs. *-ist*). He begins by explaining why it is useful to be familiar with the spelling of these word parts; they can help you spell words because they have a consistent spelling across many different words, and they also provide clues to the meaning of words.

Then he presents each suffix, with sample words and the meaning of each suffix:

- *-est*, the superlative, as in *biggest*, *smallest*, *widest*, and so on; the most big, the most small, the most wide, and so on
- *-ist*, a person who does something, as in *artist*, someone who does art
- *-en*, to become, as in *weaken*, to become weak
- *-ful*, full of something, as in *fearful*, full of fear
- *-ity*, the state of, a suffix that changes an adjective to a noun, as in *pure/purity* or *simple/simplicity*; the state of being pure, the state of being simple
- *-ment*, the action or result of, a suffix that changes a verb into a noun, as in *pay/payment*, *move/movement*; the action of paying, the action of moving

Mr. Morello emphasizes that to be a suffix and to be spelled accordingly, the morpheme must have the appropriate meaning in the context of the word. For example, the word *muffin* sounds like it might end in the suffix *-en* but does not because in this word, *muff* is not a base word and the second syllable does not have anything to do with becoming something. Leaving the spelling of the suffixes available for students to see, he then dictates several words for students to write using the appropriate suffix (e.g., *thankful*, *deepen*, *latest*). Students have learned basic spelling rules, such as those for adding a suffix to a one-syllable base word (e.g., consonant doubling and dropping silent *e*), so he includes some words that require knowledge of these rules. Unlike Ms. Rosen's work with Tanya on word-specific spellings, Mr. Morello is trying to develop students' abilities to spell a wide variety of multisyllabic words with these suffixes. Therefore, he uses a range of base words that he knows students have the skills to spell rather than focusing on a smaller subset of specific words, as Ms. Rosen does.

In a later lesson, Mr. Morello provides further practice for students on spelling words with these suffixes and using them appropriately. Form 9.2 (page 233) shows a sample practice activity. Ultimately, students are expected to recall the spelling of the suffixes from memory and apply them correctly in spelling multisyllabic words, both in dictation activities and their other writing.

Teaching Students How to Determine the Gist of a Passage

Many students with poor reading comprehension have difficulties determining the gist, or main idea, of an informational passage. Educators can explicitly teach students to look for specific clues to the gist. Both Tanya and Lucas can benefit from this type of instruction, although the grade level of the texts used would differ for each of them, since Lucas reads at a more advanced level than Tanya (i.e., sixth grade vs. third grade). Specific grade expectations for both students also would differ.

Figure 9.2 displays a list of clues to the gist of a passage—that is, a paragraph or a few interrelated paragraphs—for students. Here is some additional detail about each type of clue:

- **Passage structure.** As discussed in Chapter 2, five common types of informational text structure are descriptive, cause–effect, problem–solution, sequence, and

> **To help determine the gist, or main idea, of a passage, look for the clues below:**
>
> 1. **Use passage structure.** Five types of passage structure are descriptive, problem–solution, cause–effect, sequence, and compare–contrast. You can use signal words to help figure out the type of passage structure. For example, signal words for cause–effect include *because, so, as a result, therefore,* and *consequently.*
> 2. **Look for headings and subheadings.** These often outline the key points of an informational text and provide important clues to the gist.
> 3. **Check the first and last sentence of a passage.** Sometimes one of these sentences will sum up the gist of a passage.
> 4. **Look for frequently repeated content words.** If a content word is repeated often in a passage, it usually has something to do with the gist.
> 5. **Consider emboldened words.** In informational texts, words shown in bold font generally are important vocabulary or concepts that relate to the gist of the passage.
> 6. **Pay attention to summary sentences or paragraphs.** Sometimes an informational text will have a sentence or paragraph that sums up the key points of a passage, usually at the end. These kinds of sentences and paragraphs may be signaled by words such as *in summary, to sum up, overall, on the whole,* and *in general.*

FIGURE 9.2. Some clues to the gist of a passage.

compare–contrast. Furthermore, signal words provide clues to the type of text structure (see Table 2.5 in Chapter 2). Text structure provides clues to the gist because it indicates the focus of the passage. For example, a problem–solution text structure focuses on a problem and one or more solutions to the problem; a compare–contrast passage compares two things and describes similarities and differences between them. Students also should understand that informational passages do not always fit neatly into one of these structures, which is why considering the additional clues below is important.

• **Headings and subheadings.** Many informational texts have headings and subheadings that organize the content of the text into key topics and can therefore be useful in determining the gist of passages. For instance, a U.S. history passage with the subheading *Turning Point: The Battle of Gettysburg* is likely going to have a gist that explains how the battle of Gettysburg was a turning point in the American Civil War.

• **First and last sentence of a passage.** Sometimes the first sentence of a passage conveys the gist, for example, *Certain defining characteristics are found in all mammals,* followed by details about these characteristics. Alternatively, this kind of sentence may come at the end of a passage: *These defining characteristics are found in all mammals.* Either way, the gist of the passage likely involves the defining characteristics of mammals.

• **Frequently repeated content words.** Content words repeated often in a passage typically have something to do with the gist. Consider, for instance, the Gettysburg example noted earlier. If the subheading were missing or more vague, frequent repetition of the words *battle* and *Gettysburg* in the passage would at least indicate that the gist of the passage has something to do with the battle of Gettysburg.

- **Emboldened words.** In an informational passage, words are sometimes emboldened because they signal the introduction of a new vocabulary word or concept, such as *photosynthesis* in a science text or *emancipation* in a text about the Civil War. These kinds of words often have something to do with the gist of a passage.

- **Summary sentences or paragraphs.** These sentences and paragraphs, usually found at the end of a passage, may be signaled by words such as *in summary, to sum up,* or *overall.* By definition, these kinds of sentences relate to the gist because they sum up key points of a passage. If present, it is important to attend to them.

Clues to the gist should be taught using texts that exemplify the different clues, including texts that students are reading in school. Teaching the clues in the context of group activities and class discussions can be especially valuable because students can learn from each other, as well as from the teacher, and they may find these activities more engaging (Fletcher et al., 2019; Vaughn et al., 2022). These activities can also help make visible the kind of thinking that students need to do to determine the key points of a passage.

A Graphic Organizer for the Gist and Details of a Passage

Graphic organizers are effective for teaching various text structures (NRP, 2000). When students are first learning these structures, graphic organizers tailored to the specific type of text structure—descriptive, problem–solution, and so on—are particularly useful (see, e.g., Cartwright, 2015; Hennessey, 2021; Oakhill et al., 2015). Once students have learned about different text structures as well as other clues to the gist, teachers may find a broader type of organizer helpful. This kind of organizer is displayed in Form 9.3 (page 234). (See Stevens & Austin, 2022, for an alternative approach to teaching the gist with additional graphic organizers.)

The top of Form 9.3 displays various clues to the gist for students to reference, along with a box for students to write the gist of the passage. If students read a passage and already grasp the gist, they do not need to belabor the clues; they can write the gist in the appropriate box right away. However, if students are uncertain about the gist, they should try the clues at the top, checking off the clues they have used, until they think they know the gist and can write it down.

The organizer also has bullet points for key details from the passage relating to the gist. Teachers should encourage students to put at least some of these points in their own words, rather than simply copying them from the passage because doing so will usually lead to deeper processing and understanding. Figure 9.3 displays a sample informational text passage, and Figure 9.4 illustrates how a student might fill in the organizer for this passage.

Teachers should introduce the graphic organizer in Form 9.3 with modeling based on a sample text. Students can then use the organizer as part of a partner or group activity in intervention, with students reading another passage and filling in the gist and key details, and with guidance and feedback from the teacher. Alternatively, the organizer could sometimes be completed independently, such as during homework.

COVID-19 and the 1918 Flu

The 1918 flu and the COVID-19 pandemic occurred almost exactly 100 years apart. A **pandemic** is an infectious disease that spreads around the globe. Both pandemics involved novel viruses that had not been seen before. Both had devastating impacts, resulting in the deaths of millions of people worldwide.

There were other similarities between the two pandemics. As in the COVID-19 pandemic, during the 1918 flu, people were urged to wear masks and avoid crowds. Many people ignored this advice. During both pandemics, there were serious concerns about hospitals becoming overwhelmed by large numbers of sick people.

Nevertheless, there were some important differences between the COVID-19 pandemic and the 1918 flu. By 2019, scientists had learned from prior pandemics, including the 1918 flu, and they understood the value of shutting down public spaces as early as possible to limit the spread of disease. A COVID vaccine was developed quickly, but there were no flu vaccines in 1918.

Also, more people perished globally in the 1918 flu pandemic than from COVID. Currently infectious disease specialists estimate that at least 50 million people, worldwide, died of the 1918 flu. As of October 2023, according to the World Health Organization, nearly 7 million people globally have died from COVID-19, over a million of those in the United States. In the 1918 flu, mortality was especially high among healthy young adults, whereas this is not the case for COVID-19.

FIGURE 9.3. Sample informational passage on pandemics.

Eventually, students can learn how to combine multiple gist statements for a series of passages from the same text into a summary of that text. For content classes, the organizer could help students prepare for tests involving the content of class readings.

SL Intervention Plans
for Advanced-Stage Readers with MRD

The intervention plan from Chapter 8, shown in Table 8.2 for early-stage readers with MRD, can also be used for advanced-stage readers with this profile. For the latter, the opening sections of the intervention plan that are focused on word reading will emphasize more advanced skills in this area (e.g., advanced morphology, generalizations for dividing long words, flexibility training) rather than basic skills (e.g., phoneme blending in one-syllable words, basic grapheme–phoneme relationships). Also, given the relatively better word reading of these students as compared to early stage-readers with MRD, the comprehension segment may include more silent reading of text. However, some oral reading continues to be important, so that the teacher can monitor students' accuracy of word reading in passages and provide feedback to errors. As is true for other intervention plans in this book, and as described in more detail in previous chapters, this plan can be adapted in various ways to meet the needs of individual students.

A Sample Intervention Lesson for Lucas

Table 9.3 displays a sample 50-minute intervention lesson for Lucas and his group, using the plan from Table 8.2. The lesson segment for word reading and spelling focuses on the suffixes *-ist*, *-est*, *-en*, *-ful*, *-ity*, and *-ment*, and their application in

---

GIST AND DETAILS ORGANIZER

Clues to the Gist:

Passage Structure: __ Descriptive   __ Cause–Effect __ Problem–Solution

                  __ Sequence   ✓ Compare–Contrast   __ Other

Heading or Subheading ✓

First or Last Sentence

Repetition of Content Words or Emboldened Words ✓

Summary Paragraph

Gist of Passage: *The passage compares the 1918 flu pandemic to the Covid-19 pandemic. It tells how the two pandemics were similar and different.*

Important Details:

- *A pandemic is an infectious disease that spreads all around the world.*

- *The two pandemics took place 100 years apart.*

- *Some ways they are similar are that they both killed millions of people, they both involved totally new viruses, and during each pandemic people had to wear masks and try to stay out of crowds.*

- *Some differences are that Covid mostly killed older people, but the 1918 flu killed more younger people. Also, scientists knew more about pandemics by the time Covid happened. There are vaccines for Covid but in 1918 there were no vaccines for flu.*

FIGURE 9.4. Sample graphic organizer for the pandemic passage.

spelling multisyllabic words, as described earlier in this chapter. Mr. Morello has already introduced these suffixes and provided practice activities such as those in Form 9.2; this lesson reviews the suffixes and extends them to spelling of additional multisyllabic words without any models. Mr. Morello also has the students practice flexibility in reading unfamiliar multisyllabic words, but he incorporates this practice into later segments of the lesson because he plans to discuss these words as new vocabulary from the students' text reading for the lesson.

TABLE 9.3. Sample Intervention Lesson for Lucas (with Intervention Group)

Component(s)	Activity
Word recognition and spelling (10 minutes) • Review spellings of previously taught suffixes, including -ist, -est, -en, -ment, -ful, -est, -ity. • Spell multisyllabic words with these suffixes.	• Teacher uses flash cards to quickly review sounds for previously learned suffixes, including those to be used in spelling. • Teacher displays cards for recently taught suffixes, giving sound and meaning; students point to correct suffix. • Teacher dictates six to eight multisyllabic words with these same suffixes for students to write (e.g., *royalist, deepest, document, equality*).
• Flexibility practice on multisyllabic words from the pandemic passage	• Flexibility practice to be done later in lesson (see below).
Fluency (10 minutes)	Purposeful reading of text selection on pandemics: (1) Students scan text for two to three words they are unsure how to decode; (2) teacher helps them decode these words, including flexibility practice, and discusses meaning as needed; (3) students take turns reading passage orally twice, with appropriate prosody and teacher feedback.
Language comprehension, text reading, and reading comprehension (20 minutes)	• Teacher orally reviews two to three additional words from text selection not addressed in fluency segment, with flexibility practice and discussion of meaning (e.g., *novel* meaning "totally new"), including the context sentences for each word; students encouraged to use sentence to help infer word meaning. • Teacher briefly reviews background knowledge for text selection (a novel virus can be especially devastating because no one is resistant to it; vaccines provide protection). • Teacher introduces graphic organizer for gist and details, modeling with a sample text. • Students work in pairs to determine the text structure, gist, and details of the pandemic passage, with teacher guidance and feedback.
Writing (10 minutes)	• Teacher briefly reviews structure of a compare–contrast passage and its signal words, by eliciting from students. • Students write a compare–contrast paragraph on a topic of their choosing or on one of several options provided by the teacher; complete for homework if necessary.

For the second lesson segment, the students do a purposeful fluency activity similar to the one discussed in Chapter 5, using the passage for today's reading, the one on pandemics displayed in Figure 9.3. First, Mr. Morello asks the students to scan the passage for two or three multisyllabic words that they are uncertain how to read. He shows students how to decode these words, incorporating flexibility training, which is relevant for many of the words. For instance, many students flag the word *devastating*, which could potentially be pronounced as DEE-vuh-stating, duh-VAST-uh-ting, and so on. Similarly, a few students have trouble shifting the accent pattern on *mortality*, pronouncing it as MOR-tal-itty. He also reviews the meaning of these words, providing a brief, student-friendly definition (e.g., *devastating* means "very, very bad"). Next, teacher and students take turns reading sections of the passage, with Mr. Morello going first and providing an appropriate model of reading accuracy and prosody. To give each student a chance to read, Mr. Morello has them read through the passage twice.

For the third segment of the lesson, Mr. Morello begins by discussing a couple of new vocabulary words, ones not already addressed in the fluency segment. For example, although the students can read the word *novel*, its meaning is different in this passage from the meaning with which they are most familiar, a fiction book. He highlights these words in their context sentences from the passage and encourages students to try to infer their meanings from context before providing explicit definitions of each word. He also reviews some background knowledge that is relevant to the word *novel* and to the rest of the passage—specifically, the fact that novel viruses can sometimes be devastating to a group of people because no one has built up the ability to resist them (i.e., immunity), as we do with familiar viruses such as cold viruses. However, vaccines can provide people with protection against these kinds of viruses.

Mr. Morello then introduces the graphic organizer for the gist displayed in Form 9.3, modeling its use with a sample passage different from the pandemic passage. Students already have learned the various clues to passage structure at the top of the organizer, so Mr. Morello simply draws students' attention to those but does not explain them at length. Then the students work in pairs to complete the organizer for the gist using the pandemic passage, which has a compare–contrast structure, as well as a helpful heading and an important emboldened word, *pandemic*. Mr. Morello circulates among the students, providing monitoring, guidance, and feedback as needed, while they complete the organizer.

For the final writing segment of the lesson, Mr. Morello asks the students to write a compare–contrast paragraph, at least four sentences, on a topic of their choosing. Before the students start writing, he briefly reminds them about compare–contrast text structure and its signal words as exemplified by the pandemic passage. Also, he does not want students to linger too long in deciding a topic, so he is prepared to suggest several topics if necessary, such as "Compare and contrast two movies you have seen, two books, or two sports." As students write, he monitors their work and provides suggestions, with particular attention to whether students are using compare–contrast structure and signal words in their writing. If necessary, the students complete the paragraph as homework.

Additional Considerations for Written Expression

Like early-stage readers with MRD, advanced-stage readers require multicomponent interventions for written expression, as well as for reading. For most advanced-stage readers with MRD, these interventions should include spelling. Often interventions can focus on more advanced spelling skills such as application of morphology in spelling multisyllabic words, as is appropriate for Lucas. However, because students' spelling skills lag behind their word-reading skills, some students may still require spelling intervention at the one-syllable stage, as is true for Tanya.

Because of underlying language or EF weaknesses, advanced-stage readers with MRD usually also require interventions aimed at text generation skills, organization of writing, and/or writing processes (e.g., planning). For instance, Lucas's weaknesses in vocabulary and background knowledge frequently manifest in his writing, as well as his reading. Activities focused on applying vocabulary and background knowledge learned in the context of reading, to his writing, can benefit both areas. Tanya's problems in EF tend to make planning and organization of writing especially difficult for her, so she needs some emphasis on explicit teaching of these writing processes. Multicomponent interventions for writing can also benefit multiple components of students' reading. For example, as discussed earlier in this chapter, better spelling can improve students' speed of word reading, and application of passage structure in writing can improve students' reading comprehension.

Many advanced-stage readers with MRD are adolescents, in middle or high school, and must meet challenging literacy demands. In addition to SL interventions for written expression, assistive technology is often helpful in enabling students to keep up with grade-level literacy demands, in writing as well as reading.

SUMMING UP:
SL Interventions for Advanced-Stage Readers with MRD

Here are key points from this chapter:

- Advanced-stage readers with MRD require interventions focused on advanced word-reading skills beyond the one-syllable stage, as well as on the specific areas of language comprehension in which they are weak.

- Some of these students also require interventions aimed at EF skills, such as comprehension monitoring in reading and organizational strategies in writing.

- Continuation of spelling intervention is important for most of these students because spelling is often particularly difficult for them, and improvements in spelling can benefit both their writing and their reading.

- Examples of intervention activities helpful for these students include activities for learning word-specific spellings, applying morphology in spelling, and teaching clues to the gist of a passage, as well as many activities from previous chapters, if selected to meet the needs of individual students.

- These students require multicomponent interventions in writing as well as in reading.

APPLIED EXERCISES

Exercise 1

Consider the assessment data (e.g., in Figure 9.1 and Table 9.1) and other information provided for Tanya in this chapter, as well as the intervention plan in Table 8.2. Which types of word-reading skills would be important to address with Tanya in the initial segment of the intervention plan? What is an example of an intervention activity you could use for these skills? Consider activities from previous chapters as well as the current chapter.

Answer

In reading, Tanya needs a focus on multisyllabic words. She is described as having difficulties with sounds for advanced morphemes—the roots, prefixes, and suffixes common in academic vocabulary—which suggests that this could be a good area to address for her word reading. An example of an appropriate intervention activity could involve the grid shown in Table 7.1 and described in Chapter 7, with specific roots, prefixes, and suffixes chosen to be appropriate to Tanya's needs. Conor's word analysis activity from Chapter 5, shown in Figure 5.5, could also be helpful, if focused on the specific morphemes and decoding skills that Tanya has been taught.

Exercise 2

Consider the type and level of text that might be most helpful to use with Tanya. What type/level would you want to use in intervention? In encouraging independent reading?

Answer

Tanya's word-reading skills are sufficiently well developed that she does not require decodable text, but text difficulty level is an important consideration. For intervention, in which she has the support of a teacher, grade-3 text (Tanya's highest instructional level) would likely be appropriate. However, with preteaching and support from her interventionist, she might sometimes be able to read more difficult texts and perhaps some grade-appropriate texts. For independent reading, easier texts (e.g., grade 2) should probably be used, although Tanya might be able to read somewhat more challenging texts independently if she were highly motivated to read the text, and if the text involved an area in which she had strong background knowledge. As described for Dashawn in Chapter 8, ongoing progress monitoring assessments of Tanya's word accuracy and comprehension in text reading should be used to make decisions about whether the difficulty level of these texts needs adjustment.

Exercise 3

What is an example of an intervention activity that could benefit Tanya in the third, comprehension-related segment of the lesson plan? Again, consider activities from previous chapters, as well as the current chapter.

Answer

Tanya is described as having difficulties with comprehension monitoring, so activities for this area (e.g., the illogical sentences activities from Chapters 6 and 8, or the comprehension monitoring routine from Chapter 7) could all be helpful, if appropriately tailored to Tanya's text reading level and skills. Tanya could also benefit from teaching about passage structure and clues to determining the gist of a passage, as described in this chapter, if done in conjunction with appropriate reading materials.

Exercise 4

What would be an example of a helpful writing activity for Tanya?

Answer

Activities that require Tanya to apply her learned spelling words (e.g., the words with alternative spellings, such as those shown in Table 9.2) in writing exercises would be helpful. These exercises could involve dictated sentences or more extended writing, such as responding to a writing prompt. Another example of an effective writing activity would involve having Tanya apply a learned type of passage structure, such as a descriptive or compare–contrast passage, by writing her own passage with the same structure, similar to the activity in Lucas's sample lesson.

Please see Table 9.4 for a sample 60-minute intervention lesson for Tanya and her partner in intervention, Jelani. As was true for Dashawn in Chapter 8, other sample lessons with other activities could also be appropriate.

TABLE 9.4. Sample Intervention Lesson for Tanya (with Jelani)

Component(s)	Activity
Word recognition and spelling (20 minutes)	
• Review sounds for soft *c, g*. • Review sounds for previously taught morphemes (prefixes and suffixes).	• Teacher uses flash cards to quickly review sounds for soft *c* and *g* and previously learned morphemes (e.g., *un, pre, mis, dis, -able, -ible, -ment, -ous, -ful*).
• Read unfamiliar multisyllabic words.	• Teacher gives students a list of multisyllabic words (e.g., *mistreated, disgraceful, outrageous, agreeable, agreement, disagreement*); students circle prefixes and suffixes, then take turns reading words aloud; teacher provides cueing as needed.
• Practice spelling one-syllable words with /er/.	• Students complete activity shown in Form 9.1; teacher monitors and provides feedback.
Fluency (5 minutes)	Students take turns rereading a familiar (previously read) section of a grade-3 trade book orally, with appropriate prosody; rereading is untimed, but teacher progress monitors word accuracy, phrasing, and prosody of reading.
Language comprehension, text reading, and reading comprehension (25 minutes)	• Teacher reviews the importance of thinking about meaning when reading and some fix-up strategies for when comprehension fails (e.g., rereading). • Teacher gives students several paragraphs from the next section of their grade-3 trade book with illogical or inconsistent sentences inserted (similar to Figure 8.5). • Students read silently to find illogical or inconsistent sentences and take turns explaining why they don't make sense, with further discussion as needed. • Students then take turns reading orally from the original version of the grade-3 text, with teacher feedback to word-reading errors, and with questioning and discussion, including both literal and inferential types of questions.
Writing (10 minutes)	• Teacher dictates three sentences using previously learned spelling words, including words with alternative spellings, and basic writing conventions. • Students write another sentence that uses one of their current spelling words in a grammatically correct sentence that shows the meaning of the word.

Practice Activity for Spelling Words with /er/

er, ir, or ur?

Directions: Write *er*, *ir*, or *ur* in the blank to correctly spell a real word that fits the meaning of the sentence. Then write the entire word in the blank.

1. When Dan tripped on the stairs, he h_____t his leg.   _____

2. A g_____m can sometimes make you sick.   _____

3. The cowboys drove the h_____d of cattle into the field.   _____

4. Someone stole my mother's p_____se.   _____

5. Lisa wants to be a n_____se when she grows up.   _____

6. You have to st_____ the gravy while it is cooking.   _____

7. At the end of the t_____m, report cards go out.   _____

8. She wore her new sk_____t to the party.   _____

9. Matt was th_____d in line.   _____

10. On Sundays they go to ch_____ch.   _____

11. After working in the garden, his hands were covered in d_____t.   _____

12. There was a sharp c_____ve in the road.   _____

Practice Activity for Spelling Words with Specific Morphemes

-est, -ist, -en, -ful, -ment, or *-ity*?

Directions (Part 1): Choose the correct morpheme from the list above to make a real word that has the base word shown in parentheses. Write the word in the blank on the right.

1. Molly loved music and was a talented _____ (violin).   _____

2. It was a hot day, so the ice cream quickly began to _____ (soft).   _____

3. During the night a _____ (power) storm leveled the town.   _____

4. Of the three brothers, Rick was the _____ (old).   _____

5. After the election, the mayor made a brief _____ (state).   _____

6. Mark was a _____ (final) on the singing show.   _____

7. The problem is hard to solve because of its _____ (complex).   _____

8. When I told her my secret, she looked at me in _____ (amaze).   _____

9. Lee is the _____ (strong) player on the team.   _____

10. I have to _____ (sharp) my pencil.   _____

Directions (Part 2): Using the morphemes at the top of the page, write a real word that has the base word shown. Then write a complete sentence that shows the meaning of the word.

1. fear

2. tall

3. equal

4. type

Graphic Organizer for the Gist and Details of a Passage

GIST AND DETAILS ORGANIZER

Clues to the Gist:

<u>Passage Structure:</u>   __ Descriptive   __ Cause–Effect   __ Problem–Solution

__ Sequence   __ Compare–Contrast   __ Other

<u>Heading or Subheading</u>

<u>First or Last Sentence</u>

<u>Repetition of Content Words or Emboldened Words</u>

<u>Summary Paragraph</u>

Gist of Passage:

Important Details:

- _____
- _____
- _____
- _____

References

Adams, M. J., Fillmore, L. W., Goldenberg, C., Oakhill, J. Paige, D., Rasinski, T., & Shanahan, T. (2020). *Comparing reading research to program design: An examination of Teachers College Units of Study.* Student Achievement Partners.

Adlof, S. M. (2020). Promoting reading achievement in children with developmental language disorders: What can we learn from research on specific language impairment and dyslexia? *Journal of Speech, Language, and Hearing Research, 63,* 3277–3292.

Al Otaiba, S., Allor, J. H., & Stewart, J. (2022). Structured literacy interventions for phonemic awareness and basic word recognition skills. In L. Spear-Swerling (Ed.), *Structured literacy interventions: Teaching students with reading difficulties, K–6* (pp. 23–42). Guilford Press.

Apel, K., Masterson, J. J., & Brimo, D. (2012). Spelling assessment and intervention: A multiple linguistic approach to improving literacy outcomes. In A. G. Kamhi & H. W. Catts (Eds.), *Language and reading disabilities* (3rd ed., pp. 152–169). Pearson.

Archer, A. L., Gleason, M. M., & Vachon, V. L. (2003). Decoding and fluency: Foundation skills for struggling older readers. *Learning Disability Quarterly, 26,* 89–101.

Archer, A. L., & Hughes, C. A. (2011). *Explicit instruction: Effective and efficient teaching.* Guilford Press.

Armbruster, B. B., & Anderson, T. H. (1985). Producing "considerate" expository text: Or easy reading is damned hard writing. *Journal of Curriculum Studies, 17,* 247–263.

August, D., Carlo, M., Dressler, C., & Snow, C. (2005). The critical role of vocabulary development for English language learners. *Learning Disabilities Research and Practice, 20,* 50–57.

Baker, S., Lesaux, N., Jayanthi, M., Dimino, J., Proctor, C. P., Morris, J., et al. (2014). *Teaching academic content and literacy to English learners in elementary and middle school* (NCEE 2014-4012). Institute of Education Sciences, U.S. Department of Education. http://ies.ed.gov/ncee/wwc/publications_reviews.aspx

Barquero, L. A., & Cutting, L. E. (2021). Introduction to the special issue on advances in the understanding of reading comprehension deficits. *Annals of Dyslexia, 71,* 211–217.

Barth, A. E., & Elleman, A. (2017). Evaluating the impact of a multistrategy inference intervention for middle-grade struggling readers. *Language, Speech, and Hearing Services in Schools, 48,* 31–41.

Beck, I. L., McKeown, M. G., & Kucan, L. (2002). *Bringing words to life: Robust vocabulary instruction.* Guilford Press.

Biemiller, A. (2009). *Words worth teaching: Closing the vocabulary gap.* SRA/McGraw-Hill.

Brady, S. (2011). Efficacy of phonics teaching for reading outcomes: Indications from post-NRP research. In S. Brady, D. Braze, & C. Fowler (Eds.), *Explaining individual differences in reading: Theory and evidence* (pp. 69–96). Psychology Press.

Brady, S. (2020). A 2020 perspective on research findings on alphabetics (phoneme awareness and phonics): Implications for instruction. *Reading League Journal, 1,* 20–28.

Brady, S., Gillis, M., Smith, T., Lavalette, M., Liss-Bronstein, L., Lowe, E., et al. (2009). First grade teachers' knowledge of phonological awareness and code concepts: Examining gains from an intensive form of professional development. *Reading and Writing: An Interdisciplinary Journal, 22,* 425–455.

Brown, K. J., Patrick, K. C., Fields, M. K., & Craig, G. T. (2021). Phonological awareness materials in Utah kindergartens: A case study in the science of reading. *Reading Research Quarterly, 56,* 249–272.

Brown, M. C., Sibley, D. E., Washington, J. A., Rogers, T. T., Edwards, J. R., MacDonald, M. C., et al. (2015). Impact of dialect use on a basic component of learning to read. *Frontiers in Psychology, 6,* 1–17.

Brown, V. L., Hammill, D. D., & Wiederholt, J. L. (2009). *Test of Reading Comprehension* (4th ed.). Western Psychological Services.

Brown-Chidsey, R., & Steege, M. W. (2005). *Response to intervention: Principles and strategies for effective practice.* Guilford Press.

Capin, P., Cho, E., Miciak, J., Roberts, G., & Vaughn, S. (2021). Examining the reading and cognitive profiles of students with significant reading comprehension difficulties. *Learning Disabilities Quarterly, 44,* 183–196.

Cardenas-Hagan, E. (2020). Teaching literacy skills to English learners. In E. Cardenas-Hagan (Ed.), *Literacy foundations for English learners: A comprehensive guide to evidence-based instruction* (pp. 3–30). Brookes.

Carlisle, J. F. (2010). An integrative review of the effects of instruction in morphological awareness on literacy achievement. *Reading Research Quarterly, 45,* 464–487.

Carnine, D. W., Silbert, J., Kame'enui, E. J., & Tarver, S. G. (2009). *Direct instruction reading* (5th ed.). Pearson.

Cartwright, K. B. (2015). *Executive skills and reading comprehension: A guide for educators.* Guilford Press.

Castiglioni-Spalten, M., & Ehri, L. (2003). Phonemic awareness instruction: Contribution of articulatory segmentation to novice beginners' reading and spelling. *Scientific Studies of Reading, 7,* 25–52.

Catts, H. W., Adlof, S. M., Hogan, T. P., & Weismer, S. E. (2005). Are specific language impairment and dyslexia distinct disorders? *Journal of Speech, Language, and Hearing Research, 48*(6), 1378–1396.

Catts, H. W., Adlof, S. M., & Weismer, S. E. (2006). Language deficits in poor comprehenders: A case for the simple view of reading. *Journal of Speech, Language, and Hearing Research, 49,* 278–293.

Catts, H. W., Compton, D. L., Tomblin, J. B., & Bridges, M. S. (2012). Prevalence and nature of late-emerging poor readers. *Journal of Educational Psychology, 104,* 166–181.

Chall, J. S. (1983). *Stages of reading development.* McGraw-Hill.

Chi, M., Glaser, R., & Farr, M. (1988). *The nature of expertise.* Erlbaum.

Christensen, C. A., & Bowey, J. A. (2005). The efficacy of orthographic rime, grapheme–phoneme correspondence, and implicit phonics approaches to teaching decoding skills. *Scientific Studies of Reading, 9,* 327–349.

Clarke, P. J., Truelove, E., Hulme, C., & Snowling, M. J. (2014). *Developing reading comprehension*. Wiley.

Cole, J. (1992). *The magic school bus on the ocean floor*. Scholastic.

Coleman, J. J., Venediktov, R. A., Troia, G. A., & Wang, B. P. (2013). *Impact of literacy intervention on the achievement outcomes of children with developmental language disorders: A systematic review*. National Center for Evidence-Based Practice in Communication Disorders, American Speech–Language–Hearing Association.

Common Core State Standards Initiative. (2023). *Common Core State Standards Initiative: Preparing America's students for college and career*. www.corestandards.org

Compton, D. L., Miller A. C., Elleman, A. M., & Steacy, L. M. (2014). Have we forsaken reading theory in the name of "quick fix" interventions for children with reading disability? *Scientific Studies of Reading, 18, 55–73.*

Connor, C. M., & Morrison, F. (2016). Individualizing student instruction in reading: Implications for policy and practice. *Policy Insights from the Behavioral and Brain Sciences, 3, 54–61.*

Connor, C. M., Morrison, F. J., Fishman, B., Giuliani, S., Luck, M., Underwood, P., et al. (2011). Testing the impact of child characteristics by instruction interactions on third graders' reading comprehension by differentiating literacy instruction. *Reading Research Quarterly, 46,* 189–221.

Coyne, M. D., & Loftus-Rattan, S. (2022). Structured literacy interventions for vocabulary. In L. Spear-Swerling (Ed.), *Structured literacy interventions: Teaching students with reading difficulties, K–6* (pp. 114–135). Guilford Press.

Cummins, J. (1981). The role of primary language development in promoting educational success for language minority students. In California State Department of Education (Ed.), *Schooling and language minority students: A theoretical rationale* (pp. 3–49). California State University.

Cutting, L. E., Clements-Stephens, A., Pugh, K. R., Burns, S., Cao, A., Pekar, J. J., et al. (2013). Not all reading disabilities are dyslexia: Distinct neurobiology of specific comprehension deficits. *Brain Connectivity, 3,* 199–211.

Cutting, L. E., Materek, A., Cole, C., Levine, T., & Mahone, E. M. (2009). Effects of fluency, oral language, and executive function on reading comprehension performance. *Annals of Dyslexia, 59,* 34–54.

Cutting, L. E., & Scarborough, H. S. (2006). Prediction of reading comprehension: Relative contributions of word recognition, language proficiency, and other cognitive skills can depend on how comprehension is measured. *Scientific Studies of Reading, 10,* 277–299.

Daane, M. C., Campbell, J. R., Grigg, W. S., Goodman, M. J., & Oranje, A. (2005). *Fourth-grade students reading aloud: NAEP 2002 Special Study of Oral Reading* (NCES 2006-469). U.S. Government Printing Office.

dePaola, T. (1975). *Strega Nona*. Simon & Schuster.

Dodd, J. L., Ocampo, A., & Kennedy, K. S. (2011). Perspective taking through narratives: An intervention for students with ASD. *Communication Disorders Quarterly, 33,* 23–33.

Duke, N. K., & Pearson, P. D. (2002). Effective practices for developing reading comprehension. In A. E. Farstrup & S. J. Samuels (Eds.), *What research has to say about reading instruction* (3rd ed., pp. 205–242). International Reading Association.

Dunn, D. M. (2019). *Peabody Picture Vocabulary Test* (5th ed.). NCS Pearson.

Eason, S. H., Goldberg, L. F., Young, K. M., Geist, M. C., & Cutting, L. E. (2012). Reader–text interactions: How differential text and question types influence cognitive skills needed for reading comprehension. *Journal of Educational Psychology, 104,* 515–528.

Ehri, L. C. (2005). Learning to read words: Theory, findings, and issues. *Scientific Studies of Reading, 9,* 167–188.

Elleman, A. M. (2017). Examining the impact of inference instruction on the literal and inferential comprehension of skilled and less skilled readers: A meta-analytic review. *Journal of Educational Psychology, 109,* 761–781.

Ellis, C., Holston, S., Drake, G., Putman, H., Swisher, A., & Peske, H. (2023). *Teacher prep review: Strengthening elementary reading instruction.* National Council on Teacher Quality.

Engelmann, S. (1969). *Preventing failure in the primary grades.* Science Research Associates.

Erickson, K. (2013). Reading and assistive technology: Why the reader's profile matters. *Perspectives on Language and Literacy, 39,* 11–14.

Farley, W. (1941). *The black stallion.* Random House.

Farrall, M. L. (2012). *Reading assessment: Linking language, literacy, and cognition.* Wiley.

Filderman, M. A., Austin, C. R., Boucher, A. N., O'Donnell, K., & Swanson, E. A. (2022). A meta-analysis of the effects of reading comprehension interventions on the reading comprehension outcomes of struggling readers in third through 12th grades. *Exceptional Children, 88,* 163–184.

Fisher, P. J., & Blachowicz, C. L. Z. (2005). Vocabulary instruction in a remedial setting. *Reading and Writing Quarterly, 21,* 281–300.

Fletcher, J. M., Lyon, G. R., Fuchs, L. S., & Barnes, M. A. (2019). *Learning disabilities: From identification to intervention* (2nd ed.). Guilford Press.

Foorman, B., Beyler, N., Borradaile, K., Coyne, M., Denton, C. A., Dimino, J., et al. (2016). *Foundational skills to support reading for understanding in kindergarten through 3rd grade* (NCEE 2016-4008). U.S. Government Printing Office.

Foorman, B., Herrera, S., Dombek, J., Schatschneider, C., & Petscher, Y. (2017). *The relative effectiveness of two approaches to early literacy intervention in grades K–2* (REL 2017–251). Institute of Education Sciences, U.S. Department of Education. http://ies.ed.gov/ncee/edlabs

Frayer, D., Frederick, W. C., & Klausmeier, H. J. (1969). *A schema for testing the level of cognitive mastery.* Wisconsin Center for Education Research.

Fuchs, D., Fuchs, L. S., & Compton, D. L. (2012). Smart RTI: A next-generation approach to multilevel prevention. *Exceptional Children, 78,* 263–279.

Fuchs, L. S., & Vaughn, S. (2012). Responsiveness to intervention: A decade later. *Journal of Learning Disabilities, 45,* 195–203.

Gardner, D., & Davies, M. (2014). A new academic vocabulary list. *Applied Linguistics, 35,* 305–327.

Gatlin-Nash, B., Johnson, L., & Lee-James, R. (2020, Summer). Linguistic differences and learning to read for nonmainstream dialect speakers. *Perspectives on Language and Literacy,* pp. 28–35.

Gersten, R., Compton, D., Connor, C. M., Dimino, J., Santoro, L., Linan-Thompson, S., & Tilly, W. D. (2008). *Assisting students struggling with reading: Response to Intervention and multi-tier intervention for reading in the primary grades. A practice guide* (NCEE 2009-4045). National Center for Education Evaluation and Regional Assistance, Institute of Education Sciences, U.S. Department of Education. http://ies.ed.gov/ncee/wwc/publications/practiceguides/

Gersten, R., Haymond, K., Newman-Gonchar, R., Dimino, J., & Jayanthi, M. (2020). Meta-analysis of the impact of reading interventions for students in the primary grades. *Journal of Research on Educational Effectiveness, 13,* 401–427.

Geurts, H., & Embrechts, M. (2008). Language profiles in ASD, SLI, and ADHD. *Journal of Autism and Developmental Disorders, 38,* 1931–1943.

Gillingham, A., & Stillman, B. (1997). *The Gillingham manual: Remedial training for children with specific disability in reading, spelling, and penmanship.* Educators' Publishing Service.

Gillon, G., McNeill, B., Denston, A., Scott, A., & MacFarlane, A. (2020). Evidence-based class literacy instruction for children with speech and language difficulties. *Topics in Language Disorders, 40,* 357–374.

Gonzalez-Frey, S. M., & Ehri, L. C. (2021). Connected phonation is more effective than segmented phonation for teaching beginning readers to decode unfamiliar words. *Scientific Studies of Reading, 25,* 272–285.

Good, R. H., Kaminski, R. A., Cummings, K., Dufour-Martel, C., Petersen, K., Powell-Smith, K., et al. (2018). *Acadience Reading.* https://acadiencelearning.org

Goodman, K. S. (1976). Reading: A psycholinguistic guessing game. In H. Singer & R. Ruddell (Eds.), *Theoretical models and processes of reading* (pp. 497–508). International Reading Association.

Goodwin, A. P., & Ahn, S. (2013). A meta-analysis of morphological interventions in English: Effects on literacy outcomes for school-age children. *Scientific Studies of Reading, 17,* 257–285.

Gough, P. B., & Tunmer, W. E. (1986). Decoding, reading, and reading disability. *Remedial and Special Education, 7,* 6–10.

Graham, S., Bollinger, A., Olson, C., D'Aoust, C., MacArthur, C., McCutchen, D., et al. (2012). *Teaching elementary school students to be effective writers: A practice guide* (NCEE 2012-4058). Institute of Education Sciences, U.S. Department of Education. http://ies.ed.gov/ncee/wwc/publications_reviews.aspx#pubsearch

Graham, S., Bruch, J., Fitzgerald, J., Friedrich, L., Furgeson, J., Greene, K., et al. (2016). *Teaching secondary students to write effectively* (NCEE 2017-4002). Institute of Education Sciences, U.S. Department of Education. https://ies.ed.gov/ncee/wwc/Docs/PracticeGuide/508_WWCPG_SecondaryWriting_122719.pdf

Graham, S., & Hebert, M. A. (2010). *Writing to read: Evidence for how writing can improve reading. A Carnegie Corporation Time to Act Report.* Alliance for Excellent Education.

Hammill, D. D., Wiederholt, J. L., & Allen, E. A. (2014). *Test of Silent Contextual Reading Fluency—Second Edition.* Pro-Ed.

Hanford, E. (2019, August 22). *At a loss for words.*

Hattie, J., & Yates, G. (2014). *Visible learning and the science of how we learn.* Routledge.

Hayes, D. P., & Ahrens, M. (1988). Vocabulary simplification for children: A special case of "motherese." *Journal of Child Language, 15,* 395–410.

Hennessey, N. L. (2021). *The reading comprehension blueprint: Helping students make meaning from text.* Brookes.

Henry, M. K. (2010). *Unlocking literacy: Effective decoding and spelling instruction* (2nd ed.). Brookes.

Herron, J., & Gillis, M. (2020). Encoding as a route to phoneme awareness and spelling: A shift in literacy instruction. *Perspectives on Language and Literacy, 46,* 17–22.

Heubusch, J. D., & Lloyd, J. W. (1998). Corrective feedback in oral reading. *Journal of Behavioral Education, 8,* 63–79.

Hiebert, E. (2022). When students perform at the below basic level on the NAEP: What does it mean and what can educators do? *The Reading Teacher, 75,* 631–639.

Hoover, W. A., & Gough, P. B. (1990). The simple view of reading. *Reading and Writing: An Interdisciplinary Journal, 2,* 127–160.

Hosp, M. K., Hosp, J. L., & Howell, K. W. (2007). *The ABCs of CBM.* Guilford Press.

Hougen, M. C., & Smartt, S. M. (Eds.). (2020). *Fundamentals of literacy instruction and assessment* (2nd ed.). Brookes.

Hudson, R. F., Anderson, E. M., McGraw, M., Ray, R., & Wilhelm, A. (2022). Structured literacy interventions for reading fluency. In L. Spear-Swerling (Ed.), *Structured literacy interventions: Teaching students with reading difficulties, K–6* (pp. 95–113). Guilford Press.

Huemer, S. V., & Mann, V. (2010). A comprehensive profile of decoding and comprehension in autism spectrum disorders. *Journal of Autism and Developmental Disorders, 40,* 485–493.

International Dyslexia Association. (2019). *Structured literacy: An introductory guide.* Author.

International Dyslexia Association. (2020). *Structured literacy: Effective instruction for children with dyslexia and related reading difficulties.* Author.

Johnston, R. S., & Watson, J. E. (2004). Accelerating the development of reading, spelling and phonemic awareness skills in initial readers. *Reading and Writing, 17,* 327–357.

Joshi, R. M., Binks, E., Hougen, M., Dahlgren, M., Ocker-Dean, E., & Smith, D. (2009). Why elementary teachers might be inadequately prepared to teach reading. *Journal of Learning Disabilities, 42,* 392–402.

Joshi, R. M., Treiman, R., Carreker, S., & Moats, L. (2008). How words cast their spell: Spelling is an integral part of learning the language, not a matter of memorization. *American Educator, 32,* 6–16.

Kearns, D. M., Lyon, C. P., & Kelley, S. L. (2022). Structured literacy interventions for reading long words. In L. Spear-Swerling (Ed.), *Structured literacy interventions: Teaching students with reading difficulties, K–6* (pp. 43–66). Guilford Press.

Keenan, J. M., & Betjemann, R. S. (2006). Comprehending the Gray Oral Reading Test without reading it: Why comprehension tests should not include passage-independent items. *Scientific Studies of Reading, 10,* 363–380.

Keenan, J. M., Betjemann, R. S., & Olson, R. K. (2008). Reading comprehension tests vary in the skills they assess: Differential dependence on decoding and oral comprehension. *Scientific Studies of Reading, 12,* 281–300.

Keenan, J. M., & Meenan, C. (2014). Test differences in diagnosing reading comprehension deficits. *Journal of Learning Disabilities, 47,* 125–135.

Kilpatrick, D. A. (2015). *Essentials of assessing, preventing, and overcoming reading difficulties.* Wiley.

Kim, J. S., Burkhauser, M. A., Relyea, J. E., Gilbert, J. B., Scherer, E., Fitzgerald, J., et al. (2023). A longitudinal randomized trial of a sustained content literacy intervention from first to second grade: Transfer effects on students' reading comprehension. *Journal of Educational Psychology, 115,* 73–98.

Kozak, S., & Martin-Chang, S. (2019). Preservice teacher knowledge, print exposure, and planning for instruction. *Reading Research Quarterly, 54,* 323–338.

Leach, J. M., Scarborough, H. S., & Rescorla, L. (2003). Late-emerging reading disabilities. *Journal of Educational Psychology, 95,* 211–224.

Learn.Genetics: Genetic Science Learning Center. (2023). *Basic genetics.* https://learn.genetics.utah.edu/content/basics

Lerner, M. D., & Lonigan, C. T. (2016). Bidirectional relations between phonological awareness and letter knowledge in preschool children revisited: A growth curve analysis of the relation between two code-related skills. *Journal of Experimental Child Psychology, 144,* 166–183.

Lesaux, N. K., & Kieffer, M. J. (2010). Exploring sources of reading comprehension difficulties among language minority learners and their classmates in early adolescence. *American Educational Research Journal, 47,* 596–632.

Li, M., Geva, E., D'Angelo, N., Koh, P. W., Chen, X., & Gottardo, A. (2021). Exploring sources of poor reading comprehension in English language learners. *Annals of Dyslexia, 71,* 299–321.

Lipka, O., Lesaux, N., & Siegel, L. (2006). Retrospective analyses of the reading development of Grade 4 students with reading disabilities: Risk status and profiles over 5 years. *Journal of Learning Disabilities, 39,* 364–378.

Lovett, M., Lacerenza, L., & Borden, S. L. (2000). Putting struggling readers on the PHAST track:

A program to integrate phonological and strategy-based remedial reading instruction and maximize outcomes. *Journal of Learning Disabilities, 33,* 458–476.

MacLachlan, P. (1985). *Sarah, plain and tall.* HarperCollins.

Mar, R. A., & Rain, M. (2015). Narrative fiction and expository nonfiction differentially predict verbal ability. *Scientific Studies of Reading, 19,* 419–433.

McCandliss, B., Beck, I. L., Sandak, R., & Perfetti, C. (2003). Focusing attention on decoding for children with poor reading skills: Design and preliminary tests of the word building intervention. *Scientific Studies of Reading, 7,* 75–104.

Moats, L. C. (1994). The missing foundation in teacher education: Knowledge of the structure of spoken and written language. *Annals of Dyslexia, 44,* 81–102.

Moats, L. C. (2017). Can prevailing approaches to reading instruction accomplish the goals of RTI? *Perspectives on Language and Literacy, 43,* 15–22.

Moats, L. C. (2020). *Speech to print: Language essentials for teachers* (3rd ed.). Brookes.

Moats, L. C. (2022). Structured language interventions for spelling. In L. Spear-Swerling (Ed.), *Structured literacy interventions: Teaching students with reading difficulties, K–6* (pp. 67–94). Guilford Press.

Mol, S. E., & Bus, A. G. (2011). To read or not to read: A meta-analysis of print exposure from infancy to early adulthood. *Psychological Bulletin, 137,* 267–296.

Murray, M. S., Munger, K. A., & Hiebert, E. H. (2014). An analysis of two reading intervention programs: How do the words, texts, and programs compare? *Elementary School Journal, 114,* 479–500.

Nation, K. (2005). Children's reading comprehension difficulties. In M. J. Snowling & C. Hulme (Eds.), *The science of reading: A handbook* (pp. 248–266). Blackwell.

Nation, K., Clarke, P., Wright, B., & Williams, C. (2006). Patterns of reading ability in children with autism spectrum disorder. *Journal of Autism and Developmental Disorders, 36,* 911–919.

Nation, K., & Snowling, M. (1997). Assessing reading difficulties: The validity and utility of current measures of reading skill. *British Journal of Educational Psychology, 67,* 359–370.

National Center for Education Statistics. (2019). *National Assessment of Educational Progress: The NAEP reading achievement levels by grade.* https://nces.ed.gov/nationsreportcard/reading/achieve.aspx

National Center on Improving Literacy. (2022). *The science of reading: The basics.* https://improvingliteracy.org/brief/science-reading-basics

National Reading Panel. (2000). *Teaching children to read: An evidence-based assessment of the scientific research literature on reading and its implications for reading instruction.* National Institutes of Health.

NCS Pearson. (2020). *Wechsler Individual Achievement Test* (4th ed.). Author.

Nelson, N. (2010). *Language and literacy disorders: Infancy through adolescence.* Allyn & Bacon.

Norbury, C., & Nation, K. (2011). Understanding variability in reading comprehension in adolescents with autism spectrum disorders: Interactions with language status and decoding skill. *Scientific Studies of Reading, 15,* 191–210.

Nouwens, S., Groen, M. A., Kleemans, T., & Verhoeven, L. (2021). How executive functions contribute to reading comprehension. *British Journal of Educational Psychology, 91,* 169–192.

Oakhill, J., Cain, K., & Elbro, C. (2015). *Understanding and teaching reading comprehension: A handbook.* Routledge.

O'Connor, R. E., Bocian, K. M., Beach, K. D., Sanchez, V., & Flynn, L. (2013). Special education in a four-year response to intervention (RtI) environment: Characteristics of students with learning disability and grade of identification. *Learning Disabilities Research and Practice, 28,* 98–112.

O'Connor, R. E., White, A., & Swanson, H. L. (2007). Repeated reading versus continuous reading: Influences on reading fluency and comprehension. *Exceptional Children, 74,* 31–46.

Ontario Human Rights Commission. (2022). *Executive summary: Right to read.* www.ohrc.on.ca/sites/default/files/right%20to%20read%20executive%20summary_ohrc%20english_0.pdf

Ouellette, G., Martin-Chang, S., & Rossi, M. (2017). Learning from our mistakes: Improvements in spelling lead to gains in reading speed. *Scientific Studies of Reading, 21,* 350–357.

Palincsar, A. S., & Brown, A. L. (1984). Reciprocal teaching of comprehension-fostering and comprehension-monitoring activities. *Cognition and Instruction, 1,* 117–175.

Pearson, P. D., Hiebert, E. H., & Kamil, M. L. (2007) Vocabulary assessment: What we know and what we need to learn. *Reading Research Quarterly, 42,* 282–296.

Phelps-Terasaki, D., & Phelps-Gunn, T. (2007). *Test of Pragmatic Language* (2nd ed.). PRO-ED.

Piasta, S. B., Connor, C. M., Fishman, B. J., & Morrison, F. J. (2009). Teachers' knowledge of literacy concepts, classroom practices, and student reading growth. *Scientific Studies of Reading, 13,* 224–248.

Pollard-Durodola, S. D. (2020). Vocabulary instruction among English learners. In E. Cardenas-Hagan (Ed.), *Literacy foundations for English learners: A comprehensive guide to evidence-based instruction* (pp. 117–145). Brookes.

Pressley, M., & Afflerbach, P. P. (1995). *Verbal protocols of reading: The nature of constructively responsive reading.* Erlbaum.

RAND Reading Study Group. (2002). *Reading for understanding: Toward an R&D program in reading comprehension.* RAND Corporation.

Raphael, T. E., & Au, K. H. (2005). QAR: Enhancing comprehension and test taking across grades and content areas. *The Reading Teacher, 59,* 206–221.

Rasinski, T., Homan, S., & Biggs, M. (2009). Teaching reading fluency to struggling readers: Method, materials, and evidence. *Reading and Writing Quarterly, 25,* 192–204.

Ray, K., Dally, K., Rowlandson, L., Tam, K. I., & Lane, A. E. (2022). The relationship of handwriting ability and literacy in kindergarten: A systematic review. *Reading and Writing, 35,* 1119–1155.

Riedel, B. W. (2007). The relation between DIBELS, reading comprehension, and vocabulary in urban first-grade students. *Reading Research Quarterly, 42,* 546–567.

Rivera, M. O., Moughamian, A. C., Lesaux, N. K., & Francis, D. J. (2008). *Language and reading interventions for English language learners and English language learners with disabilities.* RMC Research Corporation, Center on Instruction.

Roberts, T. A., & Sadler, C. D. (2019). Letter sound characters and imaginary narratives: Can they enhance motivation and letter sound learning? *Early Childhood Research Quarterly, 46,* 97–111.

Roberts, T. A., Vadasy, P. F., & Sanders, E. A. (2020). Preschool instruction in letter names and sounds: Does contextualized or decontextualized instruction matter? *Reading Research Quarterly, 55,* 573–600.

Saddler, B. (2012). *Teacher's guide to effective sentence writing.* Guilford Press.

Sargiani, R., Ehri, L. C., & Maluf, M. (2022). Teaching beginners to decode consonant–vowel syllables using grapheme–phoneme subunits facilitates reading and spelling as compared with teaching whole-syllable decoding. *Reading Research Quarterly, 57,* 629–648.

Scarborough, H. S. (2001). Connecting early language and literacy to later reading (dis)abilities: Evidence, theory, and practice. In S. B. Neuman & D. K. Dickinson (Eds.), *Handbook of early literacy research* (pp. 97–125). Guilford Press.

Scarborough, H. S. (2005). Developmental relationships between language and reading: Reconciling a beautiful hypothesis with some ugly facts. In H. W. Catts & A. Kamhi (Eds.), *The connections between language and reading disabilities* (pp. 3–24). Erlbaum.

Scarborough, H. S., Ehri, L. C., Olson, R. K., & Fowler, A. E. (1998). The fate of phonemic awareness beyond the elementary school years. *Scientific Studies of Reading, 2,* 115–142.

Schrank, F. A., McGrew, K. S., & Mather, N. (2014). *Woodcock–Johnson IV.* Riverside.

Seidenberg, M. (2017). *Language at the speed of sight.* Basic Books.

Sesma, H. W., Mahone, E. M., Levine, T., Eason, S. H., & Cutting, L. E. (2009). The contribution of executive skills to reading comprehension. *Child Neuropsychology, 15,* 232–246.

Shanahan, T. (2020). What constitutes a science of reading instruction? *Reading Research Quarterly, 55,* 1–13.

Shanahan, T., Callison, K., Carriere, C., Duke, N. K., Pearson, P. D., Schatschneider, C., et al. (2010). *Improving reading comprehension in kindergarten through 3rd grade: A practice guide* (NCEE 2010-4038). Institute of Education Sciences, U.S. Department of Education. whatworks.ed.gov/publications/practiceguides

Slingerland, B. (1994). *A multisensory approach to language arts for specific language disability children: A guide for primary teachers.* Educators' Publishing Service.

Smith, S. L., & Haynes, C. W. (2022). Structured language interventions for written expression. In L. Spear-Swerling (Ed.), *Structured literacy interventions: Teaching students with reading difficulties, K–6* (pp. 189–214). Guilford Press.

Spear-Swerling, L. (2004). Fourth-graders' performance on a state-mandated assessment involving two different measures of reading comprehension. *Reading Psychology, 25,* 121–148.

Spear-Swerling, L. (2009). A literacy tutoring experience for prospective special educators and struggling second graders. *Journal of Learning Disabilities, 42,* 431–443.

Spear-Swerling, L. (2018). Structured literacy and typical literacy practices: Understanding differences to create instructional opportunities. *Teaching Exceptional Children, 51,* 201–211.

Spear-Swerling, L. (2022a). Multicomponent structured literacy interventions for mixed reading difficulties. In L. Spear-Swerling (Ed.), *Structured literacy interventions: Teaching students with reading difficulties, K–6* (pp. 215–236). Guilford Press.

Spear-Swerling, L. (2022b). An introduction to structured literacy and poor-reader profiles. In L. Spear-Swerling (Ed.), *Structured literacy interventions: Teaching students with reading difficulties, K–6* (pp. 1–22). Guilford Press.

Spear-Swerling, L. (Ed.). (2022c). *Structured literacy interventions: Teaching students with reading difficulties, K–6.* Guilford Press.

Spear-Swerling, L., & Brucker, P. (2004). Preparing novice teachers to develop basic reading and spelling skills in children. *Annals of Dyslexia, 54,* 332–364.

Spear-Swerling, L., & Brucker, P. (2006). Teacher-education students' reading abilities and their knowledge about word structure. *Teacher Education and Special Education, 29,* 113–123.

Spear-Swerling, L., Brucker, P., & Alfano, M. (2010). Relationships between sixth-graders' reading comprehension and two different measures of print exposure. *Reading and Writing: An Interdisciplinary Journal, 23,* 73–96.

Spear-Swerling, L., & Cheesman, E. (2012). Teachers' knowledge base for implementing response-to-intervention models in reading. *Reading and Writing: An Interdisciplinary Journal, 25,* 1691–1723.

Spencer, M., Richmond, M. C., & Cutting, L. (2020). Considering the role of executive function in reading comprehension: A structural equation modeling approach. *Scientific Studies of Reading, 24,* 179–199.

Spencer, M., & Wagner, R. K. (2018). The comprehension problems of children with poor reading comprehension despite adequate decoding: A meta-analysis. *Review of Educational Research, 88,* 366–400.

Spencer, T. D., & Petersen, D. B. (2020). Narrative intervention: Principles to practice. *Language, Speech, and Hearing Services in Schools, 51,* 1081–1096.

Stanovich, K. E. (2000). *Progress in understanding reading: Scientific foundations and new frontiers*. Guilford Press.

Stevens, E. A., & Austin, C. R. (2022). Structured reading comprehension intervention for students with reading difficulties. In L. Spear-Swerling (Ed.), *Structured literacy interventions: Teaching students with reading difficulties, K–6* (pp. 162–188). Guilford Press.

Stevens, E. A., Walker, M. A., & Vaughn, S. (2017). The effects of reading fluency interventions on the reading fluency and reading comprehension performance of elementary students with learning disabilities: A synthesis of the research from 2001 to 2014. *Journal of Learning Disabilities, 50*, 576–590.

Swan, M., & Smith, B. (Eds.). (2001). *Learner English: A teacher's guide to interference and other problems* (2nd ed.). Cambridge University Press.

The Reading League. (2022). *Science of reading: Defining guide*. www.thereadingleague.org/what-is-the-science-of-reading

Torgesen, J., Wagner, R., & Rashotte, C. (2012). *Test of Word Reading Efficiency* (2nd ed.). Pearson.

Treiman, R. (2017). Learning to spell words: Findings, theories, and issues. *Scientific Studies of Reading, 21*, 265–276.

Tridas, E. (2020). Components of literacy instruction for English learners. In E. Cardenas-Hagan (Ed.), *Literacy foundations for English learners: A comprehensive guide to evidence-based instruction* (pp. 31–42). Brookes.

University of Oregon. (2018–2019). *Dynamic Indicators of Basic Early Literacy Skills (DIBELS)* (8th ed.). University of Oregon. https://dibels.uoregon.edu

Vaughn, S., Denton, C. A., & Fletcher, J. M. (2010). Why intensive interventions are necessary for students with severe reading difficulties. *Psychology in the Schools, 47*, 432–444.

Vaughn, S., Gersten, R., Dimino, J., Taylor, M. J., Newman-Gonchar, R., Krowka, S., et al. (2022). *Providing reading interventions for students in Grades 4–9* (WWC 2022007). Institute of Education Sciences, U.S. Department of Education. https://ies.ed.gov/ncee/wwc/Docs/PracticeGuide/WWC-practice-guide-reading-intervention-full-text.pdf

Vaughn, S., Wanzek, J., Murray, C. S., & Roberts, G. (2012). *Intensive interventions for students struggling in reading and mathematics: A practice guide*. RMC Research Corporation, Center on Instruction. https://files.eric.ed.gov/fulltext/ED531907.pdf

Wagner, R. K., Beal, B., Zirps, F. A., & Spencer, M. (2021). A model-based meta-analytic examination of specific reading comprehension deficit: How prevalent is it and does the simple view of reading account for it? *Annals of Dyslexia, 71*, 260–281.

Wanzek, J., Al Otaiba, S., & McMaster, K. L. (2020). *Intensive reading interventions for the elementary grades*. Guilford Press.

Washington, J. A., & Seidenberg, M. S. (2021). Teaching reading to African American children: When home and school language differ. *American Educator, 45*, 26–33.

Wei, Y., Spear-Swerling, L., & Mercurio, M. (2021). Motivating students with disabilities to read. *Intervention in School and Clinic, 56*, 155–162.

Westby, C. (2012). Assessing and remediating text comprehension problems. In A. G. Kamhi & H. W. Catts (Eds.), *Language and reading disabilities* (3rd ed., pp. 189–247). Pearson.

Wexler, J., Vaughn, S., Edmonds, M., & Reutebuch, C. K. (2008). A synthesis of fluency interventions for secondary struggling readers. *Reading and Writing: An Interdisciplinary Journal, 21*, 317–347.

Wexler, N. (2019). *The knowledge gap*. Avery.

Whalon, K. (2018). Enhancing the reading development of learners with autism spectrum disorder. *Seminars in Speech and Language, 39*, 144–157.

Whalon, K., Al Otaiba, S., & Delano, M. (2009). Evidence-based reading instruction for individuals with autism spectrum disorders. *Focus on Autism and Other Developmental Disabilities, 24,* 3–16.

Whitehouse, A., Line, E., Watt, H., & Bishop, D. (2009). Qualitative aspects of developmental language impairment relate to language and literacy outcome in adulthood. *International Journal of Language and Communication Disorders, 44,* 489–510.

Wiederholt, J. L., & Bryant, B. R. (2012). *Gray Oral Reading Test* (5th ed.). PRO-ED.

Wiig, E., Semel, E., & Secord, W. (2013). *Clinical evaluation of language fundamentals* (5th ed.). Pearson.

Wilson, B. A. (2018). *Wilson Reading System* (4th ed.). Wilson Language Training Corporation.

Zipoli, R. P. (2017). Unraveling difficult sentences: Strategies to support reading comprehension. *Intervention in School and Clinic, 52,* 218–227.

Zipoli, R. P., & Merritt, D. D. (2017). Risk of reading difficulty among students with a history of speech or language impairment: Implications for Student Support Teams. *Preventing School Failure: Alternative Education for Children and Youth, 61,* 95–103.

Zipoli, R. P., & Merritt, D. M. (2022). Structured literacy interventions for oral language comprehension. In L. Spear-Swerling (Ed.), *Structured literacy interventions: Teaching students with reading difficulties, K–6* (pp. 136–151). Guilford Press.

Index

Note. *f* or *t* following a page number indicates a figure or a table.